Becoming Reinaldo Arenas

Para Riley,
Con mil gracias y
un fuerte abrazo,
Jose
17 abril 2013

Becoming Reinaldo Arenas

FAMILY, SEXUALITY, AND THE CUBAN REVOLUTION

Jorge Olivares

Duke University Press · Durham and London · 2013

© 2013 Duke University Press
All rights reserved
Printed in the United States of America on acid-free paper ∞
Designed by Courtney Leigh Baker
Typeset in Galliard by Keystone Typesetting
Library of Congress Cataloging-in-Publication Data
appear on the last printed page of this book.

For Marc, with love

·CONTENTS·

·ACKNOWLEDGMENTS·

I am fortunate to be part of a circle of Cuban friends and scholars with whom I share not only a love of country but also a passion for its literature. In one way or another, they have left their imprint on *Becoming Reinaldo Arenas*, for which I am profoundly grateful. More than thirty years ago Nivia Montenegro suggested that we interview the recently exiled Reinaldo Arenas; unbeknownst to me at the time, the seed for this book was then planted. My heartfelt thanks go to Monte, from whom I have learned much about Cuba and Arenas, as I have from another friend and *cubanólogo*, Enrico Mario Santí. Lesbia Varona, librarian extraordinaire at the University of Miami's Cuban Heritage Collection, has made available to me, with her legendary generosity, countless materials without which I could not have written this book. Graciella Cruz-Taura and Rosa Perelmuter, enthusiastic cheerleaders of this project, offered many encouraging words. Roberto Ignacio Díaz, with whom I have a *comte* and a *comtesse* in common, has been a princely interlocutor and fellow traveler since our paths crossed years ago in central Maine. A special mention goes to Gustavo Pérez Firmat, my most engaging and toughest critic, who has meticulously read every word that I have ever written on Reinaldo Arenas. My immense gratitude goes to him for his insightful comments, keen suggestions, and gentle prodding during this long journey.

During the many years that it took to write *Becoming Reinaldo Arenas*, I was also surrounded by other friends and colleagues who in multiple ways, big and small, helped to make this book a reality: Silvia Bermúdez, Artie Greenspan, Christiane Guillois, Steven Maynard, Luis Millones, Mary Anne Pérez Firmat, Ulla Reidel, Hanna Roisman, Joseph Roisman, and my poker buddies Lisa Arellano, Ludger Duplessis, Carleen Mandolfo, Joyce McPhetres, Betty Sasaki, Nat Shed, Julie de Sherbinin, and Ron Turcotte. My sincere thanks go to all of them for providing support, encouragement, and nourishment (in all its varieties) and for being a constant reservoir of joy, laughter, and diversion. Betty in particular has inspired me in ways that I could not have imagined on that day, two decades ago, when I opened a fateful door in Chicago and she entered my life.

I could not have written *Becoming Reinaldo Arenas* without access to the Reinaldo Arenas Papers, a rich trove of materials in the Manuscripts Division, Department of Rare Books and Special Collections of Princeton University Library. I am deeply indebted to Reinaldo Arenas not only for his brilliant writing, which has kept me busy for years, but also for his wise and generous decision to make his papers readily available to scholars. My archival research on Arenas began in 1998, when I received a fellowship from the Friends of the Princeton University Library Fellowship Committee. During that summer, and in subsequent visits, Princeton librarians made sure that my immersion in Arenas's world was productive. I thank Princeton University Library for granting me permission to cite from several items in the Arenas collection.

I am profoundly grateful to Margarita Camacho for allowing me to quote from Arenas's published and unpublished works and correspondence. Her commitment to the dissemination of Arenas's oeuvre, a commitment shared with her late husband, the painter Jorge Camacho, is a labor of love from which Arenas scholars have greatly benefited and without which I could not have written the book you now have before you. I also thank two Arenas scholars, Perla Rozencvaig and Liliane Hasson, members of a commission that Arenas set up to advise his heirs on literary matters, for their support of my work. The composer Jorge Martín generously granted me permission to quote from the libretto of his opera *Before Night Falls*. Tomás Fernández Robaina (in Cuba) kindly arranged to have a copy of his *Misa para un ángel* reach me in Maine. Norge Espinosa Mendoza (also in Cuba) graciously granted me permission to use his words as an epigraph for one of the chapters.

I owe a special debt of gratitude to Leon Allen, who in 1993 endowed the Allen Family Chair in Latin American Literature at Colby College, which I hold. My scholarly endeavors have profited greatly from his generosity and commitment to Latin America. I also thank my home institution for its support; most recently, Colby awarded me a Sherman Fairchild Faculty Development Grant, which allowed me to travel to Fort Worth, Texas, to attend the premiere of *Before Night Falls*, the opera. The interlibrary loan staff at Colby's Miller Library handled my many requests cheerfully and efficiently, going beyond the call of duty to find obscure items. I salute them for their perseverance, patience, and professionalism.

For permission to publish material that appeared in earlier essays, I am grateful to several publishers. Chapter 2 includes a brief section from "Carnival and the Novel: Reinaldo Arenas's *El palacio de las blanquísimas mofetas*," *Hispanic Review* 53.4 (1985): 467–76; the first section of chapter 5 originally appeared as "Murderous *Mona Lisa*: Facing AIDS in Reinaldo Arenas's *Mona*," *Revista Hispánica Moderna* 56.2 (2003): 399–419. Both are reprinted with permission from the University of Pennsylvania Press. An earlier version of chapter 3 was first published in Spanish as "¿Por qué llora Reinaldo Arenas?," *MLN* 115.2 (2000): 268–98. It is revised, translated, and reprinted with permission from the Johns Hopkins University Press. Chapter 4 originally appeared as "A Twice-Told Tail: Reinaldo Arenas's 'El Cometa Halley,'" *PMLA* 117.5 (2002): 1188–206. It is reprinted with permission from the copyright owner, the Modern Language Association of America.

At Duke University Press, Senior Editor Valerie Millholland and Assistant Editor Gisela Fosado believed in my work and thoughtfully shepherded the manuscript through a painless evaluation process. I am grateful to them and also to the three reviewers who offered constructive suggestions and enthusiastically endorsed the manuscript.

I owe more than words can express to my partner, Marc Stein, who for the last seventeen years has brought joy into my life. An accomplished historian of sexuality with a keen literary sensibility, he has nurtured me and this project in innumerable ways, consistently encouraging and constructively challenging me. I dedicate this book to Marc, my coauthor in many ways, as a small token of my profound gratitude and as a testament of my enduring love.

·NOTE ON TRANSLATIONS·

To make the book more reader friendly for those not fluent in Spanish, quotations throughout are provided in English only, unless the specific wording in Spanish is important. Page references to both the Spanish original and the English translation are always provided, in this order, and are separated by a semicolon. In some instances, I have "silently" made slight revisions to existing translations. When no source is indicated, the translation is mine, either because a published version does not exist or because I offer an alternative translation. The titles of works appear in Spanish throughout the book; the English translations accompany the original titles on first mention in each chapter, but only in the case of works that have been translated.

Encountering Arenas

....

In reality, one always writes
the same book, the book of our life.
REINALDO ARENAS,
"La vida es riesgo o abstinencia"

I first encountered Reinaldo Arenas in a class called "The 'New Novel' in
Spanish America." *El mundo alucinante* (*The Ill-Fated Peregrinations of Fray
Servando*), Arenas's parodic rewriting of the memoirs of Fray Servando
Teresa de Mier, a rebellious friar of colonial Mexico, was among the novels
on the syllabus, which also included three other Cuban works: Guillermo
Cabrera Infante's *Tres tristes tigres* (*Three Trapped Tigers*), Alejo Carpentier's
El siglo de las luces (*Explosion in a Cathedral*), and José Lezama Lima's *Paradiso* (*Paradiso*). I still possess and treasure that old copy of *El mundo alucinante*, not only because it was my introduction to Arenas but also because it
is a first edition — an edition, published in Mexico in 1969, that brought
much joy and pain to Arenas. My copy of *El mundo alucinante* is liberally
marked with a green flair pen, the annotations of an eager graduate student
in his early twenties; although these markings devalue my copy of the novel
as a vendible commodity, they make it valuable to me, for they help me
reconstruct my initial connections to the book and its author.

The year was 1973 and very little was known about Arenas. My professor,
Kessel Schwartz, who had just published *A New History of Spanish American
Fiction*, which devoted only part of a paragraph to Arenas (2: 207), did not
have much to tell his students about the author of *El mundo alucinante*,
other than the fact that he had written two excellent novels — the other one,
Celestino antes del alba (*Singing from the Well*), was published in Havana in
1967 — and that Arenas was in trouble in Cuba for belonging to what the

professor elliptically referred to, with a smirk, as the "cofradía" (brother-hood). With a drawing of a friar on the front cover (Servando) and a photograph of a handsome man in his twenties on the inside cover (Reinaldo), the novel piqued my curiosity, which was encouraged by the cryptic reference to what I surmised was Arenas's homosexuality. I was intrigued by the two men who shared the two sides of the novel's front cover and who were described in the blurb, respectively, as an exceptional man and as one of the most original young writers in Latin America.

A letter to the long-dead Fray Servando, in which Arenas explains how he accidentally learned of him and how he then proceeded to research his life and work in preparation for the writing of the novel, serves as the prologue to *El mundo alucinante*. Halfway through the letter-prologue, a statement caught my eye and inspired my first green underlining in the text: "What has helped me most to apprehend you has been my discovery that you and I are the same person" (9; *The Ill-Fated Peregrinations of Fray Servando* xxi). I remember being puzzled by these words. How could Servando and Reinaldo, who lived in different epochs, be one and the same? Was there a connection between this statement, which unites friar and author, and the front cover of the novel, which also unites the two men by having the image of the friar on one side and the image of the author on the other —one on top of the other? Was Arenas suggesting a reading that would entail detecting the inscription of his own life in the narrative of the life and times of Fray Servando?

Seven years later, in 1980, a friend and I interviewed Arenas in Miami, six months after he had left Cuba. My first question harked back to my earlier ruminations about him and *El mundo alucinante*:

> One can say about you what you say about Fray Servando in the letter-prologue to *El mundo alucinante*: "one of the most important (and, sadly, most unknown) figures of the . . . literary history of the Americas." When we say that you are unknown, we refer, of course, to Reinaldo Arenas the man, not the writer. To remedy this, could you talk to us about yourself and your situation as a writer in Cuba? (Arenas, "Conversación con Reinaldo Arenas" 53)

Although Arenas preferred that day not to share specific autobiographical information, he did make this crucial assertion: "I believe that every literary work, even if it speaks about Martians, is always autobiographical" (54).

Arenas returned more than once to this view during our conversation. When asked, for instance, whether it was possible to see Reinaldo in Fortunato, the protagonist of *El palacio de las blanquísimas mofetas* (*The Palace of the White Skunks*), which had just been published in Venezuela, Arenas responded in the affirmative and explained, "One always situates oneself in a familiar context, which is the 'I' of each of us" (63). He then added that, in his works, "when re-creating the past, I am only depicting the present that I am suffering" (63). Referring specifically to the life of the rebellious friar, he disclosed that in *El mundo alucinante* he was addressing "the reality that I suffered" (61).

Anyone who has read Arenas's oeuvre, which includes his memoirs, can easily appreciate the autobiographical nature of his vast literary production. Being exercises in self-inscription, Arenas's works invite readers to approach them biographically in order to appreciate their complexity. This is not to say, however, that one must study the writer's life in ways that impose interpretive limits on our readings. Instead, one can take the writer's biography as one context among the many that are woven into the fabric of his writing — as one of multiple intertextualities that mark his oeuvre. Arenas's life story, which after all is accessible in the form of texts (his memoirs as well as correspondence and interviews), provides keys that can help unlock the secrets of his works. In Arenas, life and art are intertwined, and the confluence of the biographical and the fictional provides him with ways to confront his demons. One can learn as much about Arenas from his autofictions as from his autobiography.[1]

Arenas, if my epigraph is any indication, would agree with Guillermo Cabrera Infante, who once said, "The proper object of literary study is not the work but the author" ("En España han sido en extremo generosos conmigo" 64). I am as interested in the man behind, or within, Arenas's works as I am in the works themselves. My aim in writing this book has been to understand the figure of Reinaldo Arenas, the self-portraiture that surfaces in an oeuvre that spanned thirty years, starting with his unpublished juvenilia and ending with his posthumously published memoirs.

When Arenas and I first met, he inscribed my copies of two of his novels. In *El palacio de las blanquísimas mofetas*, he wrote, "To Jorge Olivares, with the affection of a brother in hopes and dreams." In *El mundo alucinante*, he wrote, "For Jorge Olivares, who knows how to dig deep into the twists and turns [*pericuetos*] of my hallucinatory world, which is ours." Since that day,

20 November 1980, I have asked myself many times what it is that compels me, in the words of Arenas, "to dig deep" into the "twists and turns" of his writing. It may be that in his search for his father and fatherland, a preoccupation that runs through Arenas's texts and which I examine in this book, I see elements of my own search for *padre* and *patria*, both of which I lost in my early adolescence. It may be that in his complicated relationship with his mother, which I also treat in this book, I see partial reflections of my own complicated relationship with mine. It may be that in his struggles with his gay identity and his confrontations with HIV/AIDS, which I explore in this book as well, I see some of my own struggles. When Arenas referred to me as "a brother in hopes and dreams," did he intuit a connection between us, one that, thirty years ago, I could not articulate? I leave my reader with this question and invite you to embark on your own exploration of the *vericuetos* of Arenas's *mundo alucinante*. May this book serve as a guide to your encounter with arguably the most important writer to come out of the Cuban Revolution.

In what follows, I have resisted the impulse for comprehensiveness that some critics feel when writing a monograph on a single author. I have opted, instead, to focus on close readings of a selection of Arenas's works while simultaneously exploring suggestive textual echoes that resonate across Arenas's vast oeuvre, including unpublished manuscripts and correspondence. My goal has been to disentangle a narrative web into which is woven an intricate and fascinating life story, one that begins in mid-twentieth-century Cuba with a poor, misunderstood, and lonely child as its protagonist and ends some fifty years later in the United States with an impoverished and AIDS-stricken man committing suicide in New York with Cuba on his mind. As I trace Arenas's estrangement (familial, social, political) in his writing, I examine issues of sexuality, family, exile, and nostalgia.

In chapter 1 I recount Arenas's biography and create a portrait of the cultural and sexual politics of the Cuban Revolution until 1980, when Arenas left Cuba during the Mariel boatlift. In chapter 2 I address *El palacio de las blanquísimas mofetas*, which is concerned with family trees, both personal and literary. I explore the novel's intertextual dialogue with Benito Pérez Galdós's nineteenth-century classic, *Fortunata y Jacinta* (*Fortunata and Jacinta*), from whose mode of writing the postmodern Arenas distances himself, and the novel's preoccupation with absent fathers, which it shares with the Spaniard's novel. This allows me to bring two things into focus: Arenas's critical engagement with the cultural polemics of the 1960s, about a realist aesthetic that Cuban cultural ideologues promoted in the form of socialist realism, and the "paternal erotics" that are at the core of Arenas's literary production. In chapter 3 I consider the role of the father in Arenas's life and writing alongside his relation to his fatherland. Arguing that *padre* and *patria* are intertwined, sharing a profound emotional space in Arenas, I concentrate on two texts: *Antes que anochezca* (*Before Night Falls*), Arenas's autobiography, where he lovingly recalls the encounter that he had, at age five, with his father (a scene that can be read as a "primal seduction"); and *Viaje a La Habana*, a novella in which an estranged father and son, having met apparently by chance in Cuba's capital when the exiled father returns to the island for a visit, have passionate sex. By reading these two texts together and juxtaposing them with Countess Merlin's own *Viaje a La Habana*, where she recounts a visit to her native Cuba in 1840 after having spent most of her life in Europe, I highlight Arenas's eroticized nostalgia for the father he saw only once in his life and for the fatherland that, in his thirties, he had to leave behind.

In chapter 4 I expand the discussion of the family in Arenas's oeuvre by adding the maternal figure to the mix through an analysis of the short story "El Cometa Halley" ("Halley's Comet"), a parodic continuation of Federico García Lorca's *La casa de Bernarda Alba* (*The House of Bernarda Alba*). By moving the Alba sisters from Spain to Cuba and unleashing their repressed sexualities, an exiled Arenas pursues his fantasies of sexual freedom. Subscribing to a "transvestite poetics," he metaphorically transports himself back to his homeland, where, like García Lorca during his visit to Cuba in 1930, he spent the happiest days of his life. Arenas imagines as well an alternative family constellation in which a wild and liberating mother, in contrast to García Lorca's Bernarda and to his own suffering and controlling mother, opens new worlds for her progeny. Projecting himself onto his text, Arenas modifies and rewrites his own personal story, choosing to tell one in which transgressive desires are celebrated rather than abhorred. In his writing, Arenas not only interprets his family romance in a Freudian context (absent father, domineering mother), but also uses a psychoanalytic model to offer an oedipal interpretation of the political situation of the Cuban people: Fidel Castro as a castrating and repressive mother who comes between the son and his fatherland.

In chapter 5 I broaden the treatment of sex and sexuality in Arenas by looking at the representation of AIDS, which lurks in references scattered across his fictional universe. AIDS figures more prominently in Arenas, I contend, if one reads some of his works allegorically, as can be done with *Mona* (*Mona*), a novella that Arenas wrote one year prior to his diagnosis, and *El color del verano* (*The Color of Summer*), a novel that he started writing during a hospital stay and finished shortly before his death. I conclude this chapter with an analysis of Arenas's correspondence with his mother, which I read as texts that, like *Mona* and *El color del verano*, engage in a rhetoric of indirection, the only way in which mother and son can bring themselves to express the painful reality of Arenas's illness.

I close this book with an epilogue in which I reflect on Arenas's posthumous fortunes in Cuba, where his works are selectively being "recovered" by and for the cultural establishment, and abroad, where he has become the subject of a film and an opera. Arenas may have died prematurely, but his life and work continue to have meaning for those interested in exploring family and sexuality in relation to literature, culture, and politics in and beyond Cuba.

ONE

I Scream, Therefore I Am

....

I tell my truth, as does the Jew who has suffered racism or the
Russian who has been in the Gulag, or any human being who has eyes
to see the way things really are. I scream, therefore I am.

REINALDO ARENAS,
Antes que anochezca (Before Night Falls)

The brief entry on Reinaldo Arenas in the *Diccionario de la literatura cubana*
illustrates Arenas's situation while living in Cuba. Of his literary accom-
plishments, the dictionary says only: "He received honorable mention in
the UNEAC [Unión Nacional de Escritores y Artistas de Cuba] literary
competitions in 1965, 1966 and 1968 for his novels *Celestino antes del alba*
[*Singing from the Well*] and *El mundo alucinante* [*The Ill-Fated Peregrinations
of Fray Servando*] and for his collection of short stories, still unpublished,
Con los ojos cerrados. He has been translated into English, French, Italian,
German, Portuguese and Dutch" (1: 70). What at first seems to be a rather
straightforward account of Arenas's literary achievements turns out to be an
entry filled with misleading and incorrect information. While it is true that
Arenas's peers lauded him for the two novels mentioned, they did not do so
for the collection of short stories. And contrary to what the entry says, *Con
los ojos cerrados* was indeed published, without the sanction of the Cuban
authorities, in Uruguay in 1972. Arenas had managed to smuggle the manuscript out of Cuba, as he had done before with the manuscript of *El mundo
alucinante*, his best-known novel, which was first published in a French
translation in Paris in 1968 and in its original Spanish one year later in
Mexico.[1] The dictionary also neglects to mention that the Cuban state-run
press refused to publish the award-winning *El mundo alucinante* and that
for daring to place this novel before an international readership, which

immediately hailed it as a masterpiece, and for living an openly gay life, the prize-winning and internationally acclaimed young writer not only became a persona non grata in his own country but also was incarcerated. Moreover, although the dictionary mentions the languages into which Arenas's works had been translated, it makes no reference to *El palacio de las blanquísimas mofetas* (*The Palace of the White Skunks*), the manuscript of which Arenas also had smuggled out of Cuba. Translations of this novel appeared in 1975 and 1977 in France and Germany; its original Spanish version was published in Venezuela in 1980, the year in which Arenas left Cuba and in which the *Diccionario de la literatura cubana* was published. Had the dictionary been prepared after Arenas's departure, it is likely that, instead of omissions and misinformation, there would have been complete silence. As was the case with other Cuban writers who had gone into exile (e.g., Guillermo Cabrera Infante and Severo Sarduy), Arenas would have been literally erased from this "official" account of Cuban literature.

Though Arenas was included in the *Diccionario de la literatura cubana*, he already had been banished from the literary and social landscape of Cuba during the last twelve years that he lived in his country, as much for writing works that did not celebrate the Revolution as for his homosexuality.[2] An openly gay man like Arenas was anathema to the *hombre nuevo* (new man), the man's man whom the Latin American revolutionary icon Ernesto "Che" Guevara extolled and on whose virile shoulders fell the responsibility to advance the revolutionary program.[3] In 1965, the same year that Che's influential "El socialismo y el hombre en Cuba" ("Socialism and Man in Cuba") was published, there appeared in the Cuban newspaper *El mundo* an article by the respected writer and folklorist Samuel Feijóo titled "Revolución y vicios." After making cursory comments about drugs, prostitution, gambling, and alcoholism, "vices inherited from capitalism," Feijóo focuses on "homosexuality," telling his Cuban readers that it is "one of the most abominable and harmful legacies of capitalism."[4] Feijóo then goes on to relate a conversation that he had with the Chilean literary critic Ricardo Latcham, who, in the course of lamenting "the invasion of art and literature by the sodomites," asked him to comment on "the influence of homosexuality on Cuban art":

> I told him the truth: that that legacy of capitalism still persists. But that we are fighting against it and will continue to fight until it is eradicated from a virile country that finds itself in a life-and-death

struggle against Yankee imperialism. And that this extremely virile country, with its army of men, should not and could not be expressed by homosexual or pseudo-homosexual writers and artists. Because no homosexual represents the Revolution, which is a matter for men, a matter of fists and not of feathers, of courage and not of cowardice, of integrity and not of intrigue, of creative valor and not of spineless surprises. . . . True revolutionary literature is not, and will never be, written by sodomites.

There is no other recourse, in his view, but "to annihilate" homosexuals. This is what must be done by a "nation that . . . confronts bloodthirsty Yankee imperialism with supreme virility." Feijóo concludes:

It is not about persecuting homosexuals, but about destroying their positions, their methods, their influence. This is called revolutionary social hygiene. We will have to eradicate them from their key positions at the forefront of revolutionary art and literature. If as a result we lose a dance troupe, we will do without the "sick" troupe. If we lose an exquisite writer, the cleaner the air will be. This way we will feel healthier as we create virile groups that emerge from a courageous nation. Let us break the vicious capitalist legacy.

If I have quoted at some length Feijóo's metaphorical "call to arms," it is because such words became deeds: grandiloquent rhetorical expression translated into degrading antigay repression. For 1965 was also the year that Fidel Castro not only publicly stated that he did not believe that "a homosexual could embody the conditions and requirements of conduct that would enable us to consider him a true Revolutionary, a true Communist militant" (Lockwood 124), but also authorized the creation of the Unidades Militares de Ayuda a la Producción (UMAP), work camps to which "nonconformists" (Báez) were sent beginning in November of that year.[5]

As reported in *Granma*, the Communist Party daily, the objective of the UMAP was not to punish the young men sent to the camps, but rather to "educate," "shape," and "save" them—to prevent them from becoming "parasites" or "counterrevolutionaries." Through "military discipline," they would overcome their "attitudes" and become "productive members of society" (Báez). In fact, those interned in the UMAP camps, a large number of whom were gay men, were sent there for "rehabilitation" through intense agricultural labor. "Work will make you men," the internees were told by signs posted in the camps (Almendros and Jiménez Leal 37).[6] They were subjected not only to forced labor and physicial abuse but also, in some instances, to medical experimentation, as was the case in Laguna Grande, a camp reserved exclusively for gay men, where, according to one of the internees, visiting foreign psychiatrists injected "an unknown substance" into their veins (Ronet 53).[7] There were approximately 250 UMAP camps in the province of Camagüey with a total population of about 25,000, which included such strange bedfellows as men who had sex with men, vagrants, hippies, Catholics, Seventh Day Adventists, Jehovah's Witnesses, practitioners of Afro-Cuban religions, writers, and artists.[8]

Although protests by members of the Unión Nacional de Escritores y Artistas de Cuba and by intellectuals in Europe and Latin America led to the closing of the UMAP camps in 1967, institutionalized homophobia continued.[9] Relying on traditionally antigay metaphors of infection, disease, and contamination, Abel Prieto Morales, a prominent educator who was to become Cuba's vice minister of education, published an article in 1969 in the popular magazine *Bohemia* in which he discussed the "phenomenon of homosexuality" (108).[10] With its one-word title, "Homosexualismo," printed across the page in large bold letters, the article expressed the pressing need for a program of "prophylaxis" (109), both within the family and in society at large, for the prevention of homosexuality. In Prieto Morales's view, although it would be very "simple" to execute the program in the home — "The father must behave like one and the mother must occupy within the home the place that corresponds to her" — outside the home it would entail "a major social undertaking," the primary aim of which would be to keep homosexuals, "contagious elements," away from children (109).

Prieto Morales articulates the view held most widely on the island in the 1960s on the etiology of homosexuality. In post-1959 Cuba, homosexuality was primarily explained in terms of "nurture" rather than "nature," a perspective that was compatible with an interest in and commitment to its prevention and eradication. Gaspar García Galló, the distinguished pedagogue and leading figure in the Departamento de Educación, Ciencia y Cultura of the Comité Central del Partido Comunista de Cuba, voiced the prevailing position: "We believe that the justification that some pretend to make for the 'sick ones' [*enfermos*], reducing it all to a biological problem, is not valid. We believe that it is — fundamentally — a social problem: a problem of corruption" (*Nuestra moral socialista* 70). It is no coincidence that in 1963, in a speech to university students in which Fidel Castro denounced antisocial elements, including homosexuals (not mentioned by name but allusively present in the speech's language and turns of phrases), Cuba's leader highlighted the role that *ambiente* (environment) and *reblandecimiento* (softness) played in those who had the *problema* (problem) ("No cayó en el vacío el sacrificio de los mártires" 6). According to one of the available transcriptions of the speech, "Discurso pronunciado por el Comandante Fidel Castro Ruz," the audience interrupted Castro with laughter and applause, shouting that the ones with the "problem" were "those weak in the leg," "the homosexuals." The U.S. psychiatrist Irving J. Crain, having visited Cuba in 1969 and 1978, explains: "The scientific consensus in Cuba is that homosexuality is socially determined and, as society becomes more cooperative and non-exploitive, homosexuality will diminish" (16). Although the psychiatric community in Castro's Cuba later became strongly anti-Freudian, in the 1960s the notion of the Oedipus complex, a central tenet of psychoanalysis, was widely accepted. It is at the basis of Prieto Morales's program of "familial prophylaxis," which would involve altering dysfunctional home dynamics (especially the absent or passive father and the possessive or smothering mother) to prevent the development of a homosexual child.[11]

In 1971, two years after the publication of Prieto Morales's article, a program of "social prophylaxis" was proposed by the state-sponsored Primer Congreso Nacional de Educación y Cultura, which defined homosexuality as a "social pathology" ("Declaration by the First National Congress on Education and Culture" 5) and called for the removal of homosexuals from positions associated with the education of youth and the propagation of Cuban culture. One of its resolutions stated that "cultural institutions cannot serve as a platform for false intellectuals who try to convert snobbery, extravagant conduct, homosexuality and other social aberrations into expressions of revolutionary art, isolated from the masses and the spirit of the Revolution" (5). Although the recommendations of the congress regarding homosexuality did not become "official" until 1974 (see Ley 1267), their implementation was immediate, as the event was sanctioned by the nation's communist apparatus and its supreme leader, Fidel Castro, who brought the congress to a close with a rousing speech ("Only After a Revolution").

The discussions on art and literature at the congress, which convened

23–30 April 1971, had as their catalyst the "Padilla Affair." In 1968 a jury that included Cubans and non-Cubans unanimously awarded Heberto Padilla the UNEAC poetry prize for *Fuera del juego*. Although cultural ideologues at UNEAC considered the book counterrevolutionary and tried, unsuccessfully, to influence the jurors' vote, they allowed the book's publication but with a condemnatory prologue that explained UNEAC's objections to the jurors' decision. On 20 March 1971, Padilla was arrested and charged with "having plotted against the powers of the state" (Padilla, *Self-Portrait of the Other* 133). Five weeks later, when the Congreso was in session, he was released from prison and was forced to deliver an *autocrítica* (self-criticism) in which he denounced his past "errors" and those committed by friends and colleagues, some of whom were in attendance at his public declaration. Leading intellectuals from Europe and Latin America publicly denounced the treatment of Padilla and distanced themselves from Castro's Revolution, which until then they had enthusiastically supported and embraced. As a result, what otherwise would have been a national incident became an international scandal.[12]

Seeking to define the role that art, literature, and their producers should play in a socialist society and determined to exclude homosexuals from the project of nation building, the Primer Congreso Nacional de Educación y Cultura officially launched a period characterized by ideological dogmatism, cultural repression, and extreme homophobia. Ambrosio Fornet named it Quinquenio Gris ("A propósito de *Las iniciales de la tierra*" 150, 153), a five-year period of repressive measures that, according to him, began in 1971 and ended in 1976 with the creation of the Ministerio de Cultura with Armando Hart at its helm. Although there is agreement that Hart instituted policies that began to reverse those that Luis Pavón Tamayo, as president of the Consejo Nacional de Cultura, had put in place in 1971, the consensus is that the so-called Quinquenio Gris extended to the mid-1980s, having begun as early as 1968. Lasting well beyond the five years that Fornet's denomination suggests, this period has received other names, such as Decenio Negro and Trinquenio Amargo.[13] During this time, those considered to be outside the sexual, social, moral, and ideological "parameters" that defined a true revolutionary suffered ostracism, persecution, or incarceration. Homosexuals in particular, especially artists and educators, were dismissed from their jobs or given employment in places where their "contaminating" presence would not be a threat to society. Writers who did not embrace socialist realism, which imposed an ideological mold on cultural production, were silenced. They included established figures such as José Lezama Lima and Virgilio Piñera and younger writers such as Reinaldo Arenas. "Art is a weapon of the Revolution," the Primer Congreso Nacional de Educación y Cultura succinctly affirmed ("Declaration by the First National Congress on Education and Culture" 6).

Those who did not subscribe to the Congreso's dictum were accused of *diversionismo ideológico*, which in its initial application referred to the subtle penetration of capitalist ideology in socialist countries in the guise of pseudo-Marxist positions. Although in 1972 Raúl Castro called for legislation that would punish those within Cuba who committed acts of ideological deviationism, a formulation that had been used for the first time in Cuba in 1971 at the Primer Congreso Nacional de Educación y Cultura, it was not until 1974 that his wish became law, with the promulgation of Ley 1262. In Cuba, as in other socialist countries, the concept of "ideological deviationism" suffered a deviation, as it were, from its original and narrow meaning — the ideological penetration by the "enemy" from the outside — and was used to characterize any act or activity committed by people within the country that "deviated" from Cuba's moral, social, literary, artistic, and political prescriptions.[14]

In 1994 the gay writer Antón Arrufat, who in 1965 lost his job as editor of *Casa de las Américas* and in 1971 was assigned to a municipal library where he performed the menial task of packing boxes because he was not allowed to have contact with the reading public, looked back at the 1970s:

> In the seventies, called by [Virgilio] Piñera the years of civil death, that decade's bureaucracy placed us in that "strange latitude" of existence: death in life. It demanded us to die as writers and live as disciplined citizens. . . . Our books were no longer published, and those that had been published were taken away from bookstores and surreptitiously removed from the stacks of public libraries. The plays that we had written disappeared from the stage. Our names, no longer mentioned at conferences or university classes, were erased from anthologies and histories of Cuban literature written during this ill-fated period. We were not only leading a life of death: it seemed that we had never been born or had ever written anything. (42)

It was not until the mid-1980s that it became possible for Cubans on the island, including writers like Arrufat who had been silenced for their ideological deviationism, to discuss critically the 1970s—as long as it was done from within the Revolution and not from a position of political opposition or dissidence.[15]

The role of gays in Cuba's revolutionary process once again became an explosive issue in 1980. In April of that year, in reaction to the upheaval created by 10,800 disaffected Cubans who expressed their desire to emigrate by taking refuge in the Peruvian embassy in Havana, Fidel Castro declared the port of Mariel open for emigration. Setting aside a long-standing policy that prohibited ordinary Cuban nationals from traveling abroad, a frustrated and infuriated Castro lashed out at those who wished to abandon Cuba and in an unusual move allowed them to leave on boats sent from the United States (most of which were captained by Cuban Americans). Castro's "magnanimous" act was accompanied by mean-spirited references to *escoria* (scum), a label that quickly caught on as a way to characterize those who wished to leave, including homosexuals. During the Mariel boatlift, a sizable number of gay men, including some of the writers who came to be known as the "Mariel Generation," left Castro's Cuba. Reinaldo Arenas was among the approximately 125,000 Cubans who reached United States shores between April and September 1980.[16]

ON 16 JULY 1943, Reinaldo Arenas was born into abject poverty in the countryside of eastern Cuba.[17] The son of unmarried peasant parents, Arenas was raised by his mother (Oneida Fuentes) and maternal grandparents, since his father (José Antonio Arenas) abandoned Oneida and Reinaldo when his son was only a few months old. Although the family zealously tried to keep from Arenas the identity of his father, they failed in their efforts. When Arenas was five years old, he unexpectedly met his father on a riverbank, an experience that left an indelible mark on the impressionable child. This brief—and sole—encounter with his father would play a crucial role in Arenas's life and writing.

Shortly before his death in 1990, in a filmed interview in the documentary *Havana*, Arenas, visibly ill from AIDS, dons a *sombrero de yarey*, the typical straw hat worn by Cuban campesinos like his father, and then proceeds to narrate "a story that I always tell": the casual encounter with his father, who, in Arenas's words, "appeared and disappeared immediately." It may have been a fleeting occurrence, but its narrative recurrence in Arenas's oeuvre demonstrates its significance and lasting effect on the abandoned son, who, in retelling it, seems to have been working through the impact that his absent father had on his life. In *Antes que anocheza*, after recounting the scene with his father, Arenas recalls that he envied his cousins because they knew their fathers, which gave them the self-assured and confident manner that he did not have. He nevertheless at no time expressed any animosity toward his father; on the contrary, he seemed to have been in awe of him, especially his physical attributes. When asked in an interview whether his mother had managed to destroy the image of his father, Arenas quickly responded that she had not. In fact, it was toward his mother, who did not accept her son's homosexuality, that Arenas harbored feelings of resentment and from whom he felt the need to flee, which he did at age eighteen, when he moved to Havana.

Without a father and raised by a mother and grandparents who found him odd even at an early age, a misunderstood Arenas fought against the loneliness he experienced while growing up in his family's limited and limiting world by turning to the joys of nature (delighting in the falling of the rain on his naked body during tropical downpours while ecstatically hugging the trees and rolling around in the grass), sex (having intercourse with farm animals, holes in soft trees, girls and boys), and authorship (composing endless songs and writing "poetry" on tree trunks). Despite the hardships, Arenas remembers his childhood in the countryside as a "glorious time" ("Reinaldo Arenas: Aquel mar, una vez más" 155), full of magic, that kindled his creative spirit, which manifested itself during his teenage years in soap-opera inspired novels.

When Arenas was twelve years old, his family moved to Holguín, the nearest city, where he found life unbearable. Concluding that as a fatherless and poor boy he had nothing to lose except his life, fifteen-year-old Arenas joined Fidel Castro's guerrillas, who were fighting against the dictator Fulgencio Batista. An *alzado* — as the rebels were called — for only six months, he primarily performed menial tasks, such as cooking and washing for the troops. With the triumph of the Revolution in 1959, Arenas received a scholarship to attend a provincial polytechnic institute. He later enrolled at the University of Havana, from which he was expelled, according to Arenas, because of his dubious morality and political ideology.

Arenas's literary aspirations began to come to fruition in the nation's capital, in 1963, when he won a storytelling competition at the Biblioteca

Nacional. Unlike the other contestants, who, following the guidelines, memorized and told a story by an established author, Arenas memorized and told a story that he had written especially for the occasion. "Los zapatos vacíos," as the two-page manuscript was titled, impressed the jurors, among whom was the well-known poet Eliseo Diego, the head of the Departamento de Literatura Infantil y Juvenil, who immediately persuaded María Teresa Freyre de Andrade, the library's director, to hire the talented young man.[18] The bored clerk at the Instituto Nacional de Reforma Agraria soon became an assistant in the library's circulation department. With the initial guidance of Eliseo Diego and Cintio Vitier, another distinguished writer who also worked at the library, Arenas read everything he could put his hands on. Many years later Diego recalled that in one month Arenas "devoured" all the books in that library ("El silencio de los elogios" 3). Diego's hyperbolic comment captures not only Arenas's love of reading but also the admiration that the poet had for his protégé. Diego's daughter, possibly reporting what she had heard from her father, has written that Arenas's primary occupation was to read (Josefina de Diego 98). Tomás Fernández Robaina, a friend of Arenas's who was also employed at the library, remembers that the librarians turned a blind eye when their "spoiled child" was caught hiding in the stacks reading instead of carrying out his "official" duties ("Las arenas movedizas"). Diego and his colleagues at the Biblioteca Nacional, as Arenas explains in *Antes que anochezca*, owed their jobs to the magnanimity of the library's director, who protected them at a time when they were not sympathizers of the Revolution. They, in turn, extended to the incipient writer the same privileges that they enjoyed: having the opportunity to cultivate their literary talents while drawing salaries and doing very little library work.

At the Biblioteca Nacional, where he worked until 1968, Arenas was able to pursue the pleasure not only of reading but also of writing. In the mornings, before reporting for his shift in the afternoon, Arenas read and wrote for hours in the library's empty rooms. There, in one fifteen-day period, he wrote his first serious novel, *Celestino antes del alba*, which he submitted in 1965 to the inaugural Premio Nacional de Novela Cirilo Villaverde, a literary contest sponsored by UNEAC. Arenas's novel and four others received honorable mention, placing second to Ezequiel Vieta's *Vivir en Candonga*. During the jurors' deliberation and in subsequent official discussions concerning its publication, the manuscript of *Celestino antes del alba* was criticized by some who, accepting the tenets of socialist realism, objected to the novel's fantasy world. Two of the jurors, José Antonio Portuondo and Alejo Carpentier, referring to *Celestino antes del alba*, argued that they could not support awarding the prize to a novel "that had nothing to do with politics," adding that the prize-winning novel had to emphasize "the heroic thing, the politics of the Cuban Revolution" (Arenas, "Memorias de un exiliado" 42). The novel's critics were troubled also by the fact that hunger, the repression of an artist, and subtle homoerotic desire were central to the story. The resistance to *Celestino antes del alba* notwithstanding, UNEAC published it in 1967. It did not please Arenas, however, that the run was limited to two thousand copies and that of the five novels that had received honorable mention in 1965 his was the last to appear in print. According to Arenas, *Celestino antes del alba* was finally published because at the time he was *integrado* (integrated), a designation applied to those who dutifully did what was expected of them, which included not only performing well at one's job but also doing "voluntary" work. Readers of *Celestino antes del alba*, including José Lezama Lima, who soon became a mentor to Arenas, received it enthusiastically.[19]

In 1966 Arenas submitted the manuscript of another novel, *El mundo alucinante*, to the Premio Nacional de Novela Cirilo Villaverde. He again received an honorable mention, but this time he did not share the accolade with any other writer. Interestingly, no one was awarded the top prize that year. Unlike *Celestino antes del alba*, however, *El mundo alucinante* was denied publication in Cuba, which lacked publishers independent of the state. Not only was it alleged that the novel was counterrevolutionary (some read it as an allegorical denunciation of Castro's regime), but there was also concern about its "homosexual" passages. This was a serious matter, especially in the wake of the controversial publication earlier in the year of Lezama's homoerotically themed *Paradiso* (*Paradiso*), which had appeared at a time when well-positioned intellectuals and revolutionary leaders were making antigay pronouncements and when homophobia had already been institutionalized in the UMAP camps. Arenas, who was determined to publish the novel, had no other recourse but to seek publication abroad.

While on an official visit to Cuba in 1967, to attend an international art exhibition, the Cuban expatriate painter Jorge Camacho and his wife, Margarita, read *Celestino antes del alba*, liked it, and sought out its author. Their meeting with Arenas, which was the beginning of a strong friendship that lasted until Arenas's death, in 1990, provided Arenas with the opportunity to smuggle out of Cuba the manuscript of *El mundo alucinante*, which the Camachos, upon their return home to Paris, submitted along with a copy of *Celestino antes del alba* to the prestigious French publishing house Editions du Seuil. *Le Monde hallucinant* appeared in a du Seuil edition soon thereafter, in 1968, the same year that Arenas came into contact with Emmanuel Carballo, editor of Diógenes in Mexico and a frequent traveler to Cuba.[20]

At the behest of Camila Henríquez Ureña, a juror in the 1965 UNEAC literary contest who was impressed by the talent of the young author of *Celestino antes del alba*, Carballo read the manuscript of *El mundo alucinante*, considered it "the most beautiful novel written in Cuba by a young person after 1959," and decided to publish it (Carballo 537).[21] Arenas and Carballo initially made every effort to obtain approval for the Mexican publication of *El mundo alucinante* from Cuba's Instituto del Libro, a highly politicized agency in which Arenas was employed at the time.[22] They did so not because it was required but because, as Carballo has explained, they wanted to avoid conflict with the authorities. According to Carballo, the Instituto del Libro unreasonably — and maliciously — delayed its decision about whether to allow the publication in Cuba of Arenas's prize-winning novel, two fragments of which had already been published in Cuban literary journals (see "El encadenamiento del fraile" and "Estancia en Pamplona"). Having received only evasive answers from the Instituto del Libro and knowing that Arenas's novel was not officially forbidden in Cuba and that nothing prohibited Cuban authors from publishing abroad, Carballo proceeded with his plans, and the Spanish original of *El mundo alucinante* finally saw print, to Arenas's delight and Cuba's frustration, in Mexico in 1969.[23] In 1974, six years after the manuscript of *El mundo alucinante* had reached Carballo's hands, Ley 1262 was passed, which made it a crime to send and publish abroad "counterrevolutionary" texts. Until that year, Arenas had the legal right to publish anything in another country.

In March 1968, before *Le Monde hallucinant* appeared in France, a fragment of *Celestino antes del alba* was published without Arenas's knowledge in the Paris-based literary journal *Mundo nuevo*. Told that his possible hiring at the UNEAC, where he was to work as an editor, would be compromised if he did not express publicly his objection to the publication of his work in a journal that Cubans and the Latin American Left accused of being funded by the United States Central Intelligence Agency, Arenas denounced *Mundo nuevo* on 1 July 1968 in a letter that was published in the July–August issue of *La gaceta de Cuba* ("Revista *Mundo nuevo*").[24] Curiously, Arenas's letter was followed by a notice of expulsion from the UNEAC of two prominent exiled Cuban artists, the writer Guillermo Cabrera Infante and the pianist Ivette Hernández, for betraying the revolutionary cause (see "Expulsión"). Both documents were preceded by "Magia y persecución en José Martí," a long essay by Arenas. What is one to make of this textual choreography on the pages of one of Cuba's leading literary journals? If Cuban ideologues not so subtly flexed their political muscles, Arenas was not easily subdued, for he had muscles of his own — the power of his prose.

On the surface the letter to *Mundo nuevo* appears to be the denunciation that UNEAC demanded from Arenas, but a closer analysis of its language reveals it as an act of resistance. Arenas himself made this clear the next day, on 2 July 1968, in a second letter that he wrote, voluntarily this time, to Emir Rodríguez Monegal, the journal's editor ("Señor Emir Rodríguez Monegal"). Explaining the circumstances in which he had to write the "infamous letter," Arenas apologizes for it and explains the subterfuge that he used to distance himself from its content: what the letter imputes to *Mundo nuevo* is not the writer's own judgment but a comment that was published in a Cuban cultural supplement, from which Arenas craftily quoted. Moreover, he prefaced his objection to *Mundo nuevo*'s publication of his work by noting, "I have no other alternative" ("Revista *Mundo nuevo*"), an attempt to call attention to the coercion under which he wrote the letter. At a time when writers in Cuba could survive, according to Arenas, only by "shutting up, acquiescing [or] feigning to acquiesce" ("Grito, luego existo" 17), he opted here for the third alternative. In some of his essays, including the one on José Martí that appeared with the letter to *Mundo nuevo* in the same issue of *La gaceta de Cuba*, Arenas is equally devious. For instance, when he says in "Magia y persecución en José Martí" that the poet he so admires always wrote taking the necessary "precautions" (14) because he was constantly being persecuted, Arenas is arguably writing about himself. It is noteworthy that his statement about the precautions that persecuted writers have to take, which obliquely references his own situation, appears in an essay that immediately precedes his letter to *Mundo nuevo*, the writing of which involved taking such precautions.

Arenas's use of a rhetoric of indirection is also evident in "Tres mujeres y el amor," an essay on the Austrian writer Robert Musil that appeared the following year, in 1969, in *La gaceta de Cuba*. It begins by explaining that

> "unconventional conduct," "tendencies to certain excesses," "immoral and perverse" were the most common epithets used to describe Musil . . . during his life as a writer. He (like many artists) was the one who had to be the insubordinate, the nonconformist, the one who looked beyond reality (or more deeply into it) and reached alarming conclusions. (26)

Arenas goes on to argue that Musil, living in profound loneliness, produced a body of work in which he expressed his anguish and skepticism. This, according to Arenas, guaranteed "the scheming of mediocre people" and Musil's "official excommunication" (26). Seeing himself in the "immoral," "perverse," "insubordinate," and "nonconformist" Musil (analogous epithets were being used for him at the time), Arenas publicly, albeit indirectly, ponders his own "official excommunication," which was under way as he was writing about himself in the guise of two writers — Musil and Martí — whom he held in high esteem.

Although Arenas's difficulties had started in 1965, when cultural ideologues did not receive favorably the manuscript of *Celestino antes del alba*, it was not until three years later, in 1968, and especially after the publication in France of *Le Monde hallucinant*, that his "problems" in Cuba, as he put it, went from being something abstract to something absolutely real ("El mar es siempre el símbolo fundamental de la liberación" 252). Arenas's essays continued to appear in Cuban journals until 1970 (four were published that year), but his situation at the UNEAC drastically changed thereafter. Like other young writers who had fallen into disfavor, he was demoted to proofreader, and eventually those in this position were not allowed to do anything at all — just show up, attend meetings, and applaud. More significantly, Arenas became the object of constant harassment and vigilance by the secret police for writing works that deviated from the socialist realist mode and failed to celebrate the Revolution, for smuggling his manuscripts out of Cuba, and for living a promiscuous gay life.

Years later, in *Antes que anochezca*, Arenas had no qualms about telling his readers that in Cuba he regularly had sex on public beaches with multiple partners, that young men queued up outside his room waiting to have sex with him, and that by the age of twenty-five he had had sex with thousands of men. According to Arenas, same-sex sexuality was pervasive in Cuba among men; *locas* (passive partners who identify as homosexuals) and *bugarrones* (active partners who do not identify as homosexuals) regularly engaged in sex despite the repressive measures imposed by the state or, in a Foucauldian twist, precisely because of them:

> I think that the sexual revolution in Cuba actually came about as a result of the existing sexual repression. Perhaps as a protest against the regime, homosexuality began to flourish with ever-increasing defiance. Moreover, since the dictatorship was considered evil, anything it proscribed was seen in a positive light by the nonconformists, who in the sixties were already almost the majority. I honestly believe that the concentration camps for homosexuals, and the police officers disguised as willing young men to entrap and arrest homosexuals, actually resulted in the promotion of homosexual activities.
> (*Antes que anochezca* 132–33; *Before Night Falls* 107)

A dissident writer who was also publicly and defiantly gay, Arenas was targeted by those in power for not adhering to Cuba's prescribed literary, moral, political, and social norms. He continued to write incessantly, however, having to rewrite some of his manuscripts several times after they mysteriously found their way into the hands of the secret police.

Ultimately, in June 1974, Arenas was arrested on a sex charge, after two young men accused him and a friend of fondling them on a Havana beach. According to Arenas's memoirs, the four men had had consensual sex, but when Arenas's friend accused the two young men of stealing their beach bags, they retaliated by telling the police that Arenas and his friend had groped them. Not surprisingly, the police chose to believe the young men's story. Arenas was freed on bail, but in November of that year was detained without explanation. (He later wrote that he suspected that someone close to him who knew that he was planning to flee the island had informed on him.) Taking advantage of his jailers' carelessness, Arenas managed to escape from the police station. He then attempted to leave Cuba with an inner tube, as many Cubans had done before him, an act of desperation that he aborted after having been at sea for a few hours. Once back on Cuban soil, Arenas viewed dying as his only option and slashed his wrists, a suicide attempt that failed. He then traveled to eastern Cuba to try to escape via the

United States Naval Base in Guantanamo; after two unsuccessful attempts, however, he returned to Havana, where he lived as a fugitive in Lenin Park until his capture, on 9 December 1974.

Arenas was tried on charges of molesting two "boys," who, according to his account in *Antes que anochezca*, were not minors and who, inexplicably and to the chagrin of the presiding judge, refused to testify against him. Arenas was cleared of the charge of corrupting minors but was sentenced to jail for public scandal. This, Arenas claims, was a conspiracy on the part of the government to contain the sexual outlaw as well as the dissident writer who had smuggled some of his works out of the country. But by portraying him as a common — not a political — criminal, the Cuban authorities were attempting to avoid an international scandal. Arenas insists in his memoirs that he was the victim of an act of police entrapment, which was carried out in collaboration with the UNEAC and Coco Salá, the "friend" who was with Arenas the day he was arrested. Salá, unlike Arenas, did not serve a jail term, even though one of the two accusers identified him as having made the initial sexual proposition. Corroborating Arenas's account, Juan Abreu reports that the official accusation against Arenas was limited to a sexual crime; he is convinced that the political ramifications of the case were not addressed at the trial because the government wanted to avoid at all costs an "Arenas Affair," a repeat of the notorious "Padilla Affair" (*A la sombra del mar* 143, 159–60).

While in jail (from December 1974 to January 1976), Arenas signed a confession under duress in which he renounced his "homosexual condition," admitted that he was a "counterrevolutionary," regretted his "ideological weaknesses," and promised to write "optimistic novels" (*Antes que anochezca* 229; *Before Night Falls* 205). Before his capture, however, Arenas had written a communiqué, on 15 November 1974, to the International Red Cross, the United Nations, and UNESCO in which he related the gravity of his situation, noting, "I should . . . hurry up and say that what I say here is the truth, even if in the future, using torture, they make me say the opposite" ("Comunicado" 151). In a clandestine meeting at Lenin Park, Arenas gave the communiqué to Joris Lagarde, a Frenchman who knew the Camachos in France and who went to Cuba as part of a plan to help Arenas escape from the island. The plan failed and the communiqué was not published, for fear of the consequences that its publication might have on its author. In April 1975, however, a note ("Arenas disparu?") was published in the Paris newspaper *Le Figaro*, which made reference to the communiqué and to the fact that Arenas's whereabouts in the previous five months were unknown.

Arenas regarded the 1970s as the worst ten years of his life, a decade in which he experienced ostracism, imprisonment, and homelessness. Upon his release from prison in 1976, Arenas had no place to turn for work or for housing. Not unexpectedly, UNEAC refused to reinstate him in his job, invoking a law unfavorable to persons who had been incarcerated for over a year. Arenas initially relied on the generosity of friends, who gave him lodging and took up collections on his behalf. In 1977 he moved to a room in a rundown hotel in old Havana, where he lived and led a picaresque life until his departure from Cuba in 1980. Arenas survived his last years in Havana by dint of his wit and thanks to the existence of a thriving black market. He sold fruit that he and others picked in Matanzas province, wood and assorted objects from a condemned convent that he and his friends ransacked, and clothing and other items that the Camachos periodically sent him from France.

Arenas may have had no official status as a writer in his country, but in the eyes of some, especially young aspiring writers in Cuba, he became a mythical figure. Abilio Estévez remembers:

> When I first met Reinaldo Arenas, one afternoon toward the end of 1976, I had not yet read his work. . . . It made no difference that he was barely thirty-four or that a categorical and official silence surrounded his work; he was already a celebrity. Among us, the young people of the time, he had an aura of irreverence and mystery, a tropical François Villon, famous in Paris and New York, even more sacred because we had no way of reading him: any attempt to obtain one of his books was all but condemned to failure. Literary tradition has proved — examples abound — that prohibition is the first step on the way to fame. In those 1970s, years of my first dazzlements, the myth of Reinaldo Arenas had already begun. . . . He had already been in prison and . . . he lived a very dissolute, almost marginal life. He was recognized as a literary mystic. (859)

Virgilio Piñera and José Lezama Lima, among others, clandestinely made available to some of these young writers their copies of Arenas's works. Jesús Barquet recalls that Lezama, from whom he borrowed *El mundo alucinante*, derived pleasure in participating in "the mythification of that

Jean Genet" ("Rebeldía e irreverencia de Reinaldo Arenas" 33). Zoé Valdés evokes her reading of *Celestino antes del alba*, which, although published in Cuba, "nobody found anywhere, but it was read anyway, borrowed, going from hand to hand, rented at times, stolen at others" (280).

Despite the efforts to silence Arenas, he was nonetheless "heard" on the island and beyond. Since important publishers in other countries published his books in their original Spanish and in translation, Arenas was internationally recognized as a major voice in Latin American letters. In Cuba, meanwhile, he was an underground writer leading a precarious and vagabond life. His international reputation notwithstanding, Arenas, a *no-persona* (non-person) in his own country since the late 1960s, had to wait some twelve years to become a full person again.[25] For it was not until 1980, after several unsuccessful attempts to escape from Cuba, that he successfully engineered a way to leave the island during the confusion of the Mariel boatlift. Because he was an internationally acclaimed dissident writer, Arenas knew that the Cuban authorities would not willingly grant him permission to leave the island, despite the fact that he belonged to the despised and disposable "scum" that they were making every effort to expel. Arenas nonetheless went to the police station in his neighborhood, as was required, to request his exit permit, which was granted after officials there, who did not know who "Reinaldo Arenas" was, had ascertained that he was a "homosexual." As Arenas puts it in *Antes que anochezca*, "I left as just another faggot, not as a writer" (302; *Before Night Falls* 282). On 4 May 1980, having changed on his passport the "e" in his last name to an "i," Reinaldo Arenas left Cuba as "Reinaldo Arinas," a name that did not appear on the State Security list of people not authorized to leave the island, against which the passport of everyone at the port of Mariel was checked. Moments after Arenas's departure, loudspeakers at Mariel called out his name, but Arenas finally had outsmarted the Cuban regime.

It is undeniable that Arenas the writer was a product of the Cuban Revolution. Arenas himself would agree that had it not been for Castro's toppling of Batista's dictatorship, he probably would not have had the opportunity to leave his poor family in Oriente province to pursue his aspirations in Havana, where he was nurtured and mentored by Cuba's literati. But it is also very clear that the same revolution that initially opened doors to the poor young man from the provinces soon thereafter closed them. Ostracized since the late 1960s but more forcefully after the Revolution's Stalinist turn in the early 1970s, Arenas officially ceased to exist. According to Arenas, when foreign writers visiting the country sought him out, the official line they were given was that Cuba did not have a writer named Reinaldo Arenas. Even before his "true" exile in 1980, Arenas had already been exiled from his country. For his gay sexuality and his intellectual integrity, Arenas, like Lezama and Piñera, two Cuban literary giants about whom he eloquently writes in his memoirs, was banished to an internal — and what seemed to be an eternal — exile. He was an outcast in Cuba for remaining true to his convictions as a transgressive writer, a gay man, and a sexual revolutionary.

After a long and arduous sea voyage, Arenas arrived in the United States, on 6 May 1980. The first thing that he did in Key West, where United States immigration officials processed Cubans arriving from Mariel, was to make himself presentable. As he writes in *Antes que anochezca*, "I bathed, shaved, and started once again to look like a human being" (306; *Before Night Falls* 286). Beginning the textual reconstruction of his exile with a description of the transformation of his appearance, Arenas describes in this passage of his memoirs more than a routine bodily act by someone who was rescued after having been lost at sea for days. Arenas also sets in motion an erotics of exile: like a hopeful lover primping for a date, the newcomer showers, shaves, and dresses in anticipation of a crucial encounter. Anxious to forge a new life in the United States, Arenas tries to make himself attractive to whatever or whoever comes before him. For Arenas,

> the exile is a person who, having lost a loved one, keeps searching for
> the face he loves in every new face and, forever deceiving himself,
> thinks he has found it. I thought I had found that face in New York,
> when I arrived here in 1980. The city took me into its fold. I felt as if I
> had arrived in a glorified Havana, with great sidewalks, fabulous the-
> aters, a transportation system that worked marvelously, streets that
> were lively, and all kinds of people who spoke many different lan-
> guages; I did not feel like a stranger in New York. (*Antes que ano-
> chezca* 315; *Before Night Falls* 293)

In New York City, where he established residency shortly after his arrival in the United States to put distance between himself and the materialism, anti-intellectualism, homophobia, and bourgeois morality that he associated with Cuban exiles in Miami, Arenas, happily engaging in the erotic and the literary, initially found life to be "a constant celebration" (*Antes que ano-chezca* 318; *Before Night Falls* 297).[26]

Although Arenas regained in exile what he considered his lost humanity, his geographical displacement from Cuba to the United States ultimately signified a major loss, that of his beloved island, a loss the magnitude of which he soon had to confront. So attractive from afar, the United States quickly lost for Arenas its seductive charm. Having gone into exile in search of an uncertain future but at least a promising one, an expectant Arenas eventually realized that the auspicious "romance" for which he had hoped could only lead to disappointment:

> I realize that an exile has no place where he can live, because he is no-where, because the place where we started to dream, where we dis-covered the natural world around us, read our first book, loved for the first time, is always the world of our dreams. In exile one is nothing but a ghost, the shadow of someone who never achieves full reality. I ceased to exist when I went into exile. (*Antes que anochezca* 314; *Before Night Falls* 293)

Arenas did not find a home—or ever feel at home—in exile, where he constantly and achingly felt a double loss, not only that of his home, but also of his selfhood:

> What I miss the most about Cuba is . . . myself. The person I was, in a Cuban context, who lived in a small room in Havana, who would chat with his next-door neighbor, and whom his friends would visit at all hours at night. What I miss the most about Cuba is the fact that there I did not have to question my existence because I was abso-lutely sure of it. Once I went into exile, my existence is incessantly questioned. What am I? Am I Cuban, Hispanic, Latino? It is really a tragedy. What I miss the most about Cuba is, in short, the authen-ticity I have lost. ("La vida es riesgo o abstinencia" 61)

In the end, exile was for Arenas nothing more than a journey from one form of nonexistence to another.

Living in Hell's Kitchen, a seedy neighborhood in midtown Manhattan, and practicing what he called "the freedom of poverty" ("Entrevista ex-clusiva a Reinaldo Arenas" 20), Arenas survived on the modest income generated by meager book royalties, the articles he wrote for the Spanish-language press, speaking engagements, the occasional fellowship or visiting professorship, and a small annuity from Princeton University Library (the repository of his manuscripts and personal papers). His "sustenance" came from the act of writing, to which he was totally devoted and in which he found refuge from the hardships of exile. For Arenas, exile was difficult in part because of the materialism of United States culture, to which he felt other exiled Cubans too happily subscribed. Arenas also disapproved of the identity politics embraced by racial, ethnic, and sexual minorities in the United States. As if this were not enough, he missed sex with masculine "straight" men, which he had most enjoyed in Cuba.

Although in exile Arenas continued to lead a promiscuous erotic life, which included "memorable adventures" in New York's Central Park (*Antes que anochezca* 327; *Before Night Falls* 306), he became increasingly dissatisfied with both the sexual reciprocity that seemed to be the norm among gay-identified men in the United States and the greater sexual distance between gay- and straight-identified men in his new country. Arenas waxed nostalgic about his sexual life in Cuba, which was not ghettoized and which was marked, in his case, by the pursuit of "real men":

> In Cuba gays were not confined to a specific area of a club or beach. Everybody mingled and there was no division that would place the homosexual on the defensive. This has been lost in more advanced societies, where the homosexual has had to become a sort of sexual recluse and separate himself from the supposedly nonhomosexual society, which undoubtedly also excludes him. Since such divisions did not exist in Cuba, the interesting aspect of homosexuality there was that you did not have to be a homosexual to have a relationship with a man; a man could have intercourse with another man as an ordinary act. In the same way, a queen who liked another queen could easily go out and live with her. But the queen who liked real men [*hombres de verdad*] could also find a man who wanted to live or be friends with her, without in any way interfering with the heterosexual life of that man. It was not the norm for a queen to go to bed with another queen, but rather to look for a man who would fuck her and feel as much pleasure as she would when being fucked. (*Antes que anochezca* 133; *Before Night Falls* 107–8)

Arenas may have been able to have access to a sexual life without fear of persecution in the United States, but the kind of sex that he felt was available to him was, for the most part, quite unsatisfying. Cuba, for many reasons, was always on his mind.

At odds with Cuban Americans and even more so with other Latinos in the United States and at the same time disengaged from mainstream United States culture and the gay community, whose political and sexual practices he spurned, Arenas, a self-proclaimed loner, turned to where he always felt at home: the blank page. In New York, Arenas revised at a rapid pace texts that he had smuggled out of Cuba, rewrote lost and confiscated manuscripts, and penned new works. Although at first important publishers had been eager to publish these works in their original Spanish and in translation, Arenas soon discovered that some of those same publishers, partly because of his denunciations of Castro's regime, no longer warmly welcomed his works. According to Thomas Colchie, his literary agent, "In Germany and Spain there was a conspiracy not to publish him, and the same in Latin America. For people on the left in Latin America, the Cuban Revolution was a dream. It was acceptable to be a dissident in Eastern Europe, but there was no such thing as a dissident in Cuba" (qtd. in Stoffman).

Arenas's political activism involved regular participation in public events that were at times raucous, the publication of articles that were often enraged and intemperate, and the writing of spirited letters that he had no qualms about sending to what he deemed Castro-supporting newspapers, organizations, and institutions. The culmination of his political work occurred in 1988, with an open letter to Fidel Castro. Inspired by what Chileans had achieved that year with a referendum in which they expressed their views on Chile's future, Arenas and his coauthor, Jorge Camacho, demanded a plebiscite that would allow Cubans to vote on whether they wished Castro to remain in power. Although the letter failed in its goal, Arenas was proud of the support it received, as it had been signed by an impressive number of prominent figures from around the world and disseminated widely in the international media.[27]

With his characteristically caustic humor, Arenas quipped in *Antes que anochezca* that "the difference between the communist and capitalist systems is that, although both give you a kick in the ass, in the communist system you have to applaud, while in the capitalist system you can scream. And I came here to scream" (309; *Before Night Falls* 288). And it was primarily because of his sustained "screaming," in his writing and public appearances, that Arenas continued to face obstacles and opposition, which for him were in many ways reminiscent of the problems he had experienced in Cuba. As a *marielito* (a pejorative term reserved for those who left Cuba in 1980) and as a gay man to boot, he was not looked on kindly by many in the established Cuban exile community. And as a Cuban intellectual in exile, that is, as an exile from a totalitarian regime of the Left, he felt shunned—declared "invisible" — by the non-Cuban Latin American exile community, which was comprised primarily of exiles from totalitarian regimes of the Right. Cuban intellectuals residing off the island suffered a double exile, argued Arenas, for they were "condemned to disappear twice" ("La represión [intelectual] en Cuba" 92). First, he claimed, the Cuban government erased them from the cultural map of their country; and, second, leftist intellectuals residing in capitalist countries declared an all-out war to silence them. According to Arenas, this "festive" or "frivolous" Left (*Antes que anochezca* 310, 320; *Before Night Falls* 289, 299) sabotaged his public appearances, left his books out of course syllabi at major universities, made it difficult for him to publish his works, and excluded him and other Cuban writers in exile from general discussions of the Latin American exile experience. Arenas explained, "I realized that the war had started all over again, now in a much more underhanded manner; it was less terrible than Fidel's war against intellectuals in Cuba, albeit no less sinister" (*Antes que anochezca* 309; *Before Night Falls* 288).

The Cuban American poet Octavio Armand (among others) agreed with Arenas that there was a tendency among Latin American intellectuals to exclude Cubans from discussions addressing the issue of exile. Reacting to articles on exile writers by the Peruvian Julio Ortega and the Uruguayan Ángel Rama, Armand wrote in 1980, "A Cuban writer is exiled not only from his country but also from the Latin American diaspora. He is outside Cuba and outside exile. He has no right to his history and neither to the history of exile. He must be a ghost among ghosts with a vocation for statue-like immobility" ("Minicurso para borrar al escritor cubano del exilio" 87).[28] Not one with a vocation for statue-like immobility, Arenas went into action soon after arriving in the United States in what would become his first public and perhaps most contentious confrontation. Offended by the exclusion of Cuban writers from the September–December 1981 issue of *Review*, which devoted one of its sections to literature and exile but limited its scope to the Southern Cone, Arenas denounced the journal's narrow focus. That its editor, Luis Harss, had indicated that future issues would treat exile writers from other Latin American countries did not temper Arenas's reaction.

An acrimonious exchange ensued between Arenas and the contributing editor Ángel Rama, whom Arenas had met in Cuba in the late 1960s, a meeting that had resulted in the Uruguayan's smuggling out of Cuba the manuscript of *Con los ojos cerrados*, Arenas's first collection of short stories, which Rama published in Montevideo in 1972. Arenas may have been excessive in his reaction to what he considered a politically motivated decision on the part of *Review*, though Rama and the staff of the journal might not have been as sensitive — and politic — as they could have been when preparing the issue, given that the recently exiled Arenas was a frequent visitor at the Center for Inter-American Relations, the New York institution that published *Review*. One can understand why Arenas would not keep silent when encountering discussions about the Latin American exile experience that did not include Cubans living off the island, but he can be faulted for his vitriol and his baseless claim that Rama was a communist, which Arenas presented as the reason for the exclusion of Cubans from *Review*'s cluster of essays on exile.[29]

A socialist, Rama had distanced himself from Castro's Cuba in 1969, in disagreement with the regime's adoption of the Soviet model. Rama also claims to have been the only one to complain to Castro about the intolerable situation of homosexuals in the UMAP camps at a meeting of intellectuals with the Cuban leader in 1967. With regard to Arenas in particular, Rama admired him and continued to support his literary career after Arenas's departure from Cuba, as attested, for instance, by the fact that he recommended him for a Guggenheim fellowship and asked him to collaborate on an anthology that he was editing. In a long letter to Arenas, dated 30 November 1981, before the issue of *Review* came out, Rama expressed his disappointment in Arenas's indiscriminate generalizations about leftist intellectuals, advised him not to get embroiled in the passionate atmosphere typical among Cubans on and off the island, and encouraged him to dedicate himself completely to his writing. Arenas's response to Rama's letter, the patronizing tone of which may have been difficult for Arenas to take, is not known. But shortly thereafter, when the issue of *Review* appeared, Arenas lashed out at the journal and especially at Rama, an explosive reaction not uncommon with Arenas, for it would be repeated in subsequent situations in which Arenas felt affronted or aggrieved.[30]

Arenas's vast correspondence documents the difficult relationship that he had with publishers, against some of whom he directed his sarcasm and insults, calling them thieves and scoundrels. He repeatedly threatened to take legal action against them because of what he considered to be breaches of contract, meager advances and royalties, and sloppy production of his books. Although there may have been instances in which Arenas's anger was justified, his reactions were at times disproportionate. Arenas quarreled, for instance, with the Cuban writer Severo Sarduy, who for years was the editor of the Latin American list at Editions du Seuil, which published several of Arenas's works. During the process of translating *Otra vez el mar* into French, Arenas and Sarduy's relationship, which had been simultaneously professional and playful (many of their letters were quite campy), came to an ugly end. Furious because of the many erroneous translations that plagued *Encore une fois la mer* and displeased with the novel's cover, blurb, format, and typeface, Arenas assailed Sarduy, whom he held responsible for what he regarded as intentional flaws. He reacted with mordant attacks in his correspondence, unfounded accusations in his autobiography, and vicious caricatures in his fiction, depicting Sarduy as a deceitful and jealous figure who had sabotaged his work.[31]

Many others, including people who were close to him, were targets of Arenas's rage and vituperative tongue, as was the case, for instance, with Liliane Hasson, a translator with whom he had established a personal relationship. Because of a mistranslation in the French version of the novella *Viaje a La Habana*, Arenas became furious at Hasson, a reaction that, in retrospect, he categorized as "violent" and which he came to regret and for which he apologized (see *Cartas a Margarita y Jorge Camacho* 316, 318). The Colombian American writer Jaime Manrique, who was Arenas's neighbor in New York, recalls Arenas's anger when on one occasion Manrique offered Arenas what he thought was practical counsel:

> Once, in the mid-eighties, I had tried to tell him to put behind him his years of imprisonment and persecution, to forget Cuba, to accept this country as his new home and to live in the present. "You just don't understand, do you?" he had shouted, shaking with anger. "I feel like one of those Jews who were branded with a number by the

Nazis; like a concentration camp survivor. There is no way on earth I can forget what I went through. It's my duty to remember. This," he roared, hitting his chest, "will not be over until Castro is dead. Or I am dead." ("The Last Days of Reinaldo Arenas" 67)

Although Manrique disagreed with Arenas's politics, he, unlike others, was sensitive to his friend's painful history and did not take offense at Arenas's vehement response to his comment. In Manrique's case, unlike in Hasson's, no apology would be forthcoming. In matters regarding Cuba, Arenas felt that he had the right and the responsibility to behave as he did.

There is truth to Arenas's claim that, as a Cuban exile, he was often misunderstood and disparaged by many who did not share his politics. To attribute all his misfortunes, however, to a political conspiracy against him, as Arenas tended to do, is simplistic. Arenas's anti-Castro stance and his obstinacy on matters Cuban indeed accounted for many of his adversities in exile, but undoubtedly so did his caustic temperament. Arenas's close friends, who readily referred to his generosity, kindness, and humility, acknowledged that Arenas could be explosive, paranoid, and belligerent. This "other" Arenas, who in exile first surfaced publicly in sarcastic articles that he wrote about the Castro sympathizers Julio Cortázar and Gabriel García Márquez and in his dispute with Ángel Rama, was likely responsible in no small part for the difficulties that he encountered in matters personal and professional.[32] "It wasn't easy being his friend," declared Roberto Valero ("La tétrica mofeta en su palacio blanquísimo" 48), who understood Arenas's complex character, which had been shaped by a life of injustice and persecution that few have experienced and which, Arenas was convinced, few could understand. In *Antes que anochezca*, referring to himself and his friend Lázaro Gómez Carriles and the two decades that they lived under Castro, Arenas explains, "And for Cubans who, like us, suffered persecution for twenty years in that terrible world, there is really no solace anywhere. Suffering has marked us forever, and only with people who have gone through a similar experience can we perhaps find some level of understanding" (330; *Before Night Falls* 308). Unable to find solace or understanding, and attributing roadblocks that he encountered in his personal and professional life to the machinations, jealousies, and pettiness of others, Arenas found revenge in the power of the word, alienating friends and foes alike.

Despite all the turmoil in his life, Arenas never lost sight of who and what he was: a writer, first and foremost. But for him, as he explains in *Antes que anochezca*, the erotic and the literary were intertwined, since he was convinced that "the body needs to feel satisfied to give free rein to the spirit" (127; *Before Night Falls* 101).[33] If before the AIDS epidemic Arenas engaged in his writing as compulsively as he did in sex, in the mid-1980s, fearful of HIV infection, he gave up sex and channeled all his energies into his writing. In 1985 he wrote to the Camachos, "New York with the AIDS problem . . . is unbearable. . . . Fortunately my health is good . . . , but psychologically it is very depressing living in the center of the plague. . . . As you can understand, I'm leading a chaste life" (*Cartas a Margarita y Jorge Camacho* 168). A year later, in 1986, Arenas shared his fears with them: "I live in terror and have made vows of chastity. . . . You can imagine my desperation. What I do is write a lot" (177). In 1989, already suffering from AIDS, Arenas wrote to his friends, "Yesterday I rode my bike in Central Park. I even had an indecent proposition from a huge black man that unfortunately I cannot accept anymore. I have become accustomed to my monastic life and that has helped me to work a lot" (264). If declining a sexual advance must have been difficult for Arenas, feeling undesirable, as he was made to feel a few months later when he entered a public toilet, was intolerable. "Nobody paid any attention to me, and the erotic games going on proceeded undisturbed," he recalls in *Antes que anochezca*, adding, "Right then and there I thought that the best thing for me was to die" (9; *Before Night Falls* ix).

Struggling with AIDS-related illnesses, Arenas frantically immersed himself in the completion of his literary work, desperately writing, as he wrote to the Camachos on 16 May 1990, "in a struggle against death but treating her like a friend" (*Cartas a Margarita y Jorge Camacho* 293). Until the end, Arenas cared most deeply about having his finished manuscripts in print, and he entrusted his friends with the task of carrying out his dying wish. On 24 May 1990, Arenas reminded the Camachos that his writing was what gave meaning to his life, and he movingly ended this letter by imploring them to make sure that *El color del verano* (*The Color of Summer*), which he had just completed, would not be "mutilated" when published. "Que no lo mutilen" are the letter's last words (*Cartas a Margarita y Jorge Camacho* 299). An AIDS-ravaged Arenas, as if seeing himself in his body of work, hoped to spare his last novel the disfigurement that his body had to endure. Having finished the *pentagonía* and *Antes que anochezca*, Arenas committed suicide on 7 December 1990.[34] He left a suicide letter (which is appended to his autobiography):

Dear friends:

Due to my delicate state of health and to the terrible emotional depression it causes me not to be able to continue writing and struggling for the freedom of Cuba, I am ending my life. During the past few years, even though I felt very ill, I have been able to finish my literary work, to which I have devoted almost thirty years. You are the heirs of all my terrors, but also of my hope that Cuba will soon be free. I am satisfied to have contributed, though in a very small way, to the triumph of this freedom. I end my life voluntarily because I cannot continue working. Persons near me are in no way responsible for my decision. There is only one person I hold accountable: Fidel Castro. The sufferings of exile, the pain of being banished from my country, the loneliness, and the diseases contracted in exile would probably never have happened if I had been able to enjoy freedom in my country.

I want to encourage the Cuban people out of the country as well as on the Island to continue fighting for freedom. I do not want to convey to you a message of defeat but of continued struggle and of hope.

Cuba will be free. I already am. (*Antes que anochezca* 343; *Before Night Falls* 317)

Alone, in his walk-up apartment in Hell's Kitchen, Arenas ended his life, leaving a message of hope, a fitting finale for a man who would not accept defeat. At his memorial service, which was attended by a small group of friends, Thomas Colchie, his literary agent, referred to Arenas's limited readership during his years in exile and lamented to Jaime Manrique, "When he was alive, I couldn't give his books away" (qtd. in Manrique, "After Night Falls" 67). Not long before committing suicide, Arenas told his friend Armando Álvarez Bravo that his death would result in wider distribution of his work because after one dies one's defects are forgiven ("Reinaldo Arenas: 'Escribir es un acto de irreverencia'" 5D). Arenas was indeed prescient about the fate of his life's work after his death. With the posthumous publication of *Antes que anochezca* in 1992, its English translation in 1993, and, ultimately, its film adaptation by Julian Schnabel in 2000, Arenas finally — and sadly in many ways — began to enjoy in death the wide acclaim that he was denied in life.

In 1989 Arenas wrote his "Autoepitafio," a twenty-eight-line poem the last four lines of which read:

Ordenó que sus cenizas fueran lanzadas al mar
donde habrán de fluir constantemente.
No ha perdido la costumbre de soñar:
espera que en sus aguas se zambulla algún adolescente.

He arranged for his ashes to be scattered in the ocean
where they would be in constant flow.
Not having given up his habit of dreaming,
he is hopeful that an adolescent will dive into those waters.

Arenas's ashes still await their resting place — they are to be scattered in Cuban waters when Castro's regime is no longer in power — but his works are already "in constant flow" in many hearts and minds.[35] Against all odds, during a lifetime of internal and external exiles, Arenas remained true to his word, invariably faithful to his life's motto: "I scream, therefore I am." Only death silenced the eternally exiled Arenas. His writing, however, continues to scream for him, loudly and clearly expressing his views on sexuality, family, and Cuba.

TWO

Climbing the Family Tree

....

Trees have a secret life that is only revealed to
those willing to climb them.
REINALDO ARENAS,
Antes que anochezca (*Before Night Falls*)

I begin with *El palacio de las blanquísimas mofetas* (*The Palace of the White Skunks*), which first appeared in French in 1975 and German in 1977 before its publication in the original Spanish in Venezuela in March 1980, two months before Reinaldo Arenas's arrival in the United States. The manuscript of Arenas's third published novel, which is the second installment of his *pentagonía*, was smuggled out of the island, bearing the title *Resumen científico de la flora cubana*, among the books of a Frenchwoman who taught botany at the University of Havana and who admired Arenas's works (see Arenas, "Conversación con Reinaldo Arenas" 56; and Arenas, "Cronología"). It is significant that *El palacio de las blanquísimas mofetas* reached international publishers disguised as a botany book, because this novel is indeed about trees, though not the types of trees that are studied by botanists. *El palacio de las blanquísimas mofetas* is concerned with trees of a different nature: family trees, personal and literary.

Where Is My Father?

Despite its title, there is no palace and there are no skunks in *El palacio de las blanquísimas mofetas*. Instead, there is an impoverished house in Holguín, a provincial city in eastern Cuba, which is inhabited by peculiar characters: the protagonist, Fortunato, an adolescent who tries, unsuccessfully, to join Castro's revolutionary forces against the dictator Fulgencio Batista to escape from the *bestias*, or beasts, as his family members are repeatedly called; Onérica, Fortunato's single mother, now working as a maid in New York, whose letters from abroad no one reads; Celia, a crazy aunt, who thinks only about her daughter, Esther, who poisoned herself at thirteen; another aunt, Digna, who cannot forget the husband who abandoned her and left her with two mischievous children, Tico and Anisia, who spend their days playing cruel games and telling each other riddles; still another aunt, Adolfina, the oldest of five sisters, who burns herself to death after her last futile attempt to lose her virginity during a nocturnal quest for men; and the two grandparents: Jacinta, who blasphemes and prays with equal ease and whose verbal outbursts contrast with the self-inflicted silence of her husband Polo, a Spanish immigrant whose dreams of success were gradually shattered.

As this character inventory shows, *El palacio de las blanquísimas mofetas* is a family saga that lacks the authoritative presence of a patriarchal figure. Tico, Anisia, and Esther have been abandoned by their fathers; Fortunato, born out of wedlock, grows up without a father, whom he happens to see only once in his life, at age five; and Polo, the only father in the house, cedes control to his spouse and progeny, thereby ensuring the dissolution of familial order and hierarchy. The disintegration of the family unit destroys what Patricia Tobin has called the "genealogical imperative," the link in family novels between the narrative line and the dynastic line. In *El palacio de las blanquísimas mofetas* paternal and narrative authority is replaced by familial and textual anarchy: just as there is no father to enforce obedience and guarantee legitimacy, there is no central authorial voice to beget a coherent, continuous text. The plot does not unfold as a controlled succession of events, but as a fragmented and temporally disjointed recording of voices, mostly the *quejas*, or complaints, of the characters, including those of the dead whose *agonías*, or agonies, are heard from beyond the grave.[1] A basic narrator — the voice of Arenas's hometown and a caricature of the omniscient narrator of traditional novels — surfaces sporadically in an attempt to make intelligible a tale that is, in Arenas's words, "rather delirious" ("Entrevista: Reinaldo Arenas" 47). Notwithstanding the novel's complex narrative fabric, characterized by nominal elisions, the juxtaposition of incidents temporally and spatially unrelated to produce a sense of simultaneity, shifts in perspective, and polyphony, *El palacio de las blanquísimas mofetas* gradually allows the reader to apprehend the compelling — and sad — tale that it tells: the story of a fatherless son who struggles growing up in a dysfunctional household and whose life is cut short after he is tortured by Batista's men and left to die hanging from a tree on the outskirts of his hometown.

By the book's end, the reader has gained access to an enigmatic palace of words populated by strange creatures who engage in eccentric actions. In spite of its apparent nonsensicalness, the title fits the novel just right: in Arenas's topsy-turvy world, the Jamesian "house of fiction" has become a "palace of skunks."[2] This is a palace, moreover, whose resident skunks have emigrated from another house of fiction — not Henry James's but that of another master of realism, one not from the anglophone but from the hispanophone world, Benito Pérez Galdós, arguably the most highly re-garded nineteenth-century novelist in Spain. For some of the principal "skunks" in Arenas's textual palace — the "beasts" in the jungle, as it were, echoing the title of one of James's stories — are twentieth-century reincarna-tions of some of the most memorable residents in Pérez Galdós's most populous house of fiction, *Fortunata y Jacinta* (*Fortunata and Jacinta*), the novel universally regarded as the Spaniard's masterpiece.

One should not be surprised that Arenas wrote *El palacio de las blan-quísimas mofetas* in dialogue with another text. *El mundo alucinante* (*The Ill-Fated Peregrinations of Fray Servando*), his second — and best-known — novel, had been an imaginative rewriting of the memoirs of Fray Servando Teresa de Mier, a rebellious friar of colonial Mexico. This penchant for intertextuality, so cleverly deployed in *El mundo alucinante*, marked Are-nas's writing career. For instance, *La Loma del Ángel* (*Graveyard of the An-gels*) and "El Cometa Halley" ("Halley's Comet") are parodic rewritings of Cirilo Villaverde's antislavery novel *Cecilia Valdés* (*Cecilia Valdés*) and Fede-rico García Lorca's tragic play *La casa de Bernarda Alba* (*The House of Ber-narda Alba*). But, curiously, unlike *El mundo alucinante*, *La Loma del Ángel*, and "El Cometa Halley," the intertexts of which are readily made evident, Arenas's third novel does not openly acknowledge its kinship with Pérez Galdós's novel. In fact, when I first asked Arenas about the master of Span-ish realism and the presence of his masterpiece in *El palacio de las blan-quísimas mofetas*, the Cuban categorically denied any connection between the two novels and proceeded to state, "I loathe Pérez Galdós."[3] And yet, despite Arenas's protestation, *Fortunata y Jacinta* did make its way into *El palacio de las blanquísimas mofetas*.

While *El palacio de las blanquísimas mofetas* is not a sustained rewriting of *Fortunata y Jacinta*, the Cuban novel evokes the Spanish novel in the naming of some of its characters. To begin with, the names of two of the protagonists in Arenas's family romance, Fortunato and Jacinta, bring to mind the two titular characters in Pérez Galdós's novel. In *El palacio de las blanquísimas mofetas*, Pérez Galdós's attractive and sexually transgressive Fortunata undergoes a sex change, as it were, becoming the "queer" Fortunato, who, like his Galdosian counterpart, dies at the end of the narrative without having achieved his desired goal of acceptance by others. (Fortunata's goal is to have Spanish society accept her as Juanito's wife; Fortunato's goal is to have Castro's rebels accept him into the ranks of the revolutionary forces. This would allow Fortunato to have a sense of belonging, which has been denied to him by the *bestias* — his relatives — among whom he lives and who invariably make him feel like a misfit.)[4] And Jacinta, the barren wife in Pérez Galdós's novel, is transformed into a fecund matriarch, Fortunato's grandmother, who effortlessly produces offspring.

Referencing the two female protagonists of *Fortunata y Jacinta* in her discussion of *El palacio de las blanquísimas mofetas*, Julia Kushigian has noted that "the *coincidence* of Fortunato y Jacinta reinforces the Spanish family romance that is rewritten in a late twentieth-century, Cuban version" (174, emphasis added). These characters' names, however, are more than a "coincidence," for there are other links between the two novels. For instance, one of Pérez Galdós's most memorable creations in *Fortunata y Jacinta*, the affable and garrulous shopkeeper Plácido Estupiñá, also surfaces in *El palacio de las blanquísimas mofetas*. A father figure to Juanito Santa Cruz (the male protagonist of Pérez Galdós's novel), Plácido Estupiñá emerges in Arenas's novel as Fortunato's Spanish grandfather, Polo Estopiñán, the difficult and taciturn shopkeeper who, like the nineteenth-century character he re-creates, is known for eccentric verbal behavior that adversely affects his business. The "talker" Estupiñá, who "was capable of letting the best deal in the world slip through his fingers just for a bit of chit-chat" (*Fortunata y Jacinta* 144; *Fortunata and Jacinta* 35), becomes the "mute" Estopiñán, who refuses to speak with those around him, including his clients.[5] Moreover, if Pérez Galdós's novel is, according to its subtitle, *Dos historias de casadas* (*Two Stories of Married Women*), Arenas's novel is a series of stories of primarily *malcasadas*, or, in the novel's preferred term, *dejadas*, which is in essence what Fortunata and Jacinta are despite their designation as *casadas*.[6]

Although Arenas initially rejected any intertextual relationship between *El palacio de las blanquísimas mofetas* and *Fortunata y Jacinta*, he ultimately conceded, when I asked him additional questions about Pérez Galdós's masterpiece, that the Spaniard's novel might have unconsciously affected the writing of his third novel. Arenas recalled that his first exposure to *Fortunata y Jacinta* was at the Biblioteca Nacional, where a coworker made him read it, an experience that took place before he had started working on *El palacio de las blanquísimas mofetas*. Despite Arenas's dislike of Pérez Galdós's novel, he found "very interesting" the suggestive link between the Spaniard's novel and his own, recognizing that it could have been possible that *Fortunata y Jacinta* remained in his unconscious and turned up some years later in *El palacio de las blanquísimas mofetas*. Arenas went on to say, "I always felt a terrible repulsion for Pérez Galdós, and it is possible that *El palacio de las blanquísimas mofetas* may be an unconscious reaction against him." A repudiation of Pérez Galdós's mimetic enterprise, Arenas's novel, in his own words, takes up "those characters so completely realistic" and transports them "to the plane of delirium, of the imagination." It is noteworthy that Arenas, humorously comparing the prolific Pérez Galdós to a "carpenter," claimed that the Spaniard's many novels were, like chairs, "made to sit on." That is what in a literary — if not in a literal — sense *El palacio de las blanquísimas mofetas* does: it "sits" on *Fortunata y Jacinta*. As a palimpsestuous reading reveals, one can see through the text of Arenas's novel the preexisting text on which it unconsciously, and grudgingly, rests.

Arenas's antipathy for Pérez Galdós in particular and for the mimetic conventions of nineteenth-century realism in general is clearly manifest in the Cuban's many novels — not just in *El palacio de las blanquísimas mofetas* — and also in his essays and interviews. Shortly after the publication in Cuba of his first novel, *Celestino antes del alba* (*Singing from the Well*), Arenas wrote "Celestino y yo," his first of a handful of essays published in Cuba, in which he made a case for his avant-garde novel. Having lost first prize to Ezequiel Vieta's *Vivir en Candonga*, a novel written in the mode of socialist realism, the young author acknowledged not having had during the writing of *Celestino antes del alba* "the slightest intention to develop a story with a traditional plot, climax, and ending" ("Celestino y yo" 120). He distanced himself from "the superficial ones," who "swarm at an alarming rate" and to whom "everything has to be spoonfed" ("Celestino y yo" 119), which arguably alluded to, among others, the members of the jury who objected to awarding first prize to *Celestino antes del alba* when he submitted it in 1965 to the Premio Nacional de Novela Cirilo Villaverde.

With his early essays, Arenas participated in the polemics of the first decade of Castro's Cuba about the role of literature in a socialist society, insisting on the writer's responsibility to let the imagination work against the production of "the mere chronicle or simple portrait" ("Lezama o el reino de la imagen" 113).[7] From the beginning of his literary career, when the Stalinization of Cuban cultural politics was not yet official and when he was not yet totally disaffected with the Revolution, Arenas publicly argued, as did many others, against a limited concept of realism in literature, a position that put him at odds with cultural and literary ideologues who in the 1960s were promoting socialist realism.[8] Although acutely aware of the political dimension of these vigorous debates, Arenas was particularly attentive to their aesthetic implications. He recognized that nineteenth-century novelists were experimenting then in their craft as he was now in his, but he rejected as anachronistic the use of conventional realism in the twentieth century. Arenas specifically rejected socialist realism, which he regarded as dogmatic and whose adoption in Cuba had resulted in what he called "dreadful realistic novels" ("Conversation with Reinaldo Arenas" 151).[9]

If Arenas saw his novels in opposition to those of "realist" novelists like Pérez Galdós, the author of "horrible novels" and of whom he rhetorically asked, "Who reads Pérez Galdós these days?" ("Entrevista exclusiva a Reinaldo Arenas" 19), what can explain the curious link between *El palacio de las blanquísimas mofetas* and *Fortunata y Jacinta*? One may take Arenas at his word when, explaining the reason for his rewriting of *Cecilia Valdés* (Cuba's most highly regarded nineteenth-century novel) in *La Loma del Ángel*, he said, "Since I do not like the original, I write a version that I find convincing" ("Entrevista a Reinaldo Arenas" 112). But could it be more than just a corrective impulse motivated by aesthetic differences? Could there indeed be, as Arenas's musings on *El palacio de las blanquísimas mofetas* seem to suggest, an unconscious explanation for his investment in this nineteenth-century novel? It is suggestive that *Fortunata y Jacinta* has an interest in issues of paternity and, more specifically, in fatherlessness and illegitimacy. The presence of the figure of the absent father in the Spanish classic likely prompted Arenas to bond textually and emotionally with it, even as Arenas articulated his dissatisfaction with the literary mode — conventional realism — that is associated with Pérez Galdós's novel.

Fortunata y Jacinta narrates the story of Fortunata, a carefree, impulsive, and fertile woman from the lower class; and the story of Jacinta, a discreet, levelheaded, and infertile woman from the middle class. If what initially connects these two stories is the women's love for the spoiled and irresponsible Juanito Santa Cruz (he is Jacinta's husband and Fortunata's lover), what brings the stories closure is the women's love for a child over whom they bond. Before dying shortly after giving birth, Fortunata entrusts her child to Jacinta, a maternal pact that excludes the father of the child. His lover having died and his wife no longer caring for him, Juanito is last seen in the novel experiencing the "vacío de la vida" (void of life) (*Fortunata y Jacinta* 1560), a *vacío* that hints at another void, the one left by Juanito's — the father's — absence from the emotional life of his illegitimate child.[10] Suggestively, that tale of failed paternity is left untold in *Fortunata y Jacinta*, a novel that, not insignificantly, includes in its opening chapter a discussion of the role of the father in a son's upbringing.

Baldomero Santa Cruz, Juanito's father, explains to Barbarita, his wife, that his views on fatherhood differ from those of his strict father, who produced a bashful, prudish, and naïve son: a "simpleton" (*Fortunata y Jacinta* 88; *Fortunata and Jacinta* 8) who knew nothing about women and social graces. Although Baldomero admits that his father's "disciplinary rigor" (118; 23) resulted in "punishments" (118; 23) and "denials" (118; 23), he believes that "such a system had been extremely effective in bringing him up" (119; 24). He grew up to be a prosperous businessman and a good husband in an arranged marriage that, contrary to expectations, turned out well. But now, with the changing of the times, "that upbringing was not good" (89–90; 9) and Baldomero tells his wife that he wishes to raise a son who, unlike him, will experience life to the fullest:

> He's a good boy. Let him have some fun and get around. Today young men need to wake up and really see the world. These times aren't like mine, when no boy from a merchant's family got to go anywhere; they kept us tucked in till they married us off. What a difference between customs then and now! . . . Young people today have a freedom and a right to have fun that they didn't have years ago. And believe me, don't think they're any the worse for it. If you really want to know how I feel, I think it's better for boys not to be as bashful as they used to be. (88; 8)

And Baldomero adds, "I don't think Juanito will fail us in what counts" (90; 9), a confidence that his son's behavior gradually will prove unfounded. The irresponsible Juanito not only fails his father in many respects, but also fails as a father, mirroring his own father's failure. Baldomero's hands-off approach to fatherhood may have been motivated by the "boisterous paternal affection" (118; 23) that he felt for his son, but it resulted in turning him into an absent father. And when his son becomes a father at the end of the novel, he will also put distance between himself and his own son, but not for the same reasons as his father. He truly will be an absent father, an absence that the novel textually highlights with Juanito's conspicuous absence from its crucial final chapter.

Reading the account of Baldomero's and Juanito's relationships with their sons in *Fortunata y Jacinta*, a fatherless Arenas may have felt an affinity with the fatherless children in this nineteenth-century novel. Arenas may have disliked *Fortunata y Jacinta* as a novel, but because of its story of absent fathers and abandoned sons, it stayed with him and, unconsciously perhaps, made its way into *El palacio de las blanquísimas mofetas*. Arenas's concern with fathers and sons becomes even more pronounced in his later works.[11]

Fatherless children populate *El palacio de las blanquísimas mofetas*. Living in their grandparents' house, Esther, Tico, Anisia, and Fortunato, who were abandoned by their fathers, do not find a father figure in Polo, their grandfather, who, left fatherless himself at an early age, chooses not to assume the paternal role. In reaction to their loneliness and neglect, the children commit suicide (Esther), play cruel games and communicate using strange riddles (Tico and Anisia), or comfort themselves with sexual and creative activities (Fortunato). In the case of Fortunato in particular, the narrative charts the impact of his isolation and loneliness — in no small measure caused by his father's absence — on his development not just as an adolescent but also as an artist.

Fortunato's father is first mentioned in the "Prologue and Epilogue" in a multivoiced stream-of-consciousness that offers tidbits of the stories of Fortunato's relatives, familial narratives that are expanded on in the subsequent parts of the novel. Among the stories, there is one of a woman (later identified as Onérica, Fortunato's mother) and a man, Misael, who have sex under a bush in the countryside: "I go out earlier today than ever, out to where the spiny wild coffee bushes grow all in a clump, and there is Misael naked under a wild coffee bush, waiting for me" (*El palacio de las blanquísimas mofetas* 12; *The Palace of the White Skunks* 6). Misael's seduction of Onérica and their ensuing sexual trysts, to which the narrative refers a number of times from the perspective of various characters, result in the conception of Fortunato, whose birth is not narrated until much later, in the third of the five "agonies" in the second part of the novel: "And so Fortunato was born" (189; 170). Thus begins the tale of the protagonist's illegitimate birth, the telling of which in the middle of the narrative discursively underscores its centrality in Fortunato's story. Not only had Onérica not revealed her pregnancy to anyone, but now she also refuses to name the father of her child. To her mother's question, "Who is the father?," Onérica simply replies, "I don't know" (190; 171). Although the answer to Jacinta's question is not difficult for others to figure out in due course, Onérica for a while shields her son from learning his ancestry. It will take five years before Fortunato discovers the identity of his father, and this revelation, though told in a textually peripheral scene with a peculiar page layout, proves to be thematically central to the story:

My aunt Digna is an embittered woman. She denies it. She says she's not, but I've heard my grandmother say it a lot, and I believe it's the truth. She spends her whole life fighting with her kids. And some-

Once — he must have been about five years old at the time — his mother took him to an aunt's house — the Hated One's — and as they were crossing the Lirio River, a man appeared and gave him two pesos. But Onérica grabbed up a handful of rocks and started throwing them at the man. You asshole, she was screaming, you asshole! And she hit him with so many rocks that it was a wonder she didn't brain him. By the time they got to his aunt's house, Onérica was sobbing and Fortunato had realized that the man was his father.

But what made the strongest impression on him was seeing

times she takes a switch and whips those kids till they cry and sob all day long. Those times, there's really no way to stand this house. So I go out into the street, but I don't have anywhere to go. If I at least knew how to play ball. But there's no way — I just can't seem to learn how. And before I'll let other people laugh at me, I'll just not learn, either.

I really am clumsy at sports, all of them. And playing games. I've got no aim at marbles, I can never thump it right, or hit the other marbles. And when I try to hit that little piece of wood with the bat and knock it out of the yard, I just swat the air.

his mother for the first time so furious that she cried. She never complained about anything, or showed her emotions at all. . . . His mother.

So all there is to do is walk. Headed nowhere.

Or stay at home, listening to Digna squabbling and scolding and slapping her kids so hard they're half-way feeble-minded.

And screaming, "This is not life! I'm already doomed and sent to hell! Shit!" (100; 87–88)[12]

Echoing his grandmother's question to his mother, Fortunato all along may have been asking himself, "Who is my father?" At the age of five, he receives an answer upon unexpectedly meeting his progenitor on a riverbank, an answer which in turn may have triggered other questions. After the encounter with the stranger, the child may have begun to ask, "Where is my father?," since the man who turned out to be his father disappears again from his life after their brief and enigmatic exchange.

Fortunato evokes his absent father in critical moments of his life. For instance, when Batista's soldiers torture him and leave him to die hanging from a tree, he tries to come up with an "ingenious paragraph" (260; 232) that, declaimed from memory, would immunize him from the pain. What he ends up summoning is a song that his grandmother taught him when he was a child:

The song (in a great wealth of tears and self-pity) told the story of a child born fatherless, since his father had "fooled" his mother and run away. The boy "becomes a man," goes off to war, and "in revenge kills his father." The last verse of the song went like this: "And that's the way boys act who really know how to love." (260; 232)

Despite its violent content, this song ironically brings comfort to Fortunato, since at this point he focuses not on the parricide that the song depicts but on the soothing quality of the cadence of its lyrics. As he says, "Its lyrics, its catchy tune would be reverberating endlessly across that plain" (260; 232), conjuring up a "life walled about with insults, with hungers of all kinds, with humiliations of all ages past and present, with dreams and idiocies of infinite and useless variety" (260; 232). But as he goes on to admit to himself, the words to the song are "words that distance had stripped of their honest note of resentment" (260; 232). In a surprising move, then, because of his identification in Fortunato's family with the man in the song, Fortunato's father metonymically comes to be with his son in his moment of agony. Distancing himself now from the strong emotions felt by the son in the song, Fortunato seeks at this juncture not his father's demise but his company and protection, which are made possible by the "catchy tune" of *his* song.[13]

The father as protector also appears later in the text, in a scene that chronologically precedes Fortunato's death scene. On his way to Velazco to join Castro's revolutionary forces, Fortunato is stopped at a bridge by some of Batista's men who, having asked him where he is headed, let him go through when, lying, he says to them, "I'm going to see my father" (300; 269).[14] It may not be true that Fortunato has a father in Velazco but he does have one somewhere, a father for whom he searches and about whom he fantasizes, a father to whom he turns when he feels alone and in peril. As it turns out, the "lying" Fortunato indeed attempts to reunite with his father —not in Velazco but in other "lies" that he tells himself, in his fantasies and in the fictions that he, a budding novelist, incessantly writes.

Hand Jobs

Living in a household in which he is constantly demeaned and where he feels misunderstood and alienated, Fortunato finds solace in sex and in the world of the imagination. As compulsively and as privately as he masturbates, the adolescent Fortunato also writes novels, using reams of paper stolen from his grandfather. Before taking up writing, Fortunato, much to the chagrin of his grandmother, would spend his days at home reading trashy novels or putting his creativity to work by making wine, perfume, or soap bars—what Jacinta calls "filth" (128, 166; 113, 150)—out of an array of odd materials. Claiming that it gets on her nerves to see him walled up all day "like he was a little girl or something" (166; 150), Jacinta finds her grandson a job making wooden boxes at the local guava-paste factory. Forced to go out of the house, Fortunato supposedly will now be putting his hands to good— productive—use, those "hands as soft as a woman's" (234; 209) by which Fortunato's disfigured body is identified when it is found hanging from a tree at the entrance to town.

In moments of anger and frustration, Fortunato as a child would sing his heart out, interminably it seems, when alone in the woods. These songs, which were his own compositions, would be two to three hours long, and Fortunato would eventually consider them "the only real creation . . . that he would achieve his whole life long" (48; 40). This reference to Fortunato's esteemed oral creations is followed by a description of what will turn out to be a significant, and equally gratifying, revelation: the boy's discovery of masturbation, "the pleasure of rubbing his sex with his hands" (48; 40). When he first feels the delectable sexual sensation, Fortunato immediately runs from the tree under which he is lying to the privacy of the outhouse, where, fearful and yet excited, he masturbates seven more times. From that day forward, Fortunato replicates this experience daily, masturbating as uncontrollably as he sings. Sharing the solitary, as well as prolonged, experience of self-pleasuring, Fortunato's masturbating and singing can be read as related blissful activities, a connection that is suggested as well by their contiguity in this scene. As Fortunato becomes older, and now living in the city, he recognizes that he can no longer turn to his singing to cope with the oppressive and repressive reality of his daily life. He can still, however, turn to his "only refuge" (114; 100) — the bathroom — and, of course, his hands. After a hard day's work at the guava-paste factory making boxes, Fortunato goes home, where, while showering,

> his hands . . . would glide down his body, caress his skin, reach his testicles where they would linger, and then he would begin the daily, impassioned masturbation. . . . Then he felt the tremor. The shudder. A sensation of coldness would run through his skin, rise through his body. The warm whitish liquid splattered on the floor, was carried away by the current of water and disappeared into the drain. And he would feel relaxed, though at the same time frustrated, weary, irritated, and his limbs and joints would stiffen, until he could hardly walk. . . . But if you only could, if you only could. (114–15; 101)

Seeing his life as "the butt of some unbearable joke" (116; 102), Fortunato eventually succumbs to a sense of powerlessness, a "terrible sensation" (116; 102) that not even his masturbation can relieve. As he says on more than one occasion, "it was futile to masturbate again" (116; 103), a realization that disposes him to take up writing: "That was when he stole the reams of paper from his grandfather and began to write, interminably so it seemed" (117; 103). Fortunato's earlier interminable singing comes back transformed in his interminable writing. But what about Fortunato's masturbation, his

other expressive outlet? Although he does not abandon it, at times he subli-
mates it, turning to a different, yet related, *maniobra*, or hand job.

Fortunato's story belongs to a long-established literary tradition that
connects masturbation to writing.[15] Solitude and fantasy, common to both
activities, impel Fortunato to take hand to penis or to pen (or typewriter)
with equal ease. Fortunato's writing is first mentioned in the "Prologue and
Epilogue":

> While I sweat, cough, and shoo away the mosquitoes, I write. While
> I cough and cough and cough, while I sweat and sweat and fan the
> air, I write. I don't know how I managed to get my hands on a type-
> writing machine, but I've run the old man out of all paper he had in
> the shop. The old man doesn't say anything, because he won't talk,
> but he's about to pop. And Grandma wants to kill me, she's so
> furious when she sees that the old man has to send goods home with
> the people carrying them in their bare hands. While the old woman
> scolds and fights with me, I write and write and write. And I don't
> sleep. Or eat. Until finally I get over the urge to write and I throw all
> the paper down the latrine in the bathroom. The old woman catches
> me and throws a fit. Tico and Anisia pretend they don't touch the
> ground. The old man doesn't talk. Dear son. Adolfina sets herself
> afire. Life is hard. (16–17; 10)

That Fortunato's compulsive writing concludes with his throwing the written pages in the latrine cannot but make the reader wonder about the
significance of Fortunato's immediate elimination of what he has so joyfully
and frenetically produced, especially when considering that Fortunato also
eliminates something else that he produces with his hands as well: when he
masturbates in the shower he lets his ejaculate go down the *tragante*, the
drain. Since a hole in the bathroom is the recipient of Fortunato's sexual
and textual emissions, writing and masturbation converge. Moreover, like
masturbation, writing is inscribed in Arenas's novel in a discourse of shame
and disapproval. Just as Fortunato has to hide to pleasure himself, he also
has to hide to enjoy the pleasure of writing. It is revealing, then, that Fortunato's grandfather considers "filth" (211; 190) what his grandson writes.[16]

In the guava-paste factory, however, Fortunato openly puts his hands to
work, and his labor results in the production of packages the sticky contents
of which others consume and enjoy. If I have used here language that is

sexually allusive, it is because the novel, in its symbolic economy, signals an affinity between Fortunato's manual labor and his masturbatory hands. Routine, repetitive, and solitary manual work produces long and firm boxes. Day after day, "martillando y martillando" (177; 160), a hammering that echoes *masturbando y masturbando*, Fortunato uses his tools to create phallically elongated boxes. What is more, the narrative stresses Fortunato's sustained self-abuse, not only literal but also metaphorical, as the adolescent invariably *se martilla* (hammers) his fingers and hands. In this regard, Fortunato's description of his daily routine is quite evocative:

> Pull on stinking shoes, quick, at some ungodly hour before dawn, and then pull on a pair of stinking pants. Splash a little water on your face. And run to where the crate ends, crate slats, and little nails are kept, so you can start hammering the crates together. Make a thousand crates that day. . . . Hammer, hammer. And every strike of the hammer — sometimes one missed and hit a finger, or even a hand — was a blow to the trunk of the sweet-smelling tree. At every strike of the hammer, the plant shuddered, stiffened, and a shower of leaves and white flowers disappeared in bursts into the receptacle where the guava jelly was bubbling. (197–98; 175–76)

In the next to the last sentence of the quoted passage, Fortunato shifts linguistic registers, turning to figurative language to capture the essence of his work. He analogizes each blow of his hammer to a blow on "the trunk of the sweet-smelling tree," which, with each blow, "shuddered, stiffened," producing "a shower of leaves and white flowers" that "in bursts" disappeared into the "receptacle" where the guava jelly bubbled. Because of its imagery and the language that it shares with other passages in the novel, this scene is suggestively masturbatory: the object of a good whacking, a cylindrical object reaches a state of arousal that leads to the release, in bursts, of a white liquid that finds its way into an opening.[17]

Fortunato's "hand job" at the factory can be read as a sublimation of a desire to masturbate that he routinely resists each morning before he gets out of bed. On any given day, the sounds of the guava-paste factory awaken Fortunato, and as the "commotion" grows "in rhythmic speed and intensity" (203; 182), the sexually aroused adolescent contemplates generating his own competing "commotion," with its attendant rhythm and intensity:

Oh, but who could resist, at that moment when day had not yet dawned and yet the night had passed, who could resist at that moment stretching out a hand into the void, raising it gracefully, lightly, then gently arching it just at the fingertips, and then, there, in the privacy of the dark, . . . invoking a strange, foreign dance, a ballet, or emitting some shriek, some neigh, some baa, some brief death rattle perhaps, just as the sun came above the horizon. . . . But he controlled himself, he left that plan in the air, suspended, postponed, and in silence he drew back the mosquito net, and in silence he began to dress, frustrated somewhat, still sleepy, drowsy, and, as always at that hour of the day, unconsciously aroused. . . . Because there was that, too: Control yourself. Reject, deny, avoid, moments before sunrise, that which was rising and also demanded to manifest itself furiously with nonpostponable commotion. (203–4; 182)

Exercising self-control instead of pleasuring himself, Fortunato puts on his clothes and goes to the factory—a giant masturbating machine where Fortunato, in unison with the surrounding rhythmic sounds and movements, *se martilla*. (The narrative insistently points not only to the rhythmicity of the work going on in the factory but also to the distinct pungency that emanates from the production of the guava paste, a pungency that in our reading can be "smelled" as spermatic scent.)[18]

Insofar as the text links Fortunato's laboring and masturbating hands to his writer's hands, it invites the reader to speculate about a link between Fortunato's manual labor at the factory and his literary production at home. One can begin to connect Fortunato's guava-box making and novel writing by relating the nature of Fortunato's job to the nature of novel production. Fortunato, who works with wood, hammers, and nails, turns out to be a carpenter, but not a very good one. This is the trade that Arenas derisively associates with Pérez Galdós, a writer who in factory-like fashion produces "wooden" verbal artifacts—ponderous and tedious novels. Moreover, like the boxes Fortunato makes, the novels he writes are mechanically produced. Fortunato's work in the factory involves assembling precut and presized slats; similarly, his work as a novelist involves a process that does not require much skill: he puts together stories following preestablished novelistic patterns.[19] Fortunato's hands churn out comparably uninteresting products (boxes, novels) in the public sphere of the factory and in the private sphere of the home.

The connections among Fortunato's multiple uses of his hands (labor, masturbation, writing) suggest that it might be useful to take a closer look at his novels. Fortunato secretly writes, and his muse is Lolín, one of the local prostitutes, who becomes "the star" (214; 192) of his novels. A poor, innocent, and attractive young woman from another town, Lolín left her beloved family in search of a better life in Holguín, where, because of her naïveté and sentimentalism, "she would be capable of letting herself be killed, of letting herself be ruined (which is always what seems to happen in these cases) for the first man who treated her like a lady" (214; 191–92). Claiming to be in love with Lolín, the adolescent Fortunato fantasizes about their eloping together. Not one to resist peer pressure, however, Fortunato admits to himself that he should treat her the way his friends treat her—like a whore. In this way he recognizes the impossibility of sharing his desires with anyone and accepts the reality of having to confine them to the written page.

We are also told the basic outline of two of Fortunato's novels. In one of them, Fortunato and Lolín, "after a daring daylight robbery, make their escape in an enormous automobile and flee the length of the island; they make love wherever the notion strikes them, as their enemies tighten the net around them" (214; 192); in the other, "she is the remote, famous singer who comes briefly to Fortunato's small town. She looks at him once, calls him over, and makes him hers forever and ever" (214; 192). Fortunato, clearly, models his creations after the radio soap operas to which his grandmother and aunts assiduously listen. Formulaic and melodramatic, the plots of Fortunato's novels revolve around the travails and tribulations of the central characters, who, in the end, having triumphed over adversity, live happily ever after.

In his autobiographical fictions, Fortunato not only concocts story lines in which he gives agency to the Lolín-inspired female protagonist, who becomes his lover, but also projects onto the male protagonist, his double, the persona of a macho hero who defies the law and exudes (hetero)sexual potency. Fortunato, in real life, lacks not only the power and determination to free Lolín from a life of prostitution, but also his male protagonist's sexual prowess with women. In fact, in his only sexual encounter with Lolín at the local brothel, Fortunato is unable to perform and ends up masturbating. He also has difficulty achieving an erection when he attempts to pleasure himself while thinking about his girlfriends — his "beards" — but not when he relieves himself, as he does in the brothel, by conjuring up the image of his pal Abi, "tall, thin, in his tight pants" (291; 261). If for Fortunato sex with women "was really no big thing" (280; 250), that is not the case with sex with men, for a big thing does happen when Abi enters the picture. The adolescent Fortunato, who is in the process of forging a homosexual identity in a homophobic society, finds himself "eternally a fugitive from reality" (113; 99–100), living and writing by words that he simultaneously abhors and embraces: "One always had to fake, and fake that one wasn't faking" (114; 100). Fortunato writes novels that, like his life, are exercises in simulation.

El palacio de las blanquísimas mofetas alludes to another novel of adolescence whose plot the narrative does not disclose but whose title is evoked when Fortunato's writing is first mentioned. This happens in the "Prologue and Epilogue," in a passage that focuses on the doings and obsessions of Fortunato's relatives, but more specifically on those of his own, particularly his compulsive need to write. The passage ends with the following assertion: "La vida es dura" ("Life is hard") (17; 10). On one level, this statement simply encapsulates the essence of Fortunato's preceding rambling thoughts, namely, that he and his relatives do not have an easy life. On another level, this statement has wider implications; it calls to mind "¡Qué dura es la vida!," a novel that an adolescent Reinaldo Arenas, the model for Fortunato, wrote and never published. Since Arenas, like Fortunato, wrote autobiographically, the text prompts us to connect Fortunato to "¡Qué dura es la vida!," which a teenaged Arenas wrote while also working at a guava-paste factory.[20] But why does the narrative make this attribution obliquely, leaving a gap in the text by not offering a brief outline of the novel's plot as is done with the other two novels to which the narrative refers? Why does the text leave the content of this novel in the latrine, as it were, where Fortunato discards his writings, while at the same time indirectly directing the reader's attention to that hole in the house, inviting the reader to retrieve the material needed to fill in the narrative hole, which would make the novel whole?

"¡Qué dura es la vida!" tells the story of a family over a span of more than two decades, starting in 1936 and extending a bit beyond 1959, the year in which the sixteen-year-old Arenas completed the manuscript of the unpublished novel, which is dated 31 December of that year. The story goes like this: After the death of Arturo, exemplary husband and father, his widow Adelaida and their young daughter, Marta, wander aimlessly in the countryside in eastern Cuba, searching for a place to live. Antonio, a wealthy landowner, finds them, listens to their tragic story, and takes them to his farm, where Adelaida becomes a trusted housekeeper. Antonio dies some years later unaware that his wife, Isabel, has been unfaithful to him and that she and her lover at some point attempted to murder him. Antonio and Isabel's only child, Raúl, takes over the running of the farm, which the dutiful son loves but which his mother sees only as a source of income to sustain her lavish lifestyle. Because of a long and devastating drought, the family falls on hard times. Isabel turns to alcohol, goes mad, and eventually falls to her death at a dam that was built in an effort to save the farm.

Meanwhile, Raúl and Marta fall in love, get married, and have a child. When Marta is pregnant, she harbors a desire to have a miscarriage, since having a child would be an obstacle to resuming her studies at the conservatory, which she has had to put on hold because of the financial difficulties resulting from the drought. If Marta is more keen on having a singing career than on becoming a mother, Raúl is overjoyed at the prospect of fatherhood. With the birth of Raulín, their child, comes the much-needed rain, but also the death of the loving and judicious Adelaida (who has become Raúl's surrogate mother) and the rumblings of revolution. A sympathizer of the revolutionary movement, Raúl joins the rebels in their fight against the dictator ruling the country. On his triumphant return home when the revolution succeeds, Raúl finds the family farm in deep financial trouble. Despite her husband's objections, Marta pursues her singing career to fulfill her ambitions and save the farm, which she does, but her marriage to Raúl suffers in the process. Swiftly achieving national and international fame, Marta travels extensively, exacerbating her husband's resentment; Raúl takes up drinking and has an extramarital affair; and Raulín is sent off to boarding school.

In her last public performance, which takes place at a carnival celebration in Havana after one of many quarrels with her husband, Marta uncontrollably cries while singing, causing her voice to falter. In response to the audience's ungenerous reaction, Marta vows never to sing again and returns to the farm to be with her husband and son. But having no desire to continue sharing his life with Marta (in part because her success has bruised his ego), and dismissing Marta's claims that she still loves him, Raúl decides to leave her and the farm for good. A distraught Raulín, as he witnesses one of his parents' violent confrontations, falls from the top of the stairs and suffers a head injury. After his recovery at the local hospital, Raulín joins his mother at the farm, where they are last seen walking together on a path, unaccompanied by anyone else, having a conversation and holding hands.

Inspired by soap operas, as Arenas has remarked on numerous occasions, "¡Qué dura es la vida!" follows the thematics and uses the formal devices and conventions of popular melodrama. It lacks, however, the customary happy ending. The novel ends with the following words: "And there at a distance, almost lost among the shadows of the trees, one could from time to time see two figures, those of a woman and a child, hardly noticeable, on the narrow road, lit by the rays of a beautiful, lovely, and serene spring that heralds the beginning of a new life . . ." ("¡Qué dura es la vida!" 336). The narrator wistfully announces "a new life," which may or may not come to pass. The fate of the characters is uncharacteristically left untold, an indeterminacy that the closing ellipses graphically capture. The end is thus not the one the characters desire and the readers of popular melodrama expect.

It is worth reflecting on Arenas's deviation from the conventional ending by examining the conversation that Marta has with Raulín as they walk hand in hand in the final scene. Having been reassured by his mother that she will not be leaving him again, Raulín then asks her, "¿Y papá?" (And dad?). To which Marta responds, "He is not here now, but don't you worry he will come, I know that he will come back, I know it" ("¡Qué dura es la vida!" 336). Although Marta attempts to offer Raulín the "fantasy of reassurance" with which popular melodramas typically end (Prendergast 175), the dismembered family in all likelihood will not reunite.

Marta's last words in the novel recall the lyrics of "Noche azul," the bolero that she sings in her last public performance and that ends her singing career. A despondent lover's appeal to a personified blue night, Ernesto Lecuona's bolero becomes a vehicle through which Marta obliquely expresses her yearning for Raúl. She privately sings to her (k)night, the *príncipe azul* with whom she has experienced the joys and pains of love. "Come, for I'm dying of sorrow" (Orovio 59), the bolero's last plea to the blue night, not only encapsulates the sentiments of the song's lyrics; it also encapsulates Marta's as well as Raulín's sentiments about an absent man whom both mother and son deeply miss. Like his mother, Raulín aches for Raúl to come, a painful yearning that is articulated, and underscored, in the poignant question that he asks his mother in their last exchange, the heart-wrenching scene with which the novel ends.

Although Arenas has said that "¡Qué dura es la vida!" and his other early novels are "horrible" ("El mar es siempre el símbolo fundamental de la liberación" 251), one cannot completely dismiss them. They may have limited literary value, and Arenas may have legitimate grounds to disavow them, but these novels reveal much about their author, especially if read in the context of Arenas's biography and the evolution of his literary production. "¡Qué dura es la vida!" is undoubtedly awful, but the emotions in it are as authentic as literary emotions ever are. One cannot but feel the young author's inner turmoil when one reads what he wrote immediately after the novel's title page: "He puesto en ella todo mi sentir" (I've poured into it all my emotions). Melodramatic, indeed, but melodrama was the only literary mode available to the adolescent writer to explore his family situation, particularly the abandonment by his father ("And dad?," let us recall, are Raulín's last words), an issue to which Arenas will return throughout his writing career. There may be a substantial difference in literary quality between Arenas's mature novels and those that he wrote during his adolescence, but the figure of the absent father is a constant in his creative output. "Come, for I'm dying of sorrow," the sappy bolero line that captures the loss and the longing of an abandoned son (Raulín/Reinaldo), resonates in a number of Arenas's subsequent works.

El palacio de las blanquísimas mofetas is one of those works. Although not a "character" in the novel, Fortunato's father looms large in his son's emotional life, surfacing at key moments in the narrative. An absent presence, he appears through references and allusions to which one has to add the allusive presence of "¡Qué dura es la vida!" The narrative not only prompts the reader to connect this novel to Fortunato, but in so doing opens the door for other connections. As a novel within the novel, "¡Qué dura es la vida!" can be read as a *mise en abyme*, as a text that is in a specular relationship with the text that "contains" it. A family saga like *El palacio de las blanquísimas mofetas*, "¡Qué dura es la vida!" helps bring into focus a thematic element in the former that, without the specular nod, would remain perhaps unnoticed:

the protagonist's longing for his absent father. Having read "¡Qué dura es la vida!," the reader of *El palacio de las blanquísimas mofetas* must ask with Raulín, "¿Y papá?"

An "absent" novel that thematizes paternal absence, "¡Qué dura es la vida!," when read as a specular autobiographical novel authored by Fortunato, helps to bring to the fore a traumatic experience in the life of the protagonist of *El palacio de las blanquísimas mofetas* that the novel's narrative renders obliquely. Fortunato's father, although literally absent, is noticeably present in the text and in his son's life. Moreover, since "¡Qué dura es la vida!" functions as a compensation for a textual lack in *El palacio de las blanquísimas mofetas* about a familial lack (the father's absence), Fortunato's writing calls to mind another activity in which the adolescent participates that has an equally — and related — compensatory function. I am referring to Fortunato's work in the factory, which can be linked to his work as a writer. Fortunato, we are told, aims each day to make one thousand boxes and receive two pesos for his labor. Interestingly, the factory scene in which this information is revealed is followed by the only scene of Fortunato with his father, in which the five-year-old boy receives two pesos from a man who is a stranger to him and whom he will never encounter again. The presence of the two pesos in these contiguous scenes should not be read as a coincidence, as a gratuitous and inconsequential narrative detail. It invites the reader to regard the two pesos for which Fortunato works so hard in the factory as a symbolic compensation. The remuneration for Fortunato's work stands for what the abandoned son desires: the attention and love of his father.[21] Thus, in the symbolic economy of the novel, Fortunato's "erection" of the guava boxes can be read as a compensatory fantasy. The son's manual labor is a labor of love — a search for a man, his father, to whom he reaches out with his hammering, writing, and masturbating hands.

Fortunato's paternal quest reaches its culmination and termination when he decides to leave the *bestias* and join the rebels. Fortunato's departure from home is narrated in the "Fifth Agony," where his aunt Adolfina's search for male companionship is also narrated. Sharing the same textual space in a pendular narrative, Fortunato and Adolfina, aspiring "rebels," reflect one another: they embark on analogous quests. Like Adolfina's, Fortunato's "rebellion" is eroticized inasmuch as he is also after a man with a functioning "weapon" to achieve his liberating goal. As Perla Rozencvaig has put it,

"When Adolfina goes out in search of a man to lose her virginity (symbol of her sexual failure), Fortunato goes out in search of a liberating rifle (phallic symbol) to get away from his family" (89). Motivated not by revolutionary ideals but by his need to escape from a suffocating familial environment, Fortunato goes on a quest for the liberating rifle, which signifies more than a firearm that will give him access to the rebel forces. Fortunato's search for the rifle, on which this segment of the novel focuses insistently, can be related to the search that the adolescent references in his exchange with the soldiers he encounters on his way to Velazco. Fortunato is not literally in pursuit of his father, as he tells the soldiers, but his trumped-up story to get out of a compromising situation turns out to be the truth—in a symbolic sense. Like his father, however, the rifle will prove to be inaccessible and, as a result, Fortunato is left, helpless and alone, in a precarious situation.

Fortunato is apprehended in his attempt to secure the much-desired rifle. In jail, we are told, "until the man in charge showed up (a lieutenant apparently) it was just laughter, wisecracks, and a few halfhearted blows, almost accidental, playful, given him with the butt of a rifle or an elbow" (383; 345). A curious sentence then follows: "Pero luego, bajo las órdenes del jefe, y qué forma de hablar, y qué forma de caminar, y qué forma de mirar y ordenar, las cosas cambiaron" ("But then, at the leader's orders—and how he talked, how he walked, how he held his head and looked and barked out orders—things changed") (383; 345). Fortunato's torture and interrogation, encapsulated here in an apparently innocuous phrase, "things changed," seem not to matter as much as the lieutenant's demeanor and bearing, to which an admiring—and excited—Fortunato refers in a tricolon of exclamatory phrases. Not surprisingly, in the ensuing narration of his time in jail, Fortunato is more focused on the lieutenant than on the pain that the soldiers inflict on him, repeatedly referring to him as "the maybe lieutenant" (384, 385, 386; 345, 346, 347), "the surely lieutenant" (386; 348), or "the no doubt lieutenant" (387; 348) as he concentrates obsessively on the man's every move. Unable to extract a confession from Fortunato, the lieutenant, after ordering the soldiers to continue torturing him, leaves the prison cell:

> And seeing the man who had ordered his torture leaving the cell,
> Fortunato felt real fear for the first time—fear at being alone with the
> other soldiers. At least the surely lieutenant was somebody; he ex-

isted, he possessed a certain reality; but these men, these other men, were no more than clumsy, stupid machines, unreasoning, passionless animals [*animales sin razón*] with no coherent hatred. So it was impossible to reach them with reason, or to insult them. And for one moment he wanted to call out to the no doubt lieutenant, to tell him to stay, to beg him to do the torturing himself, but the man (the only man — tall, firm, cruel, enraged — real) had already disappeared down one of the hallways. (386–87; 348)

Fortunato's obsession with the prison's authority figure and his rank invites the reader to engage as well in an identifying process or guessing game. Like Fortunato, one would have to ask: Is this man indeed a lieutenant? Or could he be — or represent — something else? How is one to read as well the fact that Fortunato not only directs all his attention to the "lieutenant" but also eroticizes him, simultaneously attributing to him, despite his responsibility for Fortunato's suffering, humane feelings lacking in his subordinates? These questions can be answered if placed within the context of Fortunato's paternal fantasy. The experience in the prison, which replicates the protagonist's family dynamics, provides closure to what Richard L. Browning calls the novel's "cycle of abandonment" (61). The soldiers (*animales sin razón*), taking on the role of Fortunato's relatives (*bestias*), abuse the adolescent, who ironically idealizes (and idolizes) the man — the lieutenant/father — who in essence is responsible for his misery. In the end, Fortunato's hopes are dashed, since the lieutenant leaves him alone with the soldiers, just as his father left him alone with the *bestias* when he was a child, thereby tragically bringing to an end Fortunato's life and his fantasy of a loving father.

It all comes down to Fortunato's hands. His failure to put his hands on a weapon causes his capture, torture, and death. Caught red-handed, Fortunato is brutally killed and abandoned on the outskirts of town, his body left disfigured and unidentifiable — except for his hands. Fortunato may have failed in his last *maniobra* but his hands are left unscathed. On display, as his tortured body hangs from a tree for everyone to see, Fortunato's *manos finas* stand erect: a testimony of the adolescent's acts of resistance, defiance, and desire.[22]

Paternal Erotics

The "presence" of *Fortunata y Jacinta* and "¡Qué dura es la vida!" in *El palacio de las blanquísimas mofetas* underscores the novel's concern with paternal absence. Other texts by Arenas offer further justification for this reading of the novel. In 1970, one year after completing *El palacio de las blanquísimas mofetas*, Arenas wrote "Morir en junio y con la lengua afuera," one of three narrative poems that comprise the poetic trilogy *Leprosorio*.[23] This poem's narrator reflects on life in contemporary Cuba, an Orwellian place where "the great master . . . keeps watch" ("Morir en junio y con la lengua afuera" 87). What interests me is less the poem's denunciation of a repressive regime than the genealogy of the poetic narrator, who intertextually reveals information about his family history through an identification with Perceval, one of the knights of the Round Table, whose story was first told by Chrétien de Troyes in his twelfth-century French romance *Perceval or The Story of the Grail*. Despite the obvious differences between Perceval's glorious history and the narrator's degrading present circumstances, the narrator declares, in a direct address to Perceval, that "really your life story and mine are one and the same" (89):

> Both of us alone, searching in the fleeting night, the night that time
> will later on make sure to stretch out,
> for the changing countenance of an unknown father
> who refused to wait for us. (90)

He then asks:

> What's the point of this incessant search?
> Where's the end to this annoying pilgrimage?
> What would we do if by chance we found
> our progenitor?
>   What's there beyond the encounter?
>   How to proceed afterward? (90–91)

Both men, we are told, share a fatherless childhood with a domineering mother who "transforms herself into a *chaste virgin*" and "disguises herself as the offended one" (91). "Yes, our life stories are exactly the same" (91), says the narrator to bring the comparison with Perceval to an end. But these are not the last words on this issue. In a footnote to the poem (the longest and the last of seven footnotes), Arenas tells the story of Perceval, referring to various versions of the romance:

> Perceval, the youngest and only survivor of seven brothers killed with their father in knightly adventures, is taken to the forest, where he grows up ignorant of the adventures and duties of medieval knights — raised that way by his mother, who does not want for her surviving son the same fate of the others. But one day, the lad, "simple in spirit and pure of heart" (all encyclopedias agree on this), by chance meets some knights in the glade, gets excited about their weapons, and wants to accompany them to King Arthur's court. He abandons his mother, who, after sharing with him some parting words, "dies of sorrow." He arrives, still dressed as a peasant, in the legendary and mysterious court. There his many hallucinatory adventures begin. He encounters terror, sin, astonishment, mystery, and, of course, what is apparently love. (98)

Whether Arenas was familiar with the works of Chrétien de Troyes, Gerbert de Montreuil, and Richard Wagner, whom he mentions, or relied exclusively on encyclopedias is not clear. What Arenas makes clear, however, is that he consulted critical works on the subject and that he found them lacking in their analyses. Dismissing literary critics, Arenas ironically takes on that very role to offer his interpretation of Perceval's story:

> Although no critic has taken notice of this (the role of critics is not to see even the obvious), the two constants, the two misfortunes, that seem to dictate and justify that chain of adventures are: (a) The presence of the controlling and censorious mother who, more than the knights, is the one who pushes Perceval to flee the forest. It doesn't matter that she has died: one has to keep one's distance, one has to push away that invisible presence (that power); one has to go find freedom. (b) The search for the father, in other words, the desire to equal and surpass him. Perceval as a hero must erase — exceed — the image of the hero who preceded him and only by doing so will he be able to achieve his authenticity. Herein lies, perhaps, the essence of one of the oldest "romances" in European literature. (98)

Why does Arenas see in Perceval's story what he claims others do not?[24] In "Lezama o el reino de la imagen," an essay written a year earlier, in 1969,

Arenas argues that "the best thing about a book is not what critics tell us, and many times not even what the author sets out to do" (110), but rather the evocative power the book has on its readers. He offers a series of examples, the first of which is: "The best thing about a book is that passage whose reading retrieves for us the lost tree of childhood, the voice of the family lost in the fog of childhood" (110). When Arenas wrote this, might he have been alluding to his reading of Perceval's story and, more specifically, to the scene in which the young lad learns from his mother the details about the crucial loss that he suffered—that of his father—during childhood? The tale of a fatherless son raised in the forest by a fearful and overly protective mother who for years keeps from him the identity of his father, truncating the family tree, may have retrieved for Arenas his own tale of paternal loss, eliciting memories of the missing limb of his own truncated family tree. Reading Perceval's story may have evoked for Arenas his own fatherless and impoverished childhood in the countryside, where, like Perceval in the remote forest, he is kept ignorant about his ancestry until that momentous day in which a fortuitous encounter with his father takes place and ends the secrecy surrounding his patrilineage.

I devote chapter 3 to a detailed analysis of the only encounter between Arenas and his father, which Arenas lovingly recalls in the first chapter of *Antes que anochezca* and which inspired the only meeting between Fortunato and his father in *El palacio de las blanquísimas mofetas*. Suffice it to say, for the moment, that I read Arenas's scene with his father as told in *Antes que anocheza* as a homoerotic coming together, a joyful experience for the young son that an older Arenas may have seen reflected in the homoerotically charged scene in which the excited young Perceval meets the five handsome knights with their "weapons," who come to stand for his dead father and inspire his search for the chivalric ideal.[25] An infatuation at an early age takes Perceval, as also happens with Arenas, on a life quest that is in essence a quest for the absent father.

Looking back at Arenas's entire oeuvre, one can argue that the commentary on Perceval in the long footnote to "Morir en junio y con la lengua afuera" simultaneously offers a program for the reading of Perceval's story, Arenas's narrative poem, and Arenas's literary corpus in general. Early in his career, Arenas indirectly alerts his readers to the centrality of the mother and father in his own writing: "The presence of the controlling and censorious mother" and "the search for the father" are "the two constants" and "the essence" of *his* work. Not surprisingly, the figure of the mother has secured a prominent place in the criticism on Arenas, but the figure of the father has not, despite the author's nudge to his readers in his direction. What can account for this critical imbalance? Why haven't Arenas's critics taken notice of the crucial role of the father in his work?[26] Arenas himself is perhaps to blame, since in his literary production the figure of the father, unlike that of the mother, is not a commanding textual presence. Instead, as in *El palacio de las blanquísimas mofetas*, the father lurks between the lines. But although it is true that Arenas generally reduces the paternal function in comparison to the maternal, his intent is not, as he claims happens in Perceval's romance, "to erase" the image of the father to attain his — the son's — "authenticity." On the contrary, in some of his texts, especially among the ones he wrote later in his career, instead of enacting an erasure, a rejection, of the father, Arenas brings him to the fore, revealing a surprising, and affirming, connection between father and son. *Viaje a La Habana*, which Arenas wrote between 1983 and 1987, can be read as a response to and as a gloss of one of the questions posed in 1970 in "Morir en junio y con la lengua afuera": "What would we do if by chance we found / our progenitor?" Written almost two decades later, Arenas's response came in the form of a novella in which an estranged father and son, having met apparently by chance in Cuba's capital when the exiled father returns to the island for a visit, have passionate sex.

In 1987, the year Arenas concluded *Viaje a La Habana*, he published *La Loma del Ángel*, "a sarcastic but loving parody" (*Antes que anochezca* 12; *Before Night Falls* xiii) of Cirilo Villaverde's *Cecilia Valdés*, in which he offers a meditation on incest that is pertinent to my present discussion.[27] In "Sobre la obra," his prologue to *La Loma del Ángel*, Arenas says of *Cecilia Valdés*:

> This novel has been read as a portrait of early nineteenth-century
> Cuba and as an abolitionist tract, but it is much more than that. The
> work is not only the moral mirror of a society perverted (and made
> wealthy) by slavery, as well as the reflection of the trials and tribula-
> tions of Cuban slaves during the last century, but also a summa of ir-
> reverences, an attack on the conventions and mores of that century
> (which, by and large, are those of our own age) through a succession
> of incestuous encounters. The plot of *Cecilia Valdés* is not limited to
> the incestuous relationship between Leonardo and his half sister
> Cecilia; the entire novel is permeated by incessant, skillfully sug-

gested incestuous liaisons. What makes this text enigmatic and immortal is that when Villaverde presents us with a series of incestuous encounters — consummated or suggested — he is really portraying the eternal human tragedy — man's solitude, his incommunication, his intransferable disquiet, his quest for an ideal lover who, being ideal, can only be a mirror or reflection of ourselves. (9–10; *Graveyard of the Angels* 1)[28]

Arenas basically repeats here what he wrote in 1985 about *Cecilia Valdés* in "La literatura cubana dentro y fuera de Cuba," an unpublished essay in which he postulates that "the challenge (or enigma) posed by Villaverde is even more daring if one keeps in mind that, in contrast to pagan and Christian traditions, the author does not condemn the incestuous lovers for their supposed sin or crime" (7). What is Arenas's "challenge" to his readers with his appropriation and interpretation of Villaverde's novel? Why does Arenas express so much interest in the "incessant, skillfully suggested incestuous liaisons" in *Cecilia Valdés*, on which he elaborates in his parody? Why does Arenas admire Villaverde's decision not to condemn the incestuous lovers in his novel? If, as Arenas claims at the end of his prologue to *La Loma del Ángel*, "the conclusions my book reaches are not exactly the ones Villaverde reached in his" (10; 2), what "conclusions" does he mean? I propose that Arenas articulates one of these conclusions in one of the five chapters titled "Del amor," in which Leonardo, Cecilia's lover and half brother, offers his views on the subject of love:

> A great love means two burning, anxious bodies that find each other by means of desire and that in possessing each other become all loved and hated bodies — sister and mother, father and friends. Everything that in some way confirms our being alive and our most seditious, invincible feelings. Because a great love is, above all, a great provocation. (137; 106)[29]

Distancing itself from the conventional love story, *La Loma del Ángel* is a provocative story of the "great love" of which Leonardo speaks and of which Reinaldo, no doubt, approves: a promiscuity of bodies that excludes no one — not even the father.

When one reads *El palacio de las blanquísimas mofetas* in dialogue with other texts by Arenas, it does not seem excessive to interpret this novel as a son's eroticized quest for the father. Fortunato may not come to unite carnally with his father as is the case with the son in *Viaje a La Habana*, but his fantasy of paternal union, which the novel's symbolic economy suggests, conforms with the paternal erotics that are at the core of Arenas's oeuvre.

THREE

In Search of the Father(land)

....

A beautiful specimen of a
man, tall, dark, and handsome.
REINALDO ARENAS,
Viaje a La Habana

Reinaldo Arenas recalls in *Antes que anochezca* (*Before Night Falls*) that he began writing his memoirs in a notebook that his friend Juan Abreu had brought to him, along with a copy of the *Iliad*, in Lenin Park, a botanical garden on the outskirts of Havana, where he lived as a fugitive for a month and a half in 1974.[1] Relating his capture by the police, Arenas writes, "I was finishing the *Iliad*. I was at the point when Achilles, deeply moved, finally delivers Hector's body to Priam, a unique moment in literature" (201; 176). In jail, fearing that the other inmates would steal the book from him to turn its pages into cigarettes or use them as toilet paper, he slept "embracing the *Iliad*, smelling its pages" (207; 182). One day, much to his regret, the cherished poem disappeared. While Arenas was still in prison, Abreu made available to him another copy of the *Iliad*, and it was then that he finally finished reading it: "As soon as he left, I started reading the last canto, which I had not been able to finish after being captured in Lenin Park. After I finished it, I cried as I had not done since my imprisonment" (243; 218).

Why Did Reinaldo Arenas Cry?

If every autobiography, as Paul John Eakin argues, "is more truly understood as the revelation of the present situation of the autobiographer than as the uncovering of the past" (56), one would have to ask what portrait of Arenas emerges from the pages of an autobiography that he wrote in exile and on the brink of death. After an introduction, which addresses the author's suffering from AIDS and the book's genesis, *Antes que anochezca* proceeds chronologically in sixty-nine chapters, beginning with Arenas's childhood and adolescence in eastern Cuba, continuing with his Havana years, and concluding with his exile in the United States. His suicide letter, copies of which Arenas sent to friends and to the press, closes the text. The narrative's linearity displays, like that of all autobiographies, a textual construction of the "I," a self-figuration that is typically shaped by memory, imagination, and motivations of all sorts (explicit or implicit, conscious or unconscious). My intent here is not to establish the sincerity or falsehood of Arenas's narrative, but rather to come to an understanding of *Antes que anochezca* as a portrait of a mortally ill, exiled Cuban writer who, on his deathbed, writes the story of his life, a life that is about to end far from his father and fatherland.[2]

Appropriately titled "Las piedras," the first chapter of *Antes que anochezca* is the cornerstone of Arenas's memoirs. Here, in a brief account of the writer's childhood, Arenas's father makes his only appearance. According to Arenas, his mother had been with only one man, his father, who abandoned her shortly after she gave birth to his child. In Arenas's maternal grandparents' house, where he grew up, every effort was made to make the boy hate his father. Arenas recalls having been taught by his relatives the lyrics of a popular song about a son who kills his father for abandoning his mother:

> The boy grew up and became a man,
> And to the wars he went to fight.
> In vengeance he killed his father:
> The sons who love will do what's right. (18; *Before Night Falls* 2)

This reminiscence is followed by Arenas's narration of his only meeting — a casual encounter — with his father:

> Un día mi madre y yo íbamos caminando hacia la casa de una de mis tías. Al bajar al río vimos a un hombre que venía hacia nosotros; era un hombre apuesto, alto, trigueño. Mi madre se enfureció súbitamente; empezó a coger piedras del río y a tirárselas por la cabeza a aquel hombre que, a pesar del torrente de piedras, siguió acercándose a nosotros. Llegó hasta donde yo estaba, metió la mano en el bolsillo, me dio dos pesos, me pasó la mano por la cabeza y salió corriendo,

antes de que alguna pedrada lo descalabrase. Durante el resto del camino mi madre fue llorando y, cuando llegamos a la casa de mi tía, yo me enteré de que aquel hombre era mi padre. No lo volví a ver más, ni tampoco los dos pesos; mi tía se los pidió prestados a mi madre y no sé si se los habrá pagado. (18)

One day my mother and I were on our way to visit one of my aunts. As we walked down to the river, a man came toward us; he was handsome, tall and dark. My mother fell into a sudden rage; she began picking up stones from the riverbank and throwing them at his head, while the man, in spite of the shower of rocks, kept coming toward us. When he was close to me, he put his hand into his pocket, pulled out two pesos, and gave them to me. He then patted me on the head and ran away to avoid being hit by one of the stones. My mother cried all the way to my aunt's house, where I found out that the man was my father. I never saw him again, nor the two pesos; my aunt asked my mother to lend them to her and I do not know if she ever paid them back. (2)

Although Arenas's relatives were intent on having the child forget his father, their efforts proved futile. Many years later, ironically, the dying son confers on the father he hardly knew a privileged place in his remembrances of things past, by alluding to him in the title of the first chapter of his autobiography. Almost an anagram of *padre*, the *piedras* that long ago were thrown at his father's head are picked up as it were by the son, who tellingly places them at the head of the textual reconstruction of his life. By so doing, the illegitimate son, in an inversion of roles, confers legitimacy on his father, recognizing his crucial role as begetter of his son's biological and textual lives. Unlike the child in the parricidal song, Arenas does not kill his father; on the contrary, he keeps him alive in his memory — and in his memoirs. Moreover, in "Cronología (irónica, pero cierta)," an autobiographical sketch published in 1982, Arenas affirms that since meeting the man who turned out to be his father he has felt "a great affection" for the attractive and generous stranger, adding that "perhaps the two pesos that he gave him influenced his feeling that way."

In his telling of the scene with his father, Arenas remembers witnessing a disconcerting interaction between his mother and a stranger, a man at whom she angrily hurled stones. Dodging the stones, the stranger approached the child, lovingly patted him on his head and gave him two pesos, money that shortly thereafter found its way into someone else's hands. Arenas's account, however, differs from his mother's. In a conversation with Liliane Hasson, Oneida Fuentes is asked about Arenas and his father and whether her son's penchant for fabulation might have affected his narration of their only meeting in *Antes que anochezca*:

> — Reinaldo never tried to meet him?
> — That did not interest him.
> — And the scene with the stones in his memoirs?
> — Yes, that is all true.
> — Really? I always wondered about that. Your son had such a rich imagination. There was no way to tell!
>
> Oneida laughed heartily.
>
> — Oh, he would tell stories that would make you laugh so hard your sides hurt. What a sense of humor! He had so much imagination; we could not stop laughing. He would snipe and make fun of people's names and weaknesses, he had a talent that was really . . . fearsome. (Laughter) But that really happened. As young as he was, he threw the stones at him.
> — He did, but you didn't?
> — Me? No. His father gave him three pesos and he went away. (Hasson 24)

It is significant that Reinaldo and Oneida remember this story differently, disagreeing on a crucial point: who hurled the stones at the approaching man.[3] Unlike Hasson, I am not interested in determining the identity of the thrower. I find much more compelling an exploration of what the contending accounts reveal about the tellers of the tales.

One cannot but notice the emphasis on separation in both accounts: the desire to keep the stranger away from mother and son as if fearing that the man's presence would break up the unity of mother and child. In Oneida's version it is Reinaldo who attempts to bar the intruder access to what seems to be an idyllic two-person scene; in Reinaldo's version it is Oneida who makes every effort to put distance between them and the handsome man, with himself (the son) at first in the role of bewildered observer and later in the role of co-protagonist with the man. In one version, the son wants nothing to do with the father; in the other, the opposite seems to be the case. Although in neither version does the son or mother succeed in keeping the approaching man at bay, Oneida metonymically succeeds in doing so when she later disposes of the two (or three) pesos by lending them, never to be seen again, to one of her sisters. But if she is able to remove the man's money from her son, she is unable to remove from her son's mind the image of the man, as attested by Arenas's recollection of the scene. The casual encounter with the stranger awakens in the child feelings heretofore unknown to him; he seems to desire what his mother once desired but no longer seems to want. Beginning as a spectator of an emotionally charged scene involving his quarreling parents, the child is pulled onto center stage by the desiring and desirable stranger. This results in the ousting of the mother, who is ultimately relegated to the role that the child had — that of spectator — before he and the man make physical and emotional contact.

In her version of the scene on the riverbank, Oneida Fuentes fantasizes about the preservation of a preoedipal structure, in which the child's attachment to the mother predominates, as indicated by her insistence on the child's wish to elide the paternal presence. That Oneida privileges a version that celebrates the mother-son dyad, in which both inhabit a world of blissful symbiosis, is not surprising. In Oneida's fantasy world, Reinaldo will always choose her over his father, a man she cannot imagine ever coming between her and her son. But that is precisely what happens in her son's version, which evinces an oedipal configuration in which the son, in the end, embraces the father.[4] An aggressive and controlling mother attempts to keep the father away from the son, but the boy, who heretofore had an affectionate and erotic bond with his mother, connects affectionately and erotically with the male stranger, who breaks the relationship between mother and son. Identifying with his mother's (repressed) desire for this man, the boy transfers his object-choice from a female to a male figure, one who happens to be none other than the father who abandoned him when he was a baby.[5] With its triangular structure and its erotic undertones, the scene on the riverbank, as constructed by Arenas, re-creates his family romance, a fantasy in which his absent father makes himself present and influential, playing a major role in his son's emergence as a homosexual subject.

More specifically, the scene is a fantasy of paternal seduction, a reading suggested by the pecuniary mediation central to it. The boy's acceptance of his father's money not only establishes a "queer" connection between father and son, but also calls attention to the receptive — passive — role of the child in the encounter, an encounter that acquires an undeniable erotic resonance if one keeps in mind the psychoanalytic formulation of the relation between money and anality. Since retention of money can be traced back, if we believe Freud and others, to an anal libidinal structure, it is suggestive that the encounter between Arenas and his father is marked by money, the two pesos that the son "retains" in his memory. Like the child who experiences erotic pleasure in the retention of feces in the anal stage, "saving" that is subsequently sublimated in the "saving" of money, Arenas experiences an analogous pleasure in the mental retention of his father's money, libidinously treasuring it — and the scene in which he was its recipient — in his imaginary.[6] It therefore should not surprise us that the father-son connection mediated by money in *Antes que anochezca* is echoed and turned into an explicit anal connection in *Viaje a La Habana*, which was inspired by the scene on the riverbank where Arenas and his father once met.[7]

But there is more to Arenas's erotic recuperation of his father in his memoirs. Just a few pages later, Arenas begins the third chapter of *Antes que anochezca* with a revealing statement — "As time went on, the river became for me a place of deep mystery" (25; *Before Night Falls* 8) — adding that "this was the river that gave me a gift: an image that I will never forget" (25; 8). The memorable, indelible "image" to which Arenas refers is that of "over thirty men bathing in the nude" (25; 8), whom the erotically aroused Arenas sees cavorting in the water. But he is also alluding to the "image" of his father, the handsome stranger whom he had admiringly laid his eyes on at the same local river. Arenas's vision of his father, an experience as unforgettable as that of watching the naked swimmers, occurs at a place that for him was shrouded in mystery and where, he tells us, he had the "revelation" (25; 8) that he was attracted to men.[8]

Pertinent to this discussion of the insertion of the father into Arenas's life is a childhood fantasy game that Arenas describes at the end of the third chapter:

> At the time one of my solitary diversions was a game with jars: a number of empty glass containers of all sizes represented a family, that is, my mother, my aunts, my grandparents. Those jars suddenly turned into young swimmers who jumped into the river, while I masturbated. Then, one of the young men would find me, fall in love with me and take me into the bushes. This was paradise. (26; 9)

In this game of bodily transformations in which alluring male bodies take the place of Arenas's close relatives, the boy symbolically incorporates his father into his family constellation, assigning him, with the elimination from his game of all other family members, a privileged place in his affective and erotic life. The fantasizing child not only turns the familial figures of the mother, aunts, and grandparents into irresistible male figures, but also displaces onto the attractive young swimmers his unmentionable desire for the unmentionable — and newly discovered — member of his family. More specifically, the boy embodies his desired father in the young male body that, in the end, possesses him in his paradisiacal "solitary diversions."

Arenas's memorable encounter with his father on the riverbank, which he lovingly evokes at the threshold of his memoirs, can thus be read as a primal fantasy.[9] It has all the signs of a "primal seduction," which Jean Laplanche defines as "a fundamental situation in which an adult proffers to a child verbal, non-verbal and even behavioral signifiers which are pregnant with unconscious sexual significations" (*New Foundations for Psychoanalysis* 126). These "enigmatic signifiers" (126), explains Laplanche, "set the child a difficult, or even impossible, task of mastery and symbolization and the attempt to perform it inevitably leaves behind unconscious residues" (130). In Arenas's case, he reenacts the crucial scene on the riverbank in real and imagined encounters with other men in his life and writing, always in search of the absent but ever-present father.

Early on in his memoirs Arenas recalls two erotic experiences that also suggest the connection between the boy's paternal longing and sexual pleasure. Sharing his uncle Rigoberto's saddle when they would ride into town, the boy would have his "butt on his penis" (40; 20), and he would happily ride along, "bouncing on that huge penis, riding, as it were, on two animals at the same time" (40; 20). And more revealing perhaps is Arenas's evocation of the image of his well-endowed maternal grandfather bathing behind the well:

> For a long time afterward I was jealous of my mother and grand-
> father; in my imagination I saw her being possessed by him, and him
> raping her with his big penis and huge testicles. . . . In all honesty, I
> didn't know whether I was jealous because of my mother or because
> of my grandfather. Perhaps it was a multiple jealousy. . . . I also be-
> came jealous of my aunts, and especially of my grandmother, who

slept in her own bed, but had more rights than anyone else to enjoy those testicles. Although all this existed only in my imagination, for quite a long time I was obsessed with the vision of my naked grandfather. (31; 13–14)

These two childhood sexual episodes involving two paternal figures can be linked to the earlier episode with Arenas's father, the primal fantasy in which the boy "connects" with the handsome stranger on the riverbank. I shall spare my reader an inventory of Arenas's numerous sexual encounters, which, according to his own calculations, reached a figure of about five thousand by the time he was twenty-five years old. Certainly, however, Arenas's erotic awakening in the countryside sets the course for his adult sexual life, initially in Havana and later in exile, in which every male lover becomes, as he once said about a particular one, "sort of a father figure for me" (96; 71).[10]

In addition to Arenas's natural father, other paternal figures play a prominent role in *Antes que anochezca*. Arenas repeatedly expresses his appreciation for José Lezama Lima and Virgilio Piñera, prominent gay Cuban writers who, *in loco patris*, guided his development as a writer. Arenas pays homage to these two nurturing literary fathers not only by referring to them throughout his memoirs, but also by offering affectionate biographical sketches of each of them, which he revealingly places at the core of *Antes que anochezca*. (In an autobiography of sixty-nine chapters, chapter 34 is entirely devoted to Piñera and chapter 35 to Lezama.)

Two references to Piñera and Lezama that appear at the beginning and the end of *Antes que anochezca* are particularly meaningful. In the introduction Arenas explains that one day in 1987, having returned home from a stay in the hospital, he dragged himself to a photograph of Piñera on the wall of his apartment and demanded of him: "Listen to what I have to tell you: I need three more years of life to finish my work, which is my vengeance against most of the human race" (16; xvii). In August 1990, having survived the three years, Arenas ended his autobiography with the words "Thank you, Virgilio" (16; xvii), acknowledging his mentor for having granted him an extension of his life. If Arenas begins *Antes que anochezca* with an evocation of his biological father in "Las piedras," the autobiography's first chapter, he tellingly concludes the writing of his memoirs with another paternal evocation — and invocation — in "El fin," the appropriately titled introduction, which Arenas wrote to end the narrative of his life four months before committing suicide. A caring spiritual father, a "progenitor" of sorts, Piñera not only had demonstrated since 1966 an interest in Arenas's literary life, generously helping him in the painstaking revisions of the manuscript of *El mundo alucinante* (*The Ill-Fated Peregrinations of Fray Servando*), but also symbolically remained at Arenas's side until his death.

The full import of Arenas's last memory of Piñera in *Antes que anochezca* emerges when it is juxtaposed with Arenas's last memory of Lezama, which, not insignificantly, appears in the last chapter, "Los sueños." Arenas recalls a dream that he had about the author of *Paradiso* (*Paradiso*):

> Más adelante soñaba con Lezama, que estaba en una especie de reunión en un inmenso salón; se oía una música lejana y Lezama sacaba un enorme reloj de bolsillo; frente a él estaba su esposa, María Luisa; yo era un niño y me acercaba a él; abría sus piernas y me recibía sonriendo y le decía a María Luisa: "Mira, qué bien está, qué bien está." (335)

> Later I often dreamed of Lezama, who was at a gathering in an enormous hall; music could be heard in the distance and Lezama pulled out a large pocket watch; facing him was his wife, María Luisa. I was a boy, and when I went up to him, he would open his legs and receive me smiling, while saying to María Luisa: "Look how well he [it] is doing, how well he [it] is doing." (311)

This dream, in which a child walks toward an imposing masculine figure who invitingly opens his legs as the child approaches him, has a latent sexual content.[11] The sexualization of the encounter between man and child is intimated not only by Arenas's movement toward a sexually provocative Lezama (a provocation suggested by his alluring posture and by his pulling out an enormous and phallically suggestive pocket watch), but also by the child's reaction to the words that he hears as he makes his way toward Lezama. Assuming the role of the addressee of Lezama's utterance to María Luisa ("Mira, qué bien está, qué bien está"), the child recontextualizes these words and hears in them not only Lezama's affectionate comment about him to his wife, which is how Dolores Koch translates the passage ("Look how well he is doing, how well he is doing"), but also Lezama's enticing invitation to him "to look" at his available masculine anatomy ("Look how well it is doing, how well it is doing"). This is possible because with the absence of the subject pronoun in the Spanish original the subject of the verb could be interpreted as either *he* or *it*. Seduced by Lezama's melodious words and tantalizing body language, the child sees in all this an affirmation of same-sex desire and an invitation to its immediate gratification. Claiming for himself what was intended for Lezama's wife, the child advances toward his irresistible object of desire.

Immediately before his recounting of the dream about Lezama, Arenas writes: "Otras veces los sueños eran en colores y personajes extraordinarios se acercaban a mí, ofreciéndome una amistad que yo quería compartir; eran personajes descomunales pero sonrientes" ("At other times my dreams were in full color and extraordinary people would approach me offering me their friendship, which I accepted gladly; they were enormous creatures with smiling faces") (335; 311). These dreams, of which Arenas offers as an example the one that he has about the *descomunal* Lezama, re-create the childhood scene in which he met his father, thereby rearticulating his primal erotic fantasy. Let us recall that Arenas's father unexpectedly appears before the boy one day on a riverbank, offering not only his friendship but also his affection — an experience that from the spatial and emotional perspective of the impressionable child might have made his father as *extraordinario* and *descomunal* as the men in his dreams. Arenas's dreams are shaped by what Jean Laplanche and Jean-Bertrand Pontalis call "a phantasmatic" (*The Language of Psychoanalysis* 317), which is, in Kaja Silverman's formulation, "an unconscious fantasy or group of related fantasies which underlies a subject's dreams, symptoms, repetitive behavior, and daydreams" (161). Harking back to the foundational primal fantasy recounted in the autobiography's first chapter, Arenas's dream about Lezama suggests a phantasmatic link between a literary father and his biological father.[12] Keeping in mind Arenas's paternal longing, I find it telling that he places "encounters" with Piñera and Lezama at the beginning and at the end of *Antes que anochezca*, for they structurally frame — lovingly embracing as it were — the body of Arenas's memoirs.

I return now to Arenas's reading of the *Iliad*, since the story of Achilles and Arenas's reaction to it play a crucial role in *Antes que anochezca*. What is one to make of the fondness that Arenas had for the *Iliad*, a fondness evident not only in repeated references to it throughout *Antes que anochezca*, but also in the fact that a copy of the Homeric poem was found on his nightstand the day that he committed suicide (Hasson 172; Mayhew 16)? An explanation may be found in the last book of the *Iliad*, Arenas's reading of which, deferred a number of times, moves him to tears. Although Arenas affirms that the scene in which Achilles returns Hector's body to Priam is "a unique moment in literature" (201; 176), he is uncharacteristically laconic when referring to what is certainly for him an extraordinarily moving scene.

In book 24, where Priam negotiates with Achilles for the return of his son's body, he begins his plea with an appeal, "Achilleus like the gods, remember your father" (Homer 488), calling on the Achaean warrior's filial love in the hope that he would feel the pain of a father who misses his son. In the midst of a war that eventually will take his life, Achilles, who indeed "wept . . . for his own father" (Homer 488), gives Hector's body back to his grieving father. Like Achilles, Arenas may have been moved by Priam's words referencing a loving father-son relationship. In Arenas's case, Priam's supplication prompts in him a tearful response because it evoked for him not a caring but an absent father, a man for whom the abandoned son had secured nonetheless a special place in his heart and whom he kept intensely present in his writing. More specifically, Arenas's reading of the passage in which Achilles hands over Hector's body to the imploring Priam — a scene in which a father is reunited with his son — may have recalled for Arenas the childhood scene on the riverbank in which he and his father were fleetingly reunited, a scene with profoundly emotional significance for Arenas. Reading about a father who risks his life in search of his son, Arenas relives the pain of the absence of his own father, who on an unforgettable day unexpectedly sought out the five-year-old Arenas, offering him — albeit only momentarily — paternal love.

As he had done in Cuba in the mid-1970s, when he first read the *Iliad* and began writing *Antes que anochezca*, Arenas may have continued to see himself mirrored in the Homeric characters in the late 1980s, when in exile he resumed and concluded the writing of his autobiography with the *Iliad* still at his side. Reading Homer literally on his deathbed, Arenas likely experienced automourning — the grief of self-loss — when confronting Hector's death, as did Achilles when he lived through that experience.[13] In the *Iliad* Achilles contemplates and laments his own eventual death when he sees reflected in Priam's grief for the loss of his son the prospective grief of his own father, Peleus, who will later be told of his own son's death in Troy. In similar fashion, reflecting on — and reflected in — the process of automourning in the *Iliad*, the mortally ill Arenas also lamented his imminent death.[14] But if Achilles, finding comfort in his father's unconditional love, could imagine Peleus doing for him what Priam did for Hector, Arenas could not imagine his father doing the same for him. He knew that he would die without a grieving father to claim his body and give it a proper burial in his fatherland. Arenas, sadly, died without *padre* or *patria*.

It therefore makes sense that the *Iliad*, which has been called "the great poem of mourning" (Staten 8) and which Arenas considered "the book of books" ("La escritura como re-escritura"), would function in *Antes que anochezca* as a textual mirror, one in which Arenas would see his own life reflected.[15] Just as his reading of the *Iliad* in Cuba moved him to tears, his reading of it some years later in exile may well have elicited an equally lachrymose response: only tears could express what words could not.

Cuba Before Night Falls

In *Antes que anochezca*, recalling his first visit to Havana, where he was taken along with many other young men from the provinces to hear Fidel Castro deliver a speech on 26 July 1960 in Revolutionary Square, Arenas writes, "The fact is that this first trip to Havana was my initial contact with another world, a world of many faces, immense, fascinating. I felt that Havana was my city, that somehow I had to return" (76; *Before Night Falls* 52). Two years later, Arenas found a way to return to the capital, where he lived until his departure from Cuba in 1980. Although for political reasons Arenas was not able to set foot in his beloved country ever again, he managed to return to it by the power of his imagination. In exile Arenas wrote *Viaje a La Habana*, one last visit to the city that thirty years before had dazzled the impressionable young man from Oriente province.[16]

Viaje a La Habana opens with a letter, dated 3 November 1994, that a Cuban exile named Ismael receives in New York from his former wife, Elvia, who encourages him to visit Cuba because their son, Ismaelito, has been asking about him. The novella then proceeds in four sections, the first of which narrates Ismael's reaction to Elvia's letter, memories of his short marriage and his imprisonment in Cuba for allegedly having sexually abused a young man, and his decision to visit his country after having been away from it for fifteen years. The second part, which takes place on 23 December 1994, narrates Ismael's arrival on the island, his walk around some of his old haunts in Havana, and his meeting with a young man, Carlos, who offers to be his guide when he finds Ismael by the seashore crying for the loss of his country and his youth. The third part, which begins the next day, narrates Ismael's stroll through the capital, his visit with Carlos to Guanabo Beach, their passionate sexual encounter at the hotel, which continues into the early morning hours of 25 December, and the disappearance of Carlos and all of Ismael's personal belongings, including the gifts he brought from the United States for his family. The last part, which focuses on events just a few hours later, narrates the long and arduous walk that Ismael, wearing only a pair of shorts, takes to Elvia's apartment in the town of Santa Fe, where he comes face to face with Carlos, who is wearing the clothes that Ismael bought for Ismaelito in New York. Ismael now discovers not only that Carlos is his son, but also that the young man knew all along that Ismael was his father. Unaware of what transpired in the capital between father and son, Elvia explains to Ismael that the purpose of her letter was to lure him to Santa Fe to ask him for help in arranging Ismaelito's escape from Cuba. A Christmas dinner shared by father, mother, and son brings *Viaje a La Habana* to a close.

Viaje a La Habana is, as the title states, a voyage to Havana, but one that is both spatial and temporal, for Ismael's movement from New York to Cuba entails as well a journey to the past. To begin with, a temporal return occurs in a long flashback in the first part that narrates the protagonist's mental voyage to the Cuban capital. As Ismael watches from his New York apartment window the bewildering spectacle of a major snowstorm, he imaginatively transports himself back to the Cuba of his youth, painfully reliving in particular his farcical marriage and his only same-sex experience, for which he was imprisoned. His painful mental journey notwithstanding, Ismael ultimately lets himself envision a possible return:

> He saw himself, not as he actually had lived or believed himself to
> have lived, enslaved, humiliated, poorly dressed, unhappy and hun-
> gry, but rather as young and excited, confidently taking in an atmo-
> sphere that was not aggressive but rather complicitous and protec-
> tive; taking in, experiencing, relishing a sensation of being, of feeling,
> in his place, the only place where he really feels alive. *Because it's not
> about a landscape, the ocean, a tree or a street; it's about the fact that once
> we abandon those places where we truly were alive, where we were born,*

where we were young and lived, we abandon ourselves, we cease to exist
and, what's even worse, without dying once and for all. I will go. I have no
alternative but to return. And suddenly, all that youth, which was not
then how he saw it now, took over him, and he wanted to be that solitary and independent young man who swam in the clear waters of
the ocean. (136–37)[17]

Tempted by Elvia's exhortation to visit Cuba, Ismael imagines a return to
his country as a return to his youth, but not to the island where he had lived.
Instead, Ismael sees himself in a Cuba that would be "complicitous and
protective," one that would allow him to reclaim his authentic self, which he
had lost in the repressive reality of Castro's Cuba and the alienating reality
of exile. Although Ismael quickly recognizes that this is pure fancy, he
nonetheless convinces himself to visit his country one last time, which
would allow him to go back into exile "without memory obsessing him"
(139):

> Yes, he would go, he would go . . . to show to himself that he was
> right to abandon all that and, above all, to prove once and for all and
> forever that a return is not possible, cannot be possible, at least as
> long as time has not been abolished. . . . He would go, he would go,
> but he would go unannounced; he would arrive suddenly, loaded
> with gifts, in the town of Santa Fe to surprise them. (138)

This passage, which offers Ismael's plan for his forthcoming visit to Cuba,
also offers the narrative plan for the telling of Ismael's voyage to the island.
The reader — not Elvia or Ismaelito — will be the one taken by "surprise" by
Ismael's journey to Cuba, since he or she will eventually discover that in the
other three parts of the novella time has been abolished. Ismael goes home
again, but in the realm of fantasy, which is what *Viaje a La Habana* will turn
out to be: an imaginary voyage. Alienated from the cold North, Ismael
superimposes a nostalgic vision of his "warm country" (117) upon the "in-
hospitable" (135) snowy cityscape that his New York apartment window
frames.

The second part of the novella begins with Ismael's arrival in Havana and
with a description of his first stroll through the city:

> For Ismael, to go out suddenly into that light, into the warmth of
> that afternoon, was like abruptly regaining his youth; it felt like sud-

denly being transported to a magical time, frozen in time, his alone, where, in life-giving waves, something [*algo*] . . . penetrated his pores, his nose, his hair, the tip of his fingers, and commanded him to move forward oblivious to any sensation other than walking, seeing, being. (140)

Motivated by a desire to recover—and rewrite—the past, Ismael, as if "transported to a magical time," returns to places that he associates with his lost youth, experiencing during this nostalgic tour of the city the thrill of being penetrated by *algo*. This initial reencounter with his *patria*, which is described in sexually charged language, ends that evening with a startling and auspicious encounter on an isolated beach:

The waves continued to break, with a roar more intense each time, next to a man who, crouching down and with his hands on his face, as if hiding from darkness itself, was crying. For a while, Ismael cried almost silently, one could even say uncontrollably, oblivious to his surroundings and the place where he was. He stayed that way until he sensed that someone [*alguien*] was watching him. When he removed his hands from his face and looked up, he saw a tall shadow next to him. At first, in the darkness, Ismael couldn't see that it was someone cloaked in a cape. Immediately, Ismael stood up, apologizing. At this time of night it is dangerous to walk on the coast, said the figure. It was then that Ismael saw the young man, who wore an olive-green uniform and was cloaked in a cape of the same color. (146)

The sexualization of Ismael's reconnection with the island, figuratively suggested from the start by an indefinite *algo* that penetrates him during his initial walk through Havana, reaches its culmination—and is literalized—some pages later with Ismael's encounter with an indefinite *alguien* who, having forged a clever plan to seduce Ismael, will anally penetrate him only two days after their first meeting on the beach. Offering to be his guide, the enigmatic "figure" helps Ismael satisfy his yearning to reconnect with his *patria*. In other words, the casual encounter with the young man facilitates the search that motivates Ismael's voyage to Havana. But what, specifically, is Ismael searching for? More precisely, why does a text that is ostensibly about an exile's nostalgic return to his country involve an incestuous relationship between a father and his son? Why is the nature of this relationship not disclosed until the end of the narrative, when the identity of the enigmatic young man is revealed in a surprising anagnorisis? Why does the story take place at Christmas time, situating Ismael's return to Cuba in an equally enigmatic Christian context? These narrative elements, which revolve around an incredible coincidence that exceeds verisimilitude — Ismael's casual sexual encounter with a young man who will turn out to be his son — cease to be enigmatic if one interprets the second, third, and fourth parts of *Viaje a La Habana* as a fantasy, a desire-fulfilling reverie.[18]

Since the first part ends with Ismael's decision to go to Havana, one should not find surprising that the second part begins with his arrival in the Cuban capital: "On 23 December 1994 (but who remembers an event so insignificant and remote?) Ismael arrived in Havana" (139). Although it seems to be suggesting a chronologically precise and linear narrative, this ostensibly transparent statement puzzles the reader because of the comment in parentheses. Sounding like an afterthought, as if the narrator wished to downplay its importance, the parenthetical comment does not have the seemingly intended effect on the reader, for it not only calls attention to itself but also obliquely provides what in fact is a key that helps unlock the novella's secret. The narrator's characterization of the "event" as "insignificant" paradoxically prompts us to meditate precisely on its possible significance. Moreover, the narrator's formulation is signaling something that the adjective "remote," in its meaning of "improbable," is pointing to as well: an improbable or unreal occurrence, that is, a fantasy. The narrator's parenthetical comment thus offers unsuspected textual clues. For it not only suggests the improbability or unreality of the "event," but it does so with words in parentheses, a textual opening, as it were, that calls to mind another opening in the novella: the window that frames Ismael's fantasy, his imaginary voyage to Cuba, which is the "event" framed by the parentheses. Just as the parentheses mark a break in the narrative flow of the sentence in which they appear, the opening sentence of the novella's second part marks a break in the narrative flow of the tale in which it appears. The narrator's parenthetical comment, which at first disorients the reader, ends up orienting him or her, suggesting a reading of *Viaje a La Habana* that disorients the apparent linearity and "reality" of the story.

That Arenas's novella is a fantasy finds support in other self-referential registers in the narrative. Ismael, the protagonist, at times functions as what

Naomi Schor would term an "interpretant," the reader's specular double who guides him or her in the interpretive act (168–70). For instance, taking multiple cues from Ismael (*Viaje a La Habana* 142, 160, 165, 173), the reader must also ask what were the "real" motives behind Ismael's trip to Havana. Did Ismael return to Cuba to fulfill a desire to see his country one last time or did he do it following what he intriguingly calls a "mysterious sign" (173)? More pertinent for my purposes is Ismael's "reading" of his hotel room the morning after his sexual encounter with Carlos. When he wakes up and realizes that the young man has left with all his belongings, Ismael, "contemplating the empty room" (176), rejoicingly concludes that what happened the night before "was not a dream" (176). By putting in doubt, albeit only momentarily, the reality of the climactic scene, Ismael, with this dubitative gesture at the level of the story, invites the reader to question at the level of discourse not only the reality of this particular episode, but also, and more importantly, the reality of the entirety of Ismael's voyage to Havana. Although the reader ultimately will agree with Ismael that the two men had passionate sex at the hotel, he or she will conclude that the episode at the hotel is indeed "real" but only in the intradiegetic reality of Ismael's reverie in New York. Ismael's reading of an absence, that is, the *vacío* (emptiness) that Carlos left in his hotel room, as proof of something "real" (that Carlos and he spent the night together) both mirrors and prompts a reading that inverts Ismael's: something apparently "real" (the tale of the protagonist's voyage to Havana) is but an absence—a fantasy that fills the emotional *vacío* that Ismael feels while looking out his apartment window on a cold and snowy day in New York.

If *Viaje a La Habana* can be read as a "fantastic" voyage, where does this journey take us as readers? Toward the end of the first part, after drawing up a list of familiar reasons for Ismael's trip to Cuba, which include nostalgia for the "distinctive rhythm" (137) of the language of his country and a need to show his compatriots on the island that he has succeeded in exile, the narrator offers another reason: "Y además de todo eso, Ismael sentía una curiosidad casi morbosa por conocer a su hijo" (And besides all that, Ismael felt an almost morbid curiosity to know his son) (138). Why does the narrator characterize as "morbid" Ismael's curiosity regarding his son? Why does he use the carnally connotative verb *conocer* and not one more precise like *ver* (to see) or *reencontrarse* (to be reunited), given that Ismael and his son, although they have not been in contact for the last fifteen years, in fact "know" each other? How are we to interpret the narrator's choice of language—words that teasingly hint at something peculiar about Ismael? This provocative sentence, as it turns out, holds a key to the novella, since what ensues in the narrative is an elaboration of the satisfaction of Ismael's curiosity, a curiosity that is motivated by a desire that neither the narrator nor Ismael dares name. In Havana the sexually repressed Ismael inexplicably discards his original plans to go immediately to his former wife's house in Santa Fe and instead surrenders to the whims of the handsome and seductive young man whom he meets on the beach, thereby satisfying—unbeknownst to him—his "almost morbid curiosity to know his son." Why is this key to the novella placed at the end of a list of possible reasons for Ismael's trip to Havana, in a statement that on a first reading goes practically unnoticed? Delineating the emotional road map of Ismael's visit to Cuba, the narrator's words conform to the structuring principle of the narrative: the alternation of concealment and disclosure of information. Celibate for more than twenty years, Ismael in his fantasy gradually lets open the doors to his gay closet, also letting out in the process the "morbid" secret that he and the text diligently attempt, but ultimately fail, to contain within their emotional and narrative walls.

I now revisit three pivotal scenes in *Viaje a La Habana*: Ismael's first meeting with the attractive, as yet unidentified young man on a Havana beach; their subsequent sexual encounter at the hotel; and their reencounter, some hours later, in Elvia's apartment in Santa Fe.

Scene 1: After describing a tropical nightfall on the beach, the narrator writes, "The waves continued to break, with a roar more intense each time, next to a man who, crouching down and with his hands on his face, as if hiding from darkness itself, was crying" (146). Next, "someone cloaked in a cape" (146) approaches the crying man and the two engage in a circuitous conversation. They later walk back to the hotel together, and the young man in the cape, having offered his services as a guide, cryptically warns his interlocutor as he takes his leave, "Don't miss this opportunity or your desires will go unsatisfied" (151). Partly concealed from each other by the darkness of the evening, as well as by their attire and comportment, two strangers participate in a verbal exchange that is not entirely revealing. In what is clearly flirtatious banter, the young man promises to lead Ismael through an unexplored geography of desires. But, for the moment, those desires—like the two men's identities and bodies—remain teasingly unrevealed.

Scene 2: At the hotel a day later, Ismael opens his luggage (which we might read as the traveler's closet), displays its content for the benefit of the young man's viewing, and anxiously offers his guest some *prendas* (or "clothes"). After trying them on, the young man, who has claimed that his name is Carlos, undresses and "throws himself face up on the bed" (174), provocatively exposing, and offering, to Ismael his own enticing *prendas* (or "family jewels," another meaning of the Spanish noun). If at the beach the two men conceal their bodies and desires, at the hotel they fully expose them. But if for Ismael "the entire young man" was, as the narrator describes him in this scene, "a promised land" (174), he, like Moses, is kept from fully experiencing at this time the joy of entering paradise. Before Ismael comes to the realization that he truly has reached his "promised land" (the father-land), he will have to wander for another day.

Scene 3: In Santa Fe, in Elvia's apartment, the secret that propels the story is revealed. Ismaelito admits to having known all along that the man whom he met on an isolated beach and with whom he later had sex was his father. In so doing, he refuses to accept the ignorance that Ismael alleges. "Don't try to deceive yourself because I did not deceive you" (179), the son quickly admonishes his father. Proudly displaying "his" *prendas*, that is, fully clad in the clothes to which he is rightfully entitled, Ismaelito forces the barely clad Ismael to confront the naked truth: his fantasy of having an incestuous relationship with his son. At last, identities, bodies, and desires are laid out in the open. In his last words in the novella, responding to Elvia's request that he help Ismaelito leave Cuba, Ismael verbalizes, albeit cryptically, his secret desire: "Ismaelito sabe que yo haré cuanto pueda, y aún más, para resolver su salida" (Ismaelito knows that I'll do whatever I can, and even more, to facilitate his departure) (181). The vague but deliberate phrase "y aún más" points to Ismael's own *salida*, not from Cuba, but from a place equally oppressive, the "closet" of his queer sexuality. Returning to Cuba, Ismael not only comes out as a gay man, but also acts on his incestuous desires. But, alas, it is all a fantasy.

In *The Art of the Novel* Milan Kundera writes that "the novel's spirit is the spirit of complexity. Every novel says to the reader: 'Things are not as simple as you think'" (18). *Viaje a La Habana* is not an exception to this rule. If at first Arenas's novella seems to be a simple linear narrative about an exile's return to his native country, a more careful reading reveals that it is a fantasy — the protagonist's imaginary voyage to Havana. I must admit, however, borrowing Kundera's words, that things are not as simple as I have thus far made them appear. One cannot end a reading of *Viaje a La Habana* without considering another reading, that of *Granma*, the newspaper that participates in the circuits of desire in Arenas's novella.

To join Ismael in his hotel room, where visits from Cuban nationals are not permitted, "Carlos" devises a plan that would involve bribing two hotel employees. Ismael will conceal a hundred-dollar bill in a copy of the Cuban newspaper, which he will hand to the man at the front desk, telling him that he is expecting a militiaman (Carlos) to deliver to his room a copy of *Granma*'s morning edition. Carlos will do the same with the elevator attendant, telling him, while handing over the newspaper with the money, that it is a present from Ismael. (Given the importance that Arenas attributes to the two pesos he received from his father, one should not find surprising that money facilitates in *Viaje a La Habana* the reunion, clearly carnal in this instance, between a father and his son. The two pesos in *Antes que anochezca* appreciate in value in *Viaje a La Habana*, turning into two hundred dollars, arguably accounting not so much for economic but for emotional inflation.) The plan goes without a hitch, and Carlos, appearing at Ismael's door with *Granma* in hand, says, "I brought you a newspaper so that you would keep it as one would a very important document that every citizen must read" (170). Once inside the room, Carlos writes his name and address on a page of the newspaper, which is not mentioned again until the last scene in Santa Fe, when Ismaelito, to prove to Ismael that there had been no deception between them, tells him, "Get the newspaper that I left in your room. Do you remember that I wrote my name and address on it for you? Didn't you read it? There you'll find my real name, which is also yours, and my address, which is this one" (179–80). Heeding the young man's words, the reader cannot but regard the newspaper as "a very important document" that he or she, like the "citizen" to whom Carlos refers, "must read." The *Granma*, which goes unread in the course of the narrative, can be read as an emblem, or an interior duplication, of the text in which it is inscribed: a narrative the clues of which likewise go unread by both Ismael and the reader until the very end.[19] If the newspaper is a *mise en abyme* of the novella, and if the name written on it is, as Ismaelito tells Ismael, "my real name" but also "yours," then the question arises: In what way, mirroring the "text" inscribed on the newspaper—the name "Ismael"—does the "text" of the novella also allow a double reading? In other words, how is it possible to

CHAPTER THREE

· 84 ·

read in the novella, as in the newspaper, the presence of the father in the son? Just as, at the level of the story, *Granma* circulates unread, another text, at the level of discourse, likewise circulates unread by the reader of *Viaje a La Habana* and, like *Granma*, offers itself in due course as a key to the novella. I am referring to *Antes que anochezca*, Arenas's memoirs, in the pages of which resides the answer to the question: How can one read the father in the son? Anyone familiar with Arenas's autobiography and with *Viaje a La Habana* cannot help but perform a "circular reading" (Calinescu 455) of the two works, that is, a reading of the novella through the lens of the autobiography, and a reading of the autobiography through the lens of the novella. This reading is essential for an understanding not only of Ismael's fantasy but also of the ways in which its creator, Arenas, has projected onto the protagonist of *Viaje a La Habana* his own incestuous fantasy.

It is not difficult to recognize Arenas, as he is constructed in *Antes que anochezca*, in Ismael. Both are gay men with analogous experiences in Cuba and in exile. In fact, some episodes in *Viaje a La Habana* and *Antes que anochezca* are almost identical. For example, both men are accused of sexual corruption, brought to trial, and incarcerated in the Morro prison, where, nicknamed "the Calf," they abstain from having sex with other prisoners. In the transition from the "real" to the "fictional," not only does Arenas become Ismael, but Arenas's mother becomes Elvia, Ismael's former wife. Each being left by her husband, each woman resigns herself to her lot as a single mother caring for an only child. If Elvia is modeled on Arenas's mother and if Ismael is modeled on Arenas, on whom is Ismaelito modeled? Ismaelito, not surprisingly, is modeled on the family's absent and enigmatic member: Arenas's father. While *Viaje a La Habana* is a nostalgic journey to the past, behind Ismael's fantasy of return to his fatherland figures the author's personal childhood fantasy. For the journey to the past in *Viaje a La Habana* is a regression of sorts, an emotional voyage to the scene on the riverbank in which the five-year-old Arenas met his desiring and desirable father.

The biblical allusions in the novella contribute to the characterization of Ismael as a son figure: the name Ismael immediately calls to mind Abraham's son, who is exiled from his father's house; and the language used in some of the Havana passages to describe Ismael evokes the figure of Christ, the son of God.[20] Since the former does not need elaboration, let us turn to a consideration of the latter. Finding himself in Cuba from 23 December to

25 December, Ismael reflects on the meaning of Christmas, on "the birth of a child" (168). The mention of this "acontecimiento único" (unique event) (168), as Ismael calls it, foreshadows another event, no less unique, that will take place shortly after Ismael's reflections: Ismael and Carlos's sexual encounter, the climax and denouement of which are narrated, rather enigmatically, in language that is Christologically allusive. On his way to Santa Fe, only hours after the climactic scene at the hotel, Ismael — with a pair of shorts as his only attire, bloody feet, disheveled hair, and carrying on his shoulders a heavy piece of timber that he inexplicably picked up on his walk along the coast — is stoned and insulted by a multitude that follows him on his journey. And when Ismael reaches his former wife's house, Elvia "with true devotion washed, dried and cared for [his] bloody feet" (179). This "queer" re-creation of the passion of Christ concludes with "the father before the son" (179) at the dinner table, evoking the Christian return of the son to the father, in other words, the resurrection, to which the text alluded some pages before, when Ismael, in a moment of unbridled passion at the hotel, tells the young man, "¿No te das cuenta que yo estaba muerto y que tú me has resucitado?" (Can't you see that I was dead and that you have resurrected me?) (173).

With these associations in mind (Ismael, Christ, son), let us consider again the scene in which Ismael and Ismaelito first meet. As Ismael, overcome by emotion on arriving in Havana, inconsolably cries on an isolated beach, *alguien* suddenly appears on the scene and interrupts Ismael's crying by telling him, "At this time of night it is dangerous to walk on the coast" (146). Fearing that the person offering the advice could be "an agent provocateur" (150), Ismael ironically responds, "The advice must come from a reliable source" (150). To which the young man retorts, "You can be sure that it certainly is" (150). Like Ismael, the reader initially does not know what to make of these words or, for that matter, of the person who utters them, who inexplicably enters Ismael's life at a moment when Ismael feels alone and vulnerable. Reading this scene intertextually with *Antes que anochezca*, the reader "can be sure" to get to the "reliable source" from which this paternal advice originates. I describe the young man's advice as paternal not just because of its tone and the puerile image that is projected of the person to whom it is given (a man who, in fetal position, inconsolably cries), but also because of the physical appearance of the person who gives it: a young man "in his twenties" (147) whom, as the two men later approach a lighted area, Ismael discovers, to his surprise and delight, to be "un bello ejemplar masculino, alto, trigueño, apuesto" (a beautiful specimen of a man, tall, dark, and handsome) (149).

Alto, trigueño, apuesto. The attentive reader of *Antes que anochezca* cannot but notice that the description of the enigmatic figure who unexpectedly insinuates himself into Ismael's life is the same as the one used to describe another enigmatic figure, Arenas's father, an echo that is all the more meaningful given that in Spanish "tall, dark, and handsome" is not a set phrase, as it is in English.[21] What is more, not only was the twenty-something father who approached five-year-old Reinaldo on the riverbank "apuesto, alto, trigueño" ("handsome, tall and dark") (*Antes que anochezca* 18; *Before Night Falls* 2), but his appearance before his son, as described in the autobiography, was sudden and surprising, as was the young man's appearance before Ismael in *Viaje a La Habana*. As the reader of *Antes que anochezca* will recall, Arenas's father emerges as if out of nowhere in an isolated area, near a body of water, and, despite possible physical harm to himself, approaches his son, who, confused but appreciative, welcomes the attention of the stranger. The isolated area where Ismael and the young man meet in *Viaje a La Habana*, "a stony area and a bit of ocean" (144), calls to mind the stony river in the countryside where Arenas meets his father. In addition, the young man takes a risk when he approaches Ismael (he neglects his responsibilities as a militiaman by consorting with the "enemy," a Cuban American visiting the island), a behavior that evokes the action of Arenas's father, who also takes a risk when he approaches his son on the riverbank (he is the target of the stones being hurled by Arenas's angry mother). Arenas thus connects Castro to the figure of the castrating mother: Carlos takes a risk by going against measures of Castro's government; Arenas's father takes a risk by going against the wishes of the boy's mother.[22] And finally, the revelation in *Viaje a La Habana* and *Antes que anochezca* of the identity of the person who was to both Ismael and Arenas an attractive and enigmatic "figure" does not take place until some time after the encounter, a deferral that contributes to the creation in both texts of an aura of fantasy.[23] Led by the clues inscribed on the pages of *Granma*, how are we therefore to read the presence of the father (of Arenas) in the son (Ismaelito)?

The "fantasy" told in the second, third, and fourth parts of this novella can be regarded as a veiled re-creation of Arenas's episode with his father, a crucial experience in the writer's life whose relevance to *Viaje a La Habana* is established at the beginning of the novella. In her letter to Ismael, referring to their son, Elvia writes, "I believe that it is always important for a child to see his father at least once in his life" (115). Clearly, the mother's words reflect, and highlight, a sentiment that has its origin in one of Arenas's most profound life experiences.[24] Arenas re-creates and amplifies in *Viaje a la Habana* what was for him a life-transforming event, the "seduction scene" on the riverbank; he yields to an impulse to narrate, more elaborately in this instance, a childhood experience, a primal fantasy, that he compulsively tells. Unlike the versions in "Cronología (irónica, pero cierta)," in the documentary *Havana*, and in *El palacio de las blanquísimas mofetas* (*The Palace of the White Skunks*), versions that basically do not deviate from the one in *Antes que anochezca*, the version told in *Viaje a La Habana* fictionally expands on the paternal encounter, developing the incestuous telemachy that is only suggested in the autobiography. *Viaje a La Habana* fills in the blanks that will remain unfilled in the text of *Antes que anochezca*, for Arenas inserts in the novella an erotic dynamic between father and son that one can read only between the lines in his memoirs. Ismaelito (the son) desires and seduces Ismael (the father), who, at the end of the novella, admits his desire for his son. Even though the plot of *Viaje a La Habana* is significant in itself, by reading it with *Antes que anochezca* in mind one can also see that behind the novella's fantasy lurks another (inverted) fantasy, the one that Arenas kept close to his chest (and heart) until the writing of this novella: a father (Ismaelito as a veiled figure of Arenas's father) desires and seduces his son (Ismael as a figure of Arenas, the son), who, at the end of the novella, admits his desire for his father. After an arduous voyage (like Ismael's to Santa Fe), a voyage that soon is to come to an end (Cuba, exile, AIDS, death), Arenas confronts his wish for a father-son union, a desire that is at the core of a novella where he both inscribes and textually satisfies his paternal longing. In the guise of fiction, the son (Arenas) searches for and finds his desiring and desired father in an unforgettable return to his fatherland. Arenas's long-awaited *acontecimiento único* finally takes place in this, his last, *Viaje a La Habana*.

Continuity of the Voyages: Arenas with Merlin

To end our voyage through these texts, I explore briefly another voyage to Havana, the one on which María de las Mercedes Santa Cruz y Montalvo, Countess Merlin, goes in 1840, almost forty years after having left the island of her birth, and about which she writes in her own *Viaje a La Habana*. Born in Cuba in 1789, María de las Mercedes was reunited in Spain in 1802 with her parents, who had moved there without her just a few months after her birth. (In 1798 Merlin's father visited Cuba but returned to Spain without his daughter, who was being raised by her maternal great-grandmother.) In 1809, in Spain, she married Christophe Antoine, Count Merlin, who in 1812 took her to France, where she died in 1852. Countess Merlin visited Cuba only once, in the summer of 1840, and shortly thereafter she wrote *La Havane*, her best-known book, which she wrote in French and which appeared in 1844; that same year an abridged Spanish translation, *Viaje a La Habana*, was published.[25]

Arenas not only borrows the title of Merlin's memoirs for his novella, but also begins his *Viaje a La Habana* with an epigraph taken from the countess's book: "¡Sólo encuentro un montón de piedras sin vida y un recuerdo vivo!" (I find only a pile of lifeless stones and a living memory!) (113).[26] This "appropriation" of Merlin is not an isolated case in Arenas's oeuvre. Fascinated by her, Arenas includes Merlin as a character in two of his novels, *La Loma del Ángel* (*Graveyard of the Angels*) and *El color del verano* (*The Color of Summer*); mentions her in two other novels, *Arturo, la estrella más brillante* (*The Brightest Star*) (54; 79) and *Otra vez el mar* (*Farewell to the Sea*) (207; 180); and even uses her name as a pseudonym in his correspondence with friends ("Adorada Chelo" 102; "Delfín Prats Pupo" 82). Identifying with Merlin, with whom he shares an exilic and marginal condition, Arenas attempts to re-create and recover through his writing, as the countess had done through hers, the fatherland he left behind.[27] But there is another bond, a more intimate one, that unites the two writers: Merlin's "living memory," which, although not identified in the novella's epigraph, resonates with Arenas.

Merlin writes about her "living memory" in a section of letter 15 titled "La casa paterna." Having evoked a childhood scene in which her father, with her sitting on his lap, shows her the family's genealogical tree, Merlin concludes the evocation by saying, "Unfortunately, where's my father? I find only a pile of lifeless stones and a living memory!" (*La Habana* 116). What role does the father play in Merlin's life and works? Far from being idyllic, as the preceding extract seems to suggest and as the countess herself claims in *Mis doce primeros años*, Merlin's childhood in Cuba was marked by repeated acts of abandonment and separation. Although Merlin insists on idealizing her father despite his continuous neglect, the text of *Mis doce primeros años* unconsciously undermines her idealizing intentions. Mirroring Merlin's story of paternal inattention, the sad stories that Merlin tells of Cuban domestic slaves can be read, as Sylvia Molloy has convincingly done, as projections and corrections of her father's failings. The trauma of abandonment "accompanies" Merlin on her voyage — literal and textual — to Havana. Ostensibly made to claim her share of her father's inheritance (Méndez Rodenas, *Gender and Nationalism in Colonial Cuba* 24), Merlin's visit to the tropical island indeed had financial reasons, but it also had equally important emotional ones. The countess's return to her fatherland, from which she had been separated for four decades, may have been motivated also by a desire to reconnect, symbolically, with her father. Although in the eyes of Merlin's loved ones (and readers) Count Jaruco comes across as "una bestia" (an animal), as Eliseo Diego would regard Arenas's father a century and a half later ("El silencio de los elogios" 3), Mercedes idealizes him in her memoirs, just as Reinaldo will his own father in *Antes que anochezca*. It is therefore not surprising that Arenas, feeling Merlin's pain and paternal longing, would ask with her, "Where's my father?" But if Arenas leaves out of his epigraph this crucial question, which immediately precedes the countess's exclamation that sets the tone for the novella, he nonetheless does not stop from asking it, since that is precisely the question that he poses in his *Viaje a La Habana* and in *Antes que anochezca*. The *piedras* that Arenas evokes in the first chapter of his memoirs bring back to him, as did to Merlin the *piedras* from her father's house, a *recuerdo vivo*, that of his father, a memory rekindled by his reading of Merlin and Homer and kept alive in his own writing.

FOUR

All About Mother

....

Wouldn't you be thrilled to see me
and my daughters on our way to the whorehouse!
FEDERICO GARCÍA LORCA,
La casa de Bernarda Alba
(*The House of Bernarda Alba*)

Thus begins Reinaldo Arenas's short story "El Cometa Halley" ("Halley's Comet"):

> Very late one night in the summer of 1891 (that's right, 1891), when
> Pepe el Romano runs away with Adela's virginity, though leaving her
> behind, everything seems to have come to a most tragic end for Ber-
> narda Alba's five daughters: Adela, Pepe's lover, hangs from a noose
> fastened to the ceiling of her maiden room; Angustias keeps intact
> her forty years of chastity; and the rest of the sisters, Magdalena,
> Amelia, and Martirio, are also condemned to spinsterhood or the
> convent. (83; 138)[1]

This recapitulation of the ending of Federico García Lorca's *La casa de Bernarda Alba* is followed by the startling disclosure that things did not really
happen that way. The Cuban's provocative revelation sets in motion what
Gérard Genette would term a "corrective continuation" of the Spanish play
(175, 192–95). Giving a humorous twist to García Lorca's tragic ending,
Arenas's revised and expanded version of the history of the Alba women
begins by describing how the four older sisters disobey their mother, take
Adela down, and slap her back to life. This defiant act culminates in the
women's escape to Cuba.

After this opening account of the daughters' transatlantic emancipation from their tyrannical mother, the narrator fast-forwards almost two decades to tell us about their participation in the frenzy generated by the return of Halley's Comet in 1910. Although convinced, like most people, that the world is going to end when Earth passes through the comet's poisonous tail, the sisters do not join others in prayer for the salvation of their souls. Instead, incited by the sexually liberated Adela, who comes from Havana to die with her older sisters, the Alba women participate in a communal orgy on the streets of Cárdenas, the provincial city to which the four older siblings had moved. To everyone's surprise, the comet comes and goes, leaving the world, but not the sisters, intact. Commemorating their transformation and flaunting their liberation, Angustias, Magdalena, Amelia, and Martirio — in a joint effort with Adela — turn their house into a popular whorehouse, aptly naming it El Cometa Halley. And as the narrator not unexpectedly notes in the last line of the story, parodying the ending of García Lorca's play, "None of them died a virgin" ("El Cometa Halley" 107; "Halley's Comet" 156).[2]

This summation makes clear that the return of Halley's Comet expands the Alba sisters' horizon of experiences: sex and its pleasures, which had been barred from the maternal house in Spain, are freely welcomed into the sororal house of sexual pleasure. Insofar as Arenas's tale is a tail of sorts, a textual extension appended to the Spanish play, the comet's tail can be regarded as an emblem of Arenas's prolongation of the history of García Lorca's women. After I dovetail Arenas's and García Lorca's tales in order to explore the Alba sisters' liberating voyage to Havana, a voyage that concludes, like Ismael's in *Viaje a La Habana*, with the joyful — and, in this case, humorous — release of the characters' repressed sexual desires, I enlarge on the reading of "El Cometa Halley" by situating the story in the mother-son dynamic that figures prominently in Arenas's life and oeuvre.

The Fiery Return of the Alba Sisters

In the last scene of *La casa de Bernarda Alba*, on discovering Adela's hanging body, the servant La Poncia puts her hands around her own neck and laments, "May we never have that ending!" (199). Bernarda immediately commands everyone not to cry and, referring to Adela, declares, "She, the youngest daughter of Bernarda Alba, died a virgin. Did you hear me? Quiet, quiet, I said. Quiet!" (199; *The House of Bernarda Alba* 172). With these famous last words, the controlled and controlling Bernarda, in the female sphere of the home, attempts to assert maternal control over her daughters by proclaiming multiple expressive orifices closed. Gaping bodies, as represented by the women's clamoring mouths and Adela's penetrated vagina, have no place in Bernarda's hermetic house. Silence, finality, closure: that is what Bernarda wants but not what she gets—or so claims Arenas. According to the Cuban's narrative, García Lorca did not complete his story, leaving it "unfinished and unclear" ("El Cometa Halley" 83; "Halley's Comet" 138), because he was killed by Adela's lover, after whom García Lorca had gone in hot pursuit while the events in the Alba household were still unfolding. Although García Lorca is unsuccessful in his quest to be possessed by Pepe, he is successful in having his textual body possessed by Arenas, who gladly fills its gaps, thus fulfilling La Poncia's wish for a different ending.

That the servant enables Arenas's appropriation of García Lorca's text is revealed in the story's epigraph, which is taken from *La casa de Bernarda Alba*: "No one knows how one's life will end" ("El Cometa Halley" 83). Repeating La Poncia's warning to Bernarda about the uncertain future of the Alba women, Arenas has García Lorca obliquely authorize the continuation of the play. Beginning with a paratextual commentary about the unpredictability of endings, "El Cometa Halley" proceeds to narrate the death of the original author (García Lorca) and set the stage for the birth of his reader, our author (Arenas). By collapsing the distinction between life and fiction, the Cuban's textual performance dramatizes negotiations among author, text, and reader. Placing García Lorca in the same fictive space as his literary creations, Arenas not only has the author die at the hands of one of his characters but also calls attention to the need for an active reader to resume the writing of García Lorca's text by filling in the gaps left by the dead author. An allegory of reading, Arenas's writing of "El Cometa Halley" offers a potential ending to García Lorca's indeterminate text.

But there is more to Arenas's playful story. Deposing a canonical dramatic work, Arenas foregrounds the Alba daughters' ascent to power as they dislodge their domestically empowered mother. In other words, performing a dethronement at the level of discourse and at the level of the story, "El Cometa Halley" imaginatively displaces a tightly rule-governed play to tell, in a less restrictive literary genre, the story of the displacement of Bernarda's maternal authority. Through its emphasis on hyperbolic liberation and reversal, "El Cometa Halley" embraces a festive spirit that can be assimilated to the excessive, hybrid, topsy-turvy world of carnival. Adela's hanging body marks the end of García Lorca's play and the beginning of Arenas's story. In *La casa de Bernarda Alba* Adela's suspended state is seen as a tragic death, as a finality; in "El Cometa Halley" it is humorously seen for what it literally is: a suspension — not a termination of life but a transitory condition that leads to the animation of the lifeless Adela and the transformation of her resuscitating sisters into unlikely subversives. Besides initiating the Alba women's rebellion against Bernarda, this playfully bizarre opening scene, in which the slapping, screaming, and reproaching older sisters lower Adela's body, also sets in motion — and is emblematic of — the story's carnival logic and spirit: the systematic lowering of all that is held high.[3]

Refusing to live any longer under "the fearsome old woman's iron hand" and coming together in their desire to bring about "Bernarda Alba's fall from power" ("El Cometa Halley" 84; "Halley's Comet" 139), the five sisters disregard their mother's threats, jump out the window, escape through the stables, cross the Sierra Morena, and end up in the port city of Cádiz, where they book passage on a ship to Havana.[4] The Alba women's liberation traces a topographical trajectory, literal and metaphoric, that conforms to the story's carnivalesque thrust. If geographically the sisters' escape from their mother country follows a downward movement in Andalusia (from Córdoba through Seville to Cádiz), a corresponding vertical and horizontal displacement is suggested in their escape from their mother's house. Once Adela has been brought down, the sisters move away from the door, which is guarded by their mother, and exit through a rear window that leads to the stables, through which they have to pass to evacuate Bernarda's property. Taking into account the traditional association between the house and the human body and considering that the daughters' exit from their mother's house entails a descending backward movement, one can argue that the women's escape represents a voiding of the body. This symbolic economy, which allows us to see the Alba sisters' evacuation in physiological terms, can be read in the context of Mary Douglas's discussion of filth as "matter out of place" (40). Extricating their bodies from Bernarda's control by discharging themselves outside her house, the Alba sisters deliberately take themselves out of the ordered place in which family and culture had situated them. As a result, they become the embodiment not only of what Natalie Zemon Davis calls "female disorderliness — the female out of her place" (129), but also of symbolic impurity. More precisely, no longer in their mother's house, no longer in their place, the sisters are transformed into figurative excremental matter. Their self-expelled bodies and their movement toward and through the scatological spaces of Bernarda's stables mark the women's transgressiveness, their disrespectful departure from — and the degradation of — Bernarda's immaculate house. This initial scene in Spain thus introduces a process of carnivalesque inversion, debasement, and defilement that will culminate two decades later in the sisters' own "stable," the house of prostitution that they will make famous in Cárdenas.

If by going to Cuba in 1891 the five Alba women distance themselves from their mother, achieving a geographic separation that allows them to seek sexual pleasure, the four older ones, who repeatedly fail to attract men in their first few months in Cuba, soon succumb once again to the emotional and ideological hold that Bernarda has over them. Their transitory liberation comes to an end when they have to confront Adela's parturition, since Pepe has left their youngest sister with child. Adela's uninhibited sexuality, which is visually marked first by her pregnancy and subsequently by a child whose paternity is claimed by twenty-five men of different races, offers a public spectacle of desires that her sisters now disavow. The older sisters' reaction to Adela, which grows out of fascination and aversion, follows the logic of abjection.[5] They expel the unruly sister out of their lives in an attempt to reestablish boundaries; in other words, they aim to restore order in the Alba household by closing themselves to the threat of the abject other. To this differentiating end, they kidnap their nephew (who is christened José de Alba), move away from Havana, and settle in Cárdenas in an impenetrable and convent-like house, where Adela's name is never mentioned and where her son is spoken of as the nephew whom they brought home after his mother's death in childbirth. Angustias, Magdalena, Amelia, and Martirio, by abjecting their youngest sister, come to embody their mother's authority, reincorporating into the text the temporarily suspended oppressive maternal order. Identified in Cárdenas as "the Spanish nuns" (88; 142), the four older Alba women devote their lives to the church and to the care of their nephew. Living in a house with dark curtains and always dressed in black, the four sisters "promised themselves to stop being women" (87), thus containing their sexuality. At the same time, they control the sexuality of their nephew, who is also always dressed in black and who is allowed to leave the house only to peddle the artificial flowers and knitted goods made by his aunts.

The Alba house in Cárdenas becomes an asexual space policed by ever vigilant maternal eyes. The sisters not only re-create the house of Bernarda Alba but also subject their nephew to the same life of repression that their mother forced on them. They live in abnegation for two decades until the day when Halley's Comet and Adela return. On that day, the youngest of the five Alba sisters suddenly returns from the dead, resurrected, as it were, just as she had been when her sisters slapped her back to life. Adela's return, paralleling the comet's, constitutes an imminent danger to the older sisters' lives; specifically, she threatens their sexually repressed existence. But unlike the comet, which does not cause the anticipated "universal conflagration" ("El Cometa Halley" 93; "Halley's Comet" 146), Adela brings her sisters' world to an end with a metaphoric conflagration of sexual desire.

If at first Angustias, Magdalena, Amelia, and Martirio refuse to respond to Adela's loud and persistent knocking when she appears at their house, they eventually open the door. What they see is as menacing to them as the comet: Adela has arrived dressed in a magnificent evening gown, accessorized with a mantilla, white gloves, suede boots, and a fan of peacock feathers. The sisters' reaction is not difficult to guess: they step back in horror as Adela theatrically enters the house, "swaying her hips and gesturing to the coachman to bring down her luggage, a monumental trunk full of excellent wines, Baccarat glasses, a gramophone, and an oil painting that was an enlarged portrait [*una reproducción ampliada del retrato*] of Pepe el Romano" (96; 148).

Dressed in colorful attire, which her mother forbade, attire that makes her stand out, like the comet, in the darkness of the evening, the transgressive Adela frightens her sisters and not only because of her appearance (in the sense of both her unexpected visit and her extravagant dress). In her "monumental trunk" she carries emblems of forbidden desires that for years have been kept locked in the older women's psyches. Adela's narrative portrait, which is strategically placed in the middle of the story and which is rendered visually by Adela's appearing in the frame of her sisters' front door, significantly ends with the mention of another portrait, that of Pepe el Romano. A portrait within a portrait, Pepe's "enormous" likeness is not only sexually allusive (104; 154), because of its magnitude and its insertion in (the portrait of) Adela and her trunk, but textually emblematic as well. The *reproducción ampliada* of Pepe's portrait remands the reader to the narrative in which it is inscribed. For Arenas's story, having been written in intertextual dialogue with and as an augmentation of *La casa de Bernarda*

Alba, is, like its pictorial metonym, a provocative *reproducción ampliada* of an existing text. Throughout Arenas's story, Pepe and the cosmic tail (and tale) are linked, as the body in the portrait is figuratively constructed as a mirroring image of the distinctive attribute of the story's heavenly body. Like Halley's Comet, Pepe has returned after a long absence and commands a "tail" that the Alba women find terrifying and irresistible. Thus, in an amplified tale, with Pepe's amplified portrait as the sisters'—and the text's—guiding light, Bernarda's daughters amplify their minds and bodies.

García Lorca critics have pointed out that although Pepe sets the action of *La casa de Bernarda Alba* in motion, he never appears on-stage (Gabriele 388; Urrea 51). He is present only allusively through the women's discourse and through a picture of him that the jealous Martirio steals from Angustias in the second act, claiming later to have done so as a "broma" ("joke") (*La casa de Bernarda Alba* 166, 169, 182; *The House of Bernarda Alba* 150, 152, 160). It is in the context of the search for Pepe's missing picture that La Poncia warns Bernarda that "something big is going on here" (*La casa de Bernarda Alba* 169). Perhaps inspired by this scene in García Lorca's play and particularly by La Poncia's reaction, Arenas literally writes into his parody—his *broma*—"something big," Pepe's enormous portrait, in the presence of which other big things happen. Once inside the house, Adela executes her first act of possession in her sisters' inviolate space by hanging Pepe's portrait on one of the walls of their living room. In full view, the "splendid canvas" immediately and simultaneously captivates Angustias, Magdalena, Amelia, and Martirio: "At the sight of his image the Alba sisters were suddenly transformed" ("El Cometa Halley" 98; "Halley's Comet" 149). The women's once impenetrable house and bodies succumb to a relentless and promiscuous sexuality. For Adela, convinced that the world is about to end, turns the Alba house into a carnival stage with its full range of liberating potential: the doors are flung open and a constellation of transgressive desires let in.

The devout Alba women initially heed the admonition of the local priest, who warns them that God, angered by humanity's impiety and excess, is behind the comet's imminent destruction of the world. But in a carnival-esque shift from the spiritual to the material, Adela preaches to her sisters a religion of the flesh. Although agreeing with the priest that the comet is a "punishment" (102; 152), an inebriated Adela offers an alternative and subversive explanation:

Not for what we did, but for what we did not do. . . . We still have time, not to save our lives but to gain admission to heaven. And how does one get to heaven? . . . With hate or with love? Through abstinence or through pleasure? With sincerity or with hypocrisy? . . . We only have two hours left! . . . Let's go inside the house and pass our last minutes in loving communion. (102; 152)

During her blasphemous speech, a carnivalesque inversion of the priest's sermon, Adela is helped from falling by José, who "had been transformed into the sheer image of Pepe el Romano" (102; 152). The painting, already an object of the transgressive female gaze, now comes to life in the person of the son, whom Adela passionately kisses on the mouth, a prelude to their orgiastic sexual encounter. She then puts on a record of "Fumando espero," further stimulating the women's sexual appetite with the seductive lyrics of the phallically suggestive *cuplé*. Literally intoxicated with Adela's wine and figuratively with her words, music, and example, the Alba women make love under Pepe's enlarged portrait. Crossing various normative boundaries, the women's revelry with the young José and Adela's black coachman ignites same-sex, cross-sex, cross-class, cross-race, cross-generational, orgiastic, and incestuous desires. Like Ángel Facio in his 1972 staging of *La casa de Bernarda Alba* (Facio 15), Arenas makes explicit, for instance, the implicit lesbianism of García Lorca's Adela and Martirio; and he alludes at the end of the story to a threesome formed by these two sisters and José. By allowing his characters to express their repressed heterosexual and homosexual desires, Arenas not only outs García Lorca's play but also opens up the story in multiple ways. In moving the action from Spain to Cuba, Arenas simultaneously shifts the center of gravity from mother-daughter and sister-sister relationships to sister-sister and mother-son relationships. While I would not want to minimize the importance of the homoerotic sisterly dynamic in the text, it is worth reflecting in more detail, as I do later in this chapter, on the new element that Arenas adds to the story of the Alba women. With the resurrection of Adela and the addition of her son to the original cast of *La casa de Bernarda Alba*, Arenas privileges these two characters and directs the reader's attention to their incestuous desires. It should not surprise us that in an earlier draft of "El Cometa Halley" the mother-son incest motif is even more highlighted — as, for example, in a passage in which Adela urges her sisters to take their orgy outside and the narrator reveals that, while talking, she is being "passionately possessed by her son."[6]

Outside the Alba house, the sisters, José, and the coachman expand their promiscuous intermingling by merging with an unruly crowd of farm laborers — while Pepe's portrait still presides over their indiscriminate love-making. Just minutes before the comet positions itself at the center of the celestial vault, Adela and Martirio retrieve Pepe's image from the house, take it outdoors, and place it looking up toward the sky as if mirroring the heavenly bodies above. If Pepe and the comet are spatially associated in this scene, they are literally and discursively connected in the next. At the level of plot they share the same fate: both ultimately fade with hardly any public notice. And the paragraph in which this narrative detail is revealed is tellingly symmetrical, as it begins with the comet's disappearance and ends with the disappearance of the portrait:

> And so it did [occupy the central position in the skies]. And then it
> continued on its trajectory. And it disappeared over the horizon. And
> the sun rose. And by noon, when the Alba sisters woke up, they were
> amazed to see themselves, not in hell or in paradise but in the middle
> of the main street in Cárdenas. Totally in the buff, the sisters were
> still embracing several farm laborers, a coachman, and José de Alba,
> whose youthfulness, despite his many sexual encounters, emerged
> once more from the sweaty bodies. The only thing that had disap-
> peared in the confusion was the portrait of Pepe el Romano, though
> nobody had noticed. (105–6; 154–55)

Like the comet, Pepe's portrait disappears by morning. Moreover, also like the comet, which leaves behind a trace in the name of the sisters' brothel, the portrait leaves a trace, or tail: young José's erection looming large over the naked and sweaty bodies of the liberated Alba women.

The Alba sisters' transformation is brought home in a revealing act of naming in the last scene of the story. As the women, exhausted from a night of promiscuous sex, enter their house, a triumphant Adela removes from the front door the old sign, "VILLALBA FLOWERS AND HANDMADE KNITS," and that afternoon she replaces it with another, "HALLEY'S COMET" (106; 155). In a playfully perverse intertextual inspiration, Arenas has his characters turn their house into a whorehouse, thus realizing Bernarda's worst fears, as expressed to La Poncia: "Wouldn't you be thrilled to see me and my daughters on our way to the whorehouse!" (García Lorca, *La casa de Bernarda Alba* 170). Having put a new face on their house and on themselves, the daughters yield to, while subverting, the spirit of their mother's command to achieve "buena fachada y armonía familiar" ("proper appearances and family harmony") (*La casa de Bernarda Alba* 182; *The House of Bernarda Alba* 160).[7] Ironically, they fulfill their mother's wish, for Bernarda insists that one must always live by these words.

As in carnival, whose participants violate what are normally accepted as "impenetrable hierarchical barriers" (Bakhtin, *Problems of Dostoevsky's Poetics* 123), Arenas's characters engage in incestuous, interracial, cross-generational, and class-crossing heteroerotic and homoerotic sex. True to the transgressive logic of carnival, "El Cometa Halley" places the enjoyment of diverse forms of sexualities above normative repressions and prohibitions, a celebration of the flesh made possible by the return of the sexually indocile Adela. The youngest sister's visit to Cárdenas connects the comet's elongated tail to Pepe's amplified portrait; in their textual dissemination and in line with Arenas's male-centered worldview, the comet's tail and Pepe's enormous portrait come to represent the male element that ultimately penetrates, and carnivalistically liberates, the Alba sisters and their repressed universe.

Arenas's work reveals little awareness of many issues raised by feminist scholars, among them the complexities of prostitution. Whether prostitution is an uncomplicated source of sexual pleasure and an empowering profession, as Arenas has it, or a quintessential symbol of patriarchal exploitation, or a dangerous occupation that nonetheless gives women agency, in "El Cometa Halley," as in Arenas's imaginary more generally, patriarchal structures are reaffirmed rather than dismantled.[8] In important respects, the power achieved by the Alba sisters in their sexual liberation is illusory, for they are portrayed as becoming "women" (87) only in the presence of phallic symbols (the comet, the portrait) and only when they surrender to penetrative sex with men. By opening the brothel, the naming of which participates in the story's network of phallic resonances, the sisters defy maternal control and assert female sexual desires, but they do so by perpetuating male power. This should not be surprising, since the characters' sentimental journey echoes their author's. In Arenas's fantasy of sexual freedom, the ultimate desire is to submit, as the Alba women do, to a man.

A Son's Fantasy

Having viewed the comet's tail in Arenas's tale, I would now like to contemplate the tale behind the writing of "El Cometa Halley." What may account for Arenas's continuation of *La casa de Bernarda Alba*, particularly his linking of the lives of the Alba women with the return of the comet in 1910? Written in January 1986, Arenas's story had as its most immediate inspiration the upcoming visit of Halley's Comet, which was to make its closest outbound approach to Earth on 11 April of that year (Calder 146). In addition, Arenas may have been prompted to revisit García Lorca's play because 1986 marked the fiftieth anniversary of its writing and of the tragic death of its author, who was murdered in 1936 by the Fascists two months after completing the work (Gibson 438, 446–70). Arenas's decision to dislocate Bernarda's daughters to a sexualized Cuba may have originated in a tropical episode in García Lorca's biography, the three-month visit to the island in 1930 that introduced the Spaniard to a larger world of sexual alternatives (Walsh 273). More specifically, on this Caribbean island, a locale that García Lorca called "paradise" (Gibson 285), conveniently far away from his mother, the author of *La casa de Bernarda Alba* came to openly embrace his homosexuality. Like their original creator, who was unable to resist Cuban male bodies and who insisted that he spent the happiest days of his life in Cuba (Gibson 301), the Alba sisters, also at a safe distance from their mother, find sexual fulfillment and unqualified happiness on the irresistibly phallic island of Cuba.

Arenas's readers would not consider "El Cometa Halley" particularly remarkable, given the author's penchant for intertextuality, which is evident, for instance, in his novels *El mundo alucinante* (*The Ill-Fated Peregrinations of Fray Servando*) and *La Loma del Ángel* (*Graveyard of the Angels*). But one can ask why, other than to pay homage to a writer he admires, Arenas decides to write a parodic continuation of the story of Bernarda Alba and her daughters. Repressive motherhood and repressed sexuality, central themes of *La casa de Bernarda Alba*, undoubtedly attracted the Cuban author to the Spanish play. Arenas appropriates these themes, which are central in his oeuvre, and rewrites them from the nostalgic and painful perspective of exile.

After years of ostracism and a period of imprisonment in his native Cuba because of his political views and sexual practices, Arenas leaves the island for the United States but, like many an exile, he does not find home — or ever feel at home — once away. In an essay on José Martí, in whose life as an exile Arenas sees his own life mirrored, he observes, "Being here, away from the place we love and hate, . . . from which we had to flee to be able to continue existing as human beings, as free people, we are not completely free. Because, although we are here, in exile, we are nonetheless there in soul and image" ("Martí ante el bosque encantado" 57). Arenas finds refuge from the adversities of exile by imaginatively journeying back, through what Benigno Sánchez-Eppler calls "narrative self-repatriation" ("Reinaldo Arenas, Re-writer Revenant, and the Re-patriation of Cuban Homoerotic Desire" 158), to an otherwise unattainable Cuba.

In "El Cometa Halley" Arenas vicariously writes himself back to Cuba when he returns García Lorca, in the guise of the Alba women, to the tropical island that the Spanish writer visited and fell in love with in 1930. Returning to Cuba with — and as — Bernarda's daughters suits Arenas's literary erotics in part because this allows him to imagine being *templado* (fucked) by "hombres de verdad" ("real men") (*Antes que anochezca* 133; *Before Night Falls* 108), a possibility that Arenas associates with Cuba rather than with the United States:

> Later, in exile, I found that sexual relations can be tedious and unre-
> warding. There are categories or divisions in the homosexual world.
> The queer gets together with the queer and everybody does every-
> thing. . . . How can that bring any satisfaction? What we are really
> looking for is our opposite. The beauty of our relationships then was
> that we . . . would find that man . . . who wanted desperately to fuck
> us [*templarnos*]. . . . It is just difficult to duplicate what we had there.
> Everything here is so regulated that groups and societies have been
> created in which it is very difficult for a homosexual to find a man,
> that is, the real object of his desire. (*Antes que anochezca* 132; *Before
> Night Falls* 106–7)

Longing for the gender-differentiated sex of his Cuban years, Arenas meta-phorically transports himself back to his homeland, to a place where, like García Lorca, he spent his happiest and most sexually fulfilling days. Like García Lorca in *La casa de Bernarda Alba*, then, Arenas invites us to read his work through the lens of a "transvestite poetics," by which the reader views the heterosexual female characters as homosexual men to lay bare the text's metaphoric displacement of male homosexual desire.[9]

Having repeatedly insisted on the autobiographical dimension of his writing, Arenas would not disagree, I think, with this reading of "El Cometa Halley." Indeed, Arenas is in his text but in ways more subtle than I have suggested so far. Although it is possible to read all the Alba women and their quest for men as an allegorical representation of the woman-identified Arenas, I find the figure of Adela most intriguing. Why does Arenas bring Adela back to life, transforming her from a rebellious daughter in *La casa de Bernarda Alba* to a sexually empowering and licentious sister and mother in "El Cometa Halley"? Why does Arenas have Adela save the day by sexually emancipating not only her older sisters but also her son? Why, more to the point, does Arenas juxtapose Bernarda and Adela in their roles as mothers, one despotic and sexually repressive and the other liberating and sexually permissive? To answer these questions, I take a short detour through other texts by Arenas.

In 1981, five years before writing "El Cometa Halley," Arenas told Antonio Prieto Taboada that "in everything I have written there is a series of constants. One of the most important is the mother. The mother is of great importance to me" ("Esa capacidad para soñar" 685). Among Arenas's maternally themed works, one finds the meaningfully titled *Adiós a mamá*, a posthumous short-story collection that includes, among others, "El Cometa Halley" and the eponymous story. Having lost the original 1973 version, Arenas rewrote "Adiós a mamá" ("Goodbye Mother") in exile in 1980, six months after he left Cuba. The story centers on a Bernarda-like mother who controls her five children — four women and one man (the youngest of the five).[10] Beginning with the announcement of the mother's death, the narrative goes on to focus on her grotesque wake. Incapable of parting with their mother, the four daughters refuse to bury her and compulsively tend to her decomposing, stinking, vermin-infested body. Continuing to be ruled by their rotten mother, Ofelia, Otilia, Odilia, and Onelia completely submit to her by committing suicide; they stab themselves with her kitchen knife, then throw themselves into "the sprawling, teeming morass that is . . . mother" ("Adiós a mamá" 65; "Goodbye Mother" 58). But what about the fifth sibling, the nameless male narrator? Having been the only child who argued for the mother's burial, for which his sisters called him a traitor, the narrator, after two unsuccessful attempts at killing himself, decides not to join his mother and sisters. Instead, he flees the house and rushes to the ocean, where he plunges into the waves, proudly saying to himself, "I'm a traitor. A confirmed traitor. And happy" (79; 66).

Given its mother-focused plot, in which the youngest of five siblings rebels against a powerful matriarch, "Adiós a mamá" invites the reader to speculate about the filiation between this story and *La casa de Bernarda Alba*. Although Arenas may also have been inspired by the matriarchal household in which he lived, where his grandmother ruled over her daughters, it may not be a coincidence that "Adiós a mamá" is placed immediately before "El Cometa Halley" in the short-story collection. The textual contiguity of the two stories suggests a common Lorquian intertext.[11] One can speculate further that "El Cometa Halley" continues not only *La casa de Bernarda Alba* but also "Adiós a mamá" and not just because one follows the other in the collection. As Arenas explains in a self-conscious letter by the Tétrica Mofeta (his alter ego) in *El color del verano* (*The Color of Summer*), "My books constitute a single enormous whole in which the characters die, are reborn, appear, disappear, and travel through time — always mocking, always suffering" (345; 315). In a manner typical of Arenas, "El Cometa Halley" takes up where "Adiós a mamá" leaves off. The carnivalesque story of the rebellious child in "Adiós a mamá," which ends as the son throws himself into the sea to escape from an unbearable matriarchy, continues with the carnivalesque story of Arenas's Alba sisters, which features the women's experiences after a transatlantic voyage. Thus, García Lorca's Adela in *La casa de Bernarda Alba* metamorphoses into the figure of a son, the narrator in "Adiós a mamá," who in turn metamorphoses back into Adela in "El Cometa Halley." At the same time, although "Adiós a mamá" opens with the matriarch's death, the figure of the mother neither dies nor disappears in "El Cometa Halley." Instead, while Bernarda is left behind in Spain, the four older Alba sisters assume in Cuba, vis-à-vis their nephew, the role of the controlling mother. Eventually, however, Adela undermines their authority, bringing their stifling matriarchy to an end, and as a result a new mother — radically different — emerges, one who is an advocate for liberated pleasures and desires.

Arenas's Adela thus deviates from the customary authoritarian mother that populates the Cuban's works, a menacing figure that finds its most extreme representation in *El asalto* (*The Assault*), a novel that Arenas wrote

in 1974, a year after writing the first draft of "Adiós a mamá."[12] Both narratives, not coincidentally, thematize the son's fears of and reactions to the
impending threat of merging with the mother, physically and psychically. In
the story, when facing "the big moment to join mother" ("Adiós a mamá"
76; "Goodbye Mother" 64), the son resists and escapes; in the novel, fearing
that he will become like his mother, the son commits matricide. But, conceived, written, and published in exile a dozen years later, "El Cometa Halley" ends uncharacteristically: the son does not suffer from "matrophobia"
(Rich 235) and feel compelled to flee from the smothering figure. Instead,
son and mother happily "come together" in a tale that celebrates mother-
son incest.

The emergence of the new mother (Adela) seems odd in the context of
the familial constellation prevalent in Arenas's works, one marked by the
commanding presence of the authoritarian mother and the "absence" of the
father. To understand Adela's role, I return, briefly, to the issue of the father.
I place *absence* in quotation marks because that absence is only apparent.
Although Arenas saw his father only once, at age five, the author does not
evict the paternal figure from his literary universe. On the contrary, the
figure of the father plays a prominent, albeit oblique, role in Arenas's life
and oeuvre. As I argue in chapter 3, the cornerstone of *Antes que anochezca*,
Arenas's autobiography, is its first chapter, which briefly but movingly narrates Arenas's only encounter with his father. Suggestively titled "Las piedras," a reference to the stones that Arenas's mother throws at a handsome
young man when he attempts to bond with her simultaneously confused
and excited child, this memorable first chapter sets in motion the oedipal
dynamics of the text. This oedipal telemachy, although more veiled, figures
importantly in *El asalto* as well.

In his interview with Prieto Taboada, Arenas addresses the role of the
mother in Cuban culture:

In the world in which I lived, the mother had a patriarchal role. The
father was an adventurer who would simply conceive you and disappear (as happened in my case), but the mother was always a constant:
the one who kept watch over you, rocked you, nursed you, punished
you, criticized you, praised you. . . . In sum, the one who would forgive you or condemn you. And that is evident in what I have written.
I also believe that there is an *oedipal character* to the relationship be-

tween my mother and me, and even between Cubans in general and their mothers. The mother embodies, in the end, absolute power. In the various forms that dictatorships have had in Cuba, the dictator partly takes on the role of mother of the people. There is, as a result, a kind of sentimental blackmail: an authority almost maternal. That is what we see at present: how the dictatorship becomes a maternal power that manages us, guides us, organizes us, tells us how we must comb our hair, how we must dress, how we must speak, what we must do, what we must not do. ("Esa capacidad para soñar" 685; emphasis added)

Although we must not consider as universal the psychoanalytic postulates regarding sexual identity formation, Diana Fuss reminds us that psychoanalysis "constitutes a powerful cultural narrative that continues to shape, in both regulative and disruptive ways, representations of sexual identity" (13). Arenas is a case in point. He not only interprets his family romance in a Freudian context but also uses a psychoanalytic model to offer an oedipal interpretation of the political situation of the Cuban people. Despite Arenas's claim about his mother's centrality in his life and works, the (absent) paternal figure enjoys an equally remarkable presence, albeit allusive and elusive, in his oeuvre. Moreover, for Arenas the losses — or absences — of father and fatherland are equally poignant, since *padre* and *patria* share an emotional space in his life and writings. His exile from his fatherland and his father's absence leave a void that Arenas fills through writing. Having been denied the love of a father, Arenas redirects his filial love toward his fatherland. And in the same way that his mother, in the eyes of the innocent child, comes between him and his father, an equally repressive figure, Fidel Castro, comes between Arenas and his fatherland. Thus, for Arenas, it proves difficult if not impossible to distinguish between Castro and the castrating mother.[13]

This conflation of the mother and Castro literally takes place in *El asalto*, where the two figures who represent absolute power share the same body. In this novel, the last volume of Arenas's *pentagonía*, the nameless protagonist embarks on a homicidal search for his mother.[14] In the last scene, coming face to face with the president, Reprimerísimo, in a public square, the protagonist realizes that his mother and Reprimerísimo (an obvious double of Castro) are one and the same. As the son confronts his mother, his member swells to enormous proportions, and in a fury he sexually assaults her. After an arduous struggle, the aroused son penetrates his mother with the gigantic penis, killing her instantly: "As she is pierced, she gives a long, horrible shriek, and then she collapses. I sense my triumph—I come, and I feel the furious pleasure of discharging myself inside her. Howling, she explodes in a blast of screws, washers, tin cans, gasoline, semen, shit, and spurts of motor oil" (*El asalto* 140; *The Assault* 145). Next, as the elated citizens advance toward Reprimerísimo's agents, eventually taking over the square and destroying everything in sight, the protagonist, unseen by anyone, walks away from the crowd in the direction of the seashore. *El asalto* comes to a close with two brief sentences: "Camino hasta la arena. Y me tiendo" (I walk down to the sand. And I lie down) (141). Giving his body to the *arena* of his fatherland, the protagonist-son (a double of the author) symbolically becomes one with Arenas, the father. The narrator has reached a safe place, a place where he regains the essence of his being, that of a son— of his absent father and his beloved Cuba. And this is told, suggestively, in the final words, "me tiendo" ("I lie down"), which coupled together produce the present participle *metiendo* (inserting), a phonic verbal play that participates in the passage's sexual subtext.

If one keeps in mind Arenas's admiration for the *Iliad*, a text promiment in his memoirs, one can also read the final scene of *El asalto* as an evocation of a scene in book 23 of the Homeric poem in which the mournful Achilles, having lain down on the beach away from his men, reunites with the deceased Patroclus, whose ghost appears to him in a dream. That Patroclus, whose death leads Achilles to grieve inconsolably, has been considered a paternal figure vis-à-vis the Homeric hero—for being older, for having been named Achilles's mentor, and for having *pateres* in his name—permits the association between the beach scenes in Homer and Arenas. And if one subscribes to the view that Achilles and Patroclus have a sexual relationship, as some scholars have claimed, the Homeric connection is even more germane to my reading, since the two men's intimate lives help to advance the father-son incest motif in the final scene of Arenas's novel.[15]

Finally, this intertextual reading of the closing scene of *El asalto* is authorized by *Arturo, la estrella más brillante* (*The Brightest Star*), a novel that Arenas wrote in 1971, three years before writing *El asalto*. The happy ending of the last novel of Arenas's *pentagonía* culminates not only the five-novel cycle, but also, in keeping with Arenas's fondness for textual echoes and continuities, the creative process that Arturo initiated in the novel that bears his name. Referring to the fantastic castle that, while serving time in one of Castro's labor camps, he is constructing in his imagination for himself and the male lover for whom he is searching, Arturo explains, somewhat enigmatically, that "there were still so many marvels to be made: sands, orchids, hollows, and Patrocluses" (*Arturo, la estrella más brillante* 81; *The Brightest Star* 97). But Arturo, we are told, is murdered by a troop of soldiers led by his mother before completing his sand castle. Despite Arturo's death, his dream does not go unrealized, for like the nameless male protagonist of "Adiós a mamá," who reappears in "El Cometa Halley" in the guise of Adela, Arturo reappears in *El asalto* in the guise of this novel's nameless male protagonist, who in the end fulfills his desire to be with the man he loves. In the final scene, on the beach, the protagonist of *El asalto* finds himself in a happy place, a place where *arenas* (Arenas) and Patroclus appear and come together, joining the protagonist, not in a castle as Arturo had planned, but in an echo chamber of evocative intertextualities.

The last scene of *El asalto* also resonates with the incestuous plot of Arenas's *Viaje a La Habana*. In this novel an exiled father, persuaded by his son's mother in Cuba, returns to the island after a fifteen-year absence to reunite (sexually, as it turns out) with the son he left behind. Although metaphoric in *El asalto* and literal in *Viaje a La Habana*, the sexual reunion of father and son brings both narratives to a felicitous conclusion. But if in *El asalto* this connection is made possible only by the absence — the elimination — of the mother, in *Viaje a La Habana* it depends on her presence, since without the mother's active role father and son would not come together after years of separation. A year before completing *Viaje a La Habana*, Arenas wrote "El Cometa Halley," in which a mother also reunites father and son. In Arenas's continuation of *La casa de Bernarda Alba*, a pregnant woman who was abandoned by her lover has a son, from whom she is separated at birth. When she meets her son, eighteen years later, the mother shows him a picture of his father and introduces the young man to a life of promiscuous sex. Because of his mother's entrance into his life, the son simultaneously becomes aware of his mother's, his father's, and his own identities and desires. Although one can see in this story a subtle reworking of the father-son theme present in various texts by Arenas, two things remain enigmatic. Why, as in *Viaje a La Habana*, is the mother in "El Cometa Halley" the broker of the meeting between father and son, deviating from reality, as represented in *Antes que anochezca*, in which the mother makes every attempt to thwart their union? And why, unlike her counterpart in *Viaje a La Habana*, does the mother in "El Cometa Halley" play a central role, emerging as the tale's protagonist?

That "El Cometa Halley" and *Viaje a La Habana* were written entirely in exile may explain the portrayal in these texts of a maternal figure different from the one that Arenas had depicted earlier in his career. Completed within one year of each other and at a time when Arenas began to suspect and then confirmed that he had contracted HIV, these two fictional narratives are his way of honoring his mother, whom he suspects he will never see again.[16] Instead of a forbidding and authoritative figure, from whom the son constantly has felt the need to flee, she is now cast in the role of an understanding mother in *Viaje a La Habana* and a sexually liberated and liberating mother in "El Cometa Halley." Unlike the repressed and repressive mother protagonists in fictional texts that Arenas originally conceived in Cuba, Adela is a hedonist who literally bonds with her son through music, alcohol, and sex. In fact, she seduces him and leads him into a life of eroticism. Because of this and because José, despite his age, is characterized as sexually inexperienced, as an innocent child who undergoes his sexual awakening when his sexually aggressive mother enters his life, "El Cometa Halley" can be interpreted, more specifically, as a preoedipal fantasy. As in the preoedipal phase, the maternal figure introduces the child to sexual pleasure. No longer chaste, repressive, and frustrated, this new mother in Arenas's fantasy aggressively seeks and finds erotic fulfillment not just in others but also in her son. As in the dyad of infantile life, the son enters a world of blissful plenitude, in which he and his mother come together in a totalizing erotic communion.[17]

Although in *Antes que anochezca* Arenas describes his mother as an asexual woman who "was always faithful to my father's infidelity" and who, much to her son's dismay, "chose chastity" (19; *Before Night Falls* 3), he recalls an episode from his childhood in which he experienced his mother's sexual desires on his body:

> One of my aunts had the privilege of being allowed to listen to a soap opera; while she listened, she would pass the story on to her sisters. Sitting on my mother's lap, I remember my aunt describing the erotic scenes she heard. My mother's legs quivered and I felt the sex-

ual tension that my mother, young and anxious to make love, transmitted to me. (52–53; 30–31)

Childhood recollections such as this support reading "El Cometa Halley"
as a text that fictionalizes its author's preoedipal remembrances of things
past. In the last narrative that Arenas writes in which the maternal figure
occupies center stage, he pays homage to his preoedipal mother. And he
does this, not surprisingly, as he also pays homage to his (absent) father.
Physically absent but symbolically present through his enlarged and commanding portrait, Pepe brings to mind the other dominating image in
Arenas's life and works: that of the handsome and young *guajiro* in the
Cuban countryside who is forever remembered by his jilted lover and abandoned son. I would insist, however, that "El Cometa Halley" is primarily a
tribute to preoedipal mother love, an allegorical reenactment of the crucial
bonding phase between mother and child that the father's oedipal inter-
ference has not yet begun to disrupt.

Goodbye, Mother?

In a letter of 29 August 1989 to Jorge and Margarita Camacho, Arenas
writes about his mother, Oneida Fuentes, who was in the United States on a
twenty-day permit from Cuba. Although the dutiful son traveled from New
York to Miami to be with her, there was not, as Arenas laments to the
Camachos, "much communication of ANY SORT" (*Cartas a Margarita y
Jorge Camacho* 263). For instance, he did not say a word to her about his
precarious health. And perhaps more disheartening for Arenas was his
mother's lack of appreciation for his writing. One day, as he was diligently
working on *El color del verano*, she asked him whether he would get a real job
some day, since, as her hurt and bitter son explains, "for her to work is to
smash rocks in a chain gang" (265). Partly attributing their complicated
relationship to his illegitimate birth and accepting once and for all that his
mother "is far away from [his] life" (265), Arenas comes to a sad but irrevo-
cable determination when he writes to his friends, "En fin, *adiós a mamá*"
(In sum, *goodbye, mother*) (264). This is one more goodbye in a series of
farewells that had begun years before in Cuba, when, at a young age, Arenas
realized that he could not live with his mother. As he states in *Antes que
anochezca*:

My whole life had been a constant running away from my mother: from the country to Holguín, from Holguín to Havana; then, trying to run away from Havana to another country. . . . I had to leave my mother or become like her — that is, a poor, resigned creature full of frustrations with no urge for rebellion. Above all, I would have to smother my own being's innermost desires. (221; *Before Night Falls* 197)

When Arenas writes and underlines *adiós a mamá* in his letter to the Camachos, he not only graphically underscores the emotional import of a phrase that for him reverberates with past and present painful experiences of separation, but also deliberately calls attention to the autobiographical dimension of his writing. Like the eponymous story of *Adiós a mamá*, "El Cometa Halley" is also an *adiós a mamá*: the five Alba sisters say goodbye to their tyrannical mother, whom they leave behind in Spain.

But there is more to this goodbye in the Cuban's version of the story of Bernarda Alba and her daughters, and it has to do with the chronological deviation of Arenas's text from its intertext. "El Cometa Halley" begins, as we are insistently told, in 1891, and reaches its climax in 1910. An allegory of Spain on the eve of the civil war (Paul Julian Smith 20), *La casa de Bernarda Alba* seemingly unfolds in 1936. Why does Arenas depart from García Lorca's chronology?

Having been shaped by his harrowing experiences in revolutionary Cuba, the exiled Arenas, although inspired by the appearance of the comet in 1986, rejects setting the Alba sisters' story of sexual emancipation, a story with which he identifies, in Castro's repressive post-1959 era. Instead, Arenas antedates the events and has his narrative culminate in 1910, which not only is when Halley's Comet made its previous visit but also happens to be during the promising formative period of the young Cuban republic (founded in 1902). Though not blind to the social and economic inequalities and political corruption that plagued the early years of the republic, Arenas chooses to have his liberating story occur at this propitious moment in his country's history. The place that the 1910 comet holds in the Cuban cultural imaginary may also have contributed to Arenas's preference for 1910 instead of 1986. The curious coincidence that the comet was closest to Earth on 20 May (Giralt and Gutiérrez Lanza), eight years to the day after the founding of the republic, seized the Cuban imagination. Some Cubans claimed, for instance, that the comet's tail resembled the shape of their island. The "dazzling phenomenon" of the comet's tail indelibly marked the collective memory of a generation of Cubans, as Graziella Pogolotti has explained ("Loló, la república, el cometa" 123), and symbolized a country that was poised to embrace a dazzling future. Writing "El Cometa Halley," Arenas affirms — in the tradition of intellectuals like Renée Méndez Capote, Marcelo Pogolotti, and Loló de la Torriente before him — the comet's penetration in the Cuban imaginary.

If Cuba's history and cultural imaginary guide Arenas's manipulation of the chronology, so does the author's family history. The Cuban's corrective continuation of the Spanish play can be read as a fanciful corrective of his primal and traumatic scene of maternal separation, about which his mother wrote to him in a letter of 3 March 1986: "I just remembered that you left for Havana 24 years ago in February. We have been separated since then more each day. What we have done to suffer so much only God knows" (Fuentes, Letters to Reinaldo Arenas). Oneida Fuentes's letter alludes to the fact that Arenas was eighteen when he left her and the city of Holguín, in 1962, to begin a new life in the capital. This bit of family history is pivotal for an understanding of "El Cometa Halley."

The story's first sentence states and immediately repeats in parentheses that the tragedy Pepe brings on the Alba household takes place in 1891. By designating 1891 the year that Pepe deflowers Adela, leaving her pregnant, Arenas makes their bastard son eighteen when Halley's Comet and his mother return in 1910, a narrative detail that allows us to see Reinaldo in José. For in addition to a striking parallel between the real and fictional parental couples — in both cases, a handsome man abandons a young woman after impregnating her — there is an equally striking parallel between the two sons, who are the same age when their relationships with their mothers take crucial but inverted turns. Oneida's son is eighteen when he leaves his mother; Adela's son is eighteen when he reunites with his mother. It may not be possible to do more than speculate, but this biographical reading may be an additional tale lurking behind Arenas's comet. In a humorous but powerful story, Arenas recasts Adela as a sexually aggressive preoedipal mother and adds a son to the original cast of characters of *La casa de Bernarda Alba*, all in an attempt to imagine an alternative family constellation. Unlike Arenas's mother in real life and Bernarda Alba in García Lorca's play, who are suffering and controlling, the mother in "El Cometa Halley" is wild and liberating. Arenas fantasizes a mother who, understanding one's needs to satisfy one's "innermost desires," opens new worlds for her son. As Arenas alters García Lorca's story, he simultaneously alters and allegorically rewrites his own personal story to imagine what it would have been like if, on that day long ago, when he was eighteen, he had not been forced to say *adiós a mamá*.

FIVE

Facing AIDS

....

I am no longer I.
REINALDO ARENAS,
El color del verano
(*The Color of Summer*)

"I thought I was going to die in the winter of 1987. For months on end I had been having terrible fevers. I finally went to a doctor and he told me I had AIDS." With these words, written four months before he took his own life on 7 December 1990, Reinaldo Arenas begins *Antes que anochezca* (*Before Night Falls*), his posthumously published memoirs (9; ix). Arenas goes on to explain, in the book's introduction and in his suicide note (which was appended to the memoirs), his reasons for committing suicide: he cannot write and fight for Cuba's freedom because of the advanced stage of his illness; he has reached closure in his life as a writer, having successfully completed a literary oeuvre on which he has been working for almost thirty years; and he finds that life is not worth living if he is unable to have sex with other men, who no longer find him attractive because of his AIDS-ravaged body. Toward the end of the introduction, Arenas writes, "Now I see that I am almost coming to the end of this introduction, which is also my end, and I have not said much about AIDS. I cannot. I do not know what it is. Nobody really knows" (15; xvi). In fact, contrary to what he claims, Arenas says a great deal about AIDS in his memoirs. Although only occasionally mentioned in the sixty-nine chapters that comprise *Antes que anochezca*, AIDS is undeniably present in the elegiac tone of Arenas's autobiography.[1]

As in *Antes que anochezca*, AIDS appears in Arenas's fictional universe as a phantomlike presence, lurking in references scattered across his texts. Even in *El color del verano o Nuevo jardín de las delicias* (*The Color of Summer or The*

New Garden of Earthly Delights), Arenas's last novel, which he started writing during a hospital stay and finished shortly before his death, the specter of AIDS — though referred to, directly or indirectly, throughout the novel — is present but elusive. It is there, but not as the novel's explicit concern. That AIDS played a crucial role in the writing of *El color del verano* is undeniable, as a dedication in an early draft of the novel attests: "I dedicate this work to AIDS because without that experience I never could have written it."[2] While it is unclear why or how this dedication was expunged, its absence from the final version of *El color del verano* can be seen as emblematic of Arenas's complicated engagement with AIDS, which manifests itself as a traceable erasure.

Unlike many other AIDS-afflicted writers, Arenas chooses not to privilege AIDS as a sustained and overt theme in his voluminous literary output. "I do not know what it is," Arenas says about AIDS, explaining his reticence about the syndrome. Although he claims not to know what AIDS is, Arenas does know what the fear of AIDS is. And I contend that this terrifying fear, which haunts some of Arenas's texts, is thematized figuratively in one of the Cuban's most original and "queer" works, *Mona* (*Mona*), a novella that Arenas wrote in 1986, one year prior to his official diagnosis. Mentioned twice, briefly, in the novella's two fictional prologues, AIDS makes its way into the narrative more fully on an allegorical level, an oblique way in which Arenas faces the AIDS-disfigured body in his fiction.[3] I analyze the allegorical dimension of *Mona* taking into account larger cultural narratives about HIV/AIDS. Then, complementing my reading of Arenas's reading of Leonardo da Vinci's *Mona Lisa* in *Mona*, I look at the traces of HIV/AIDS in the character of Clara Mortera, the painter of a *Mona Lisa*–like portrait in *El color del verano*. To conclude my discussion of Arenas's rhetoric of indirection in relation to HIV/AIDS, I focus on his correspondence with his mother, Oneida Fuentes.

Mona as Allegory

Mona is a fantastic tale about a love affair between Ramón Fernández, a heterosexual Cuban exile living in New York, and Leonardo da Vinci's *Mona Lisa*, who comes to life every night by "coming out" of her framed existence at the Metropolitan Museum of Art, where the painting is on loan from the Louvre. Passing as a stunningly attractive Greek woman named Elisa, she meets Ramón at a Wendy's restaurant in Manhattan, where the Cuban works as a security guard. Their ensuing romance consists of passionate late-night sexual encounters, after which Elisa enigmatically hurries out of Ramón's apartment without disclosing her destination or her identity.

Intrigued by Elisa's behavior, Ramón surreptitiously follows her on several occasions to the Metropolitan Museum of Art, where she mysteriously disappears right before his eyes. Since Elisa does not deviate from her morning routine, Ramón imagines that she must be employed at the museum, and one day he decides to search for her everywhere in the building. While looking for Elisa among the museum's female guards in one of the galleries, he figures that she may instead be among a large group of foreign visitors gathered around a painting. He forces himself into the crowd, ultimately coming face to face not with Elisa but with *Mona Lisa*. Noticing the resemblance between his lover and the woman in the painting, Ramón, who knows little about art, thinks that she must have been the painter's model. However, upon seeing the date of the composition, 1505, Ramón surmises that the painting must be a portrait of one of Elisa's remote ancestors and that Elisa, as its fastidious owner, travels with the valuable painting, making sure each morning that it has not been stolen during the night.

Elisa, whom Ramón has constructed in his imagination as a "nymphomaniac multimillionaire" (93; 52), soon disabuses her lover of this fantasy. Although Elisa does not appreciate Ramón's curiosity as to who she is, she begrudgingly tells him not only that she and the woman in the painting are one and the same, but also that the woman in the painting is a self-portrait of the painter — as the "lusty and fascinating woman" (97; 57) who Leonardo always felt he was and wanted to be. As long as the painting exists, Elisa tells Ramón, so will she. When nobody is watching, she can concentrate, step out of the painting, and have sex with men whom Leonardo would have found desirable. Having disclosed her identity to Ramón and not trusting that he will keep her secret, Elisa has to eliminate him, but not without first forcing herself one last time on her bewildered lover, who simultaneously fears and desires her. But in the midst of their passionate encounter, the beautiful Elisa loses her concentration, forgets her murderous plan, and metamorphoses into an old, bald, toothless, stinking, and repulsive Leonardo, whom a disgusted Ramón penetrates anally before managing to escape. Some days later, convinced that his survival depends on the destruction of the painting, Ramón goes to the Metropolitan Museum of Art to hammer *Mona Lisa* to death. Seeing Ramón approaching with weapon in hand, *Mona Lisa* presses the alarm button on the wall next to the painting, which leads to the assailant's quick arrest. In jail, fearful for his life and hoping that someone will believe his story, Ramón writes what he calls his "testimony" (73, 74, 75, 107; 33, 34, 67).

Two prologues precede the Cuban's first-person narrative. The first is by his compatriot Daniel Sakuntala, who one week after his friend's death received in the mail Ramón's testimony. Written in New York in April 1987, Sakuntala's prologue contextualizes the tale and provides information about Ramón's fate. On 11 October 1986, as reported by the international press, Ramón Fernández, a twenty-seven-year-old mentally ill Cuban who left his country during the 1980 Mariel boatlift, is apprehended by the police for attempting to destroy the *Mona Lisa*. On 17 October, Sakuntala explains, the *New York Times* informs its readers about the Cuban's "strange death" (72; 31). Not having had any official visitors and having been deprived of anything that he could have used to kill himself, Ramón is inexplicably found strangled in his prison cell. (The suggestion is that Elisa was the killer.) Two days later some newspapers report the mysterious disappearance of Ramón's body from the morgue.

While the respectable press regards the incident at the museum as the actions of a deranged man who later strangles himself with his own bare hands, other publications, Sakuntala tells us, offer alternative interpretations. The yellow press proposes that "behind all that" there may be "a crime of passion" (73; 32). The New York tabloids consider it a terrorist act by an anti-Castro Cuban who was trying to destroy France's most famous art work because of his opposition to that country's socialist government. And a Cuban rag published in New Jersey sees it as a patriotic act by an exile who wished to draw French President François Mitterrand's attention to the plight of a Cuban dissident who, having been granted asylum in the French embassy in Cuba, has not yet been allowed to leave the island. Sakuntala then writes about his failure to find a publisher for his friend's testimony and his subsequent determination to pay for its publication out of his own pocket.

Sakuntala's "Foreword" is followed by a shorter "Editors' Notes," written in Monterey, California, and dated May 2025. These unidentified editors explain that Sakuntala, despite his efforts, could not publish Ramón's testimony because of his meager financial means. It is eventually published, we are told, by Ismaele Lorenzo and Vicente Echurre in New Jersey, in November 1999, after Sakuntala's mysterious disappearance in Lake Ontario, on the shores of which his clothes were found. Like Sakuntala, Lorenzo and Echurre also have disappeared, as have most of the copies of the book. The unnamed editors justify their decision to republish Ramón's testimony with their own clarifying footnotes as well as those by Sakuntala and by Lorenzo and Echurre by pointing out that copies of the 1999 edition not only are hard to find but are riddled with printing errors.[4]

Although "the case," as Sakuntala writes six months after it was first reported in the press, "appears to be closed" (73; 32), it remains unofficially open for years to come, since Ramón's story piques the curiosity of potential editors even into the twenty-first century. And curiously, as if cursed by their editorial enterprise, three of the editors (Sakuntala, Lorenzo, and Echurre) mysteriously disappear in ways reminiscent of Ramón's disappearance. Because of these enigmatic coincidences, *Mona* invites us to look "behind all that," as the yellow press did in its reporting of the case, and consider the suggestive link between the fate of the testimony's author and that of its editors. If Sakuntala, believing Ramón's tale about Elisa, rules out suicide (the official explanation) as the cause of his friend's death, then the reader may dismiss as well facile explanations for the ways in which the editors' lives come to an end. Who (or what) is responsible for the disappearance of Sakuntala, Lorenzo, and Echurre? More specifically, have these editors, as Ramón's agents, also been victimized by the dreaded Elisa?

To begin to answer these questions, I now turn to Reinaldo Arenas, who inscribes himself as a character in the novella.[5] In his preface, Sakuntala not only explains that Arenas summarily rejected the publication of Ramón's testimony in *Mariel*, a magazine he publishes, claiming that "this type of 'nineteenth-century tale' was not suitable for its pages" (74), but also interjects the apparently gratuitous information that Arenas has just died of AIDS. In their prefatory remarks, immediately after discussing Sakuntala's, Lorenzo's, and Echurre's disappearances, the editors of the 2025 edition state, "As for Reinaldo Arenas, mentioned by Mr. Sakuntala, he was a writer of the 1960s generation, justly forgotten in our century. He died of AIDS in the summer of 1987 in New York" (75–76; 35). With these self-referential comments, Arenas the writer accomplishes three things: he winks to his readers in a manner that suggests that the text that they have in their hands is not a straightforward, omniscient, third-person tale typical of the nineteenth-century, a narrative modality that he finds aesthetically unappealing; with his characteristic morbid humor, he prospectively refers to his death from an illness with which he has not yet been diagnosed; and by alluding to his death in the same passage where he discusses the editors' fates, he associates, by narrative contiguity, Sakuntala's, Lorenzo's, and Echurre's destinies with his own.[6] Because of this, the text seems to be prompting the reader to speculate about whether AIDS, the enigmatic syndrome that led to Arenas's death, may also be behind Sakuntala's, Lorenzo's, and Echurre's enigmatic disappearances.

If indeed Ramón's death is connected to Elisa, and if indeed Sakuntala's, Lorenzo's, and Echurre's disappearances are connected to Elisa and AIDS, then is it possible to establish a link between Ramón's demise and AIDS? In other words, can one posit a relation between ELISA, the woman responsible for the *marielito*'s death, and AIDS? I have used capital letters in the preceding question when referring to Arenas's female protagonist because her name, especially in this graphic rendition, evocatively participates in the novella's elaborate system of signification. An acronym for enzyme-linked immunosorbent assay, ELISA is a blood test commonly used to detect HIV infection (Grover 20–21). When considered together with Arenas's suspicion that he is HIV-positive at the time of the writing of *Mona*, with the fact that fear of Elisa is the emotion that consumes the novella's protagonist, and with the observation that "Elisa" is also an almost perfect anagram of *el sida* (Spanish for AIDS), this bit of medical information helps the case for arguing that the lethal female character in Arenas's novella stands in for HIV/AIDS.

Elisa first bursts onto the scene when she suddenly appears late one evening at Wendy's restaurant as "a truly extraordinary female specimen" (79; 37). The Cuban security guard, bewitched by Elisa's stunning beauty, declares, "Nada *raro* noté en ella esa noche" ("I noticed nothing *strange* in her that night") (80; 38; emphasis added). But, as if pressed to reconsider his initial appreciation, Ramón immediately adds, "a no ser, a veces, un extraño acento al pronunciar algunas palabras y hasta algunas frases. Así, por ejemplo, comenzaba una palabra con un tono muy femenino y suave y la terminaba con un sonido grave, casi masculino" ("except for a peculiar pronunciation of certain words and phrases. For instance, she would begin a word in a very soft, feminine tone and end it in a heavy voice, almost masculine") (80; 38). The presence of this comment early in Ramón's testimony and the choice of *raro* to describe Elisa are telling and instructive. Although it is true that *raro* is most commonly used in the sense of *extraño*, or "strange," as Dolores Koch renders it in her translation of the novella, it can also mean "queer." Just as in English the meaning of *queer* easily slips from "odd" and "abnormal" to "sexually deviant" and "gender transgressive," so does *raro* in Spanish. And this is how the text wishes us to read *raro*, since what immediately follows Ramón's initial statement is a remark about Elisa's "queer" voice, a gender-bending oral performance. Ramón is able to identify the first signs of Elisa's *rareza* (queerness) only when, looking beyond seductive surfaces, he listens to and reflects on the curious tone of the woman's words.

Just as Ramón must look beyond the surface of Elisa's appearance, *Mona*'s readers must look beyond the novella's surface, its startling plot, and listen carefully to and reflect on the curious tone of the words of the text, the intriguingly inflected articulation of the narrative. Like Elisa to Ramón, *Mona* "speaks" to its readers in an *extraño acento* — in the "other" language of allegory.[7] Indeed, as *Mona*'s readers listen to the telling of Elisa's story, they gradually come to learn that, like Elisa, who speaks for another (Leonardo), *Mona* speaks for something other: the fear of the HIV/AIDS-afflicted "queer." Arenas's tale about a sexually voracious and murderous woman who turns out to be a transgendered gay man passing as a woman allegorically presents a misogynist, homophobic, and transphobic narrative of HIV/AIDS.

While it is possible to read *Mona* as a transsexual (as opposed to a transgender) narrative, insofar as Leonardo changes into Elisa and vice versa, I do not subscribe to this reading. A quick reference to the climactic scene, in which Elisa tells Ramón who she is, may be helpful in explaining my view. On the one hand, because Ramón explicitly asks Elisa about "her sex change" (97; 57) and Elisa responds that she is the embodiment of *Mona Lisa*, Leonardo's self-portrait, in which the painter portrayed himself "as he wished to be" (97; 57), one is invited to read Elisa as a transsexual character. On the other hand, because Elisa unambiguously states in that same scene what her sex is — "I am a man" (97; 57) — and, at the moment of penetration, having just been turned back into Leonardo, insists on being called by her given male name, one is invited to read her not so much as a transsexual but as a transgender subject, meaning a person who challenges gender normativity.[8] Inasmuch as I approach Arenas's oeuvre in relation to his biography, I favor the second reading, which focuses not on corporeal disconnection but on the connection between male same-sex desire and femininity. An effeminate gay man who desired to be penetrated anally by "hombres de verdad" ("real men") (*Antes que anochezca* 133; *Before Night Falls* 108), Arenas was indeed woman-identified, but he did not yearn to become a literal woman. What I see at play, in Arenas's life and (allegorically) in *Mona*, is not the issue of transsexual embodiment but of transgender performativity. Be that as it may, what seems clear to me is that, regardless of whether one reads the Leonardo character in *Mona* as a transsexual or transgender subject, the novella is undeniably transphobic.

Ramón's testimony, the core of the narrative, begins by calling attention to a "queer" issue. The narrator-protagonist wonders about which pronoun he should use when referring to the person he once loved but now fears:

> This report is being written in a rush, and even so, I am afraid I won't be able to finish it. She knows where I am and any moment now will come to destroy me. I am saying *she*, and perhaps I should say *he*, though I don't know what to call *that thing*. From the beginning, she (or he?) ensnared me, confused me, and now is even trying to prevent me from writing this statement. But I must do it; I must do it, and in the clearest way possible. If I can finish it and someone reads it and believes it, perhaps I could still be saved. (77; 35)

At the level of plot, the reader eventually comes to understand why Ramón finds it difficult to choose between *she* and *he* when referring to his lover-turned-nemesis. But at the level of interpretation the pronominal quandary with which the narrative begins is intriguing not only because of its obvious sex and gender implications. If not a woman or a man (or if both), what does "that thing" that Ramón cannot satisfactorily designate with a personal pronoun represent? Like Ramón, I find that *she* and *he* do not adequately capture the character's essence. I take Ramón's opening remarks literally and regard Elisa/Leonardo not as a person but as a thing.[9] More specifically, that inscrutable thing that threatens the Cuban's life and from which he feels he cannot be saved turns out to be, in Ramón's own word, a "figura" (98), that is, a figuration — a symbol or representation — of HIV/AIDS.

The story of Elisa, a "monstrosity" (106; 66), as Ramón characterizes her at the end of his tale, tellingly follows the discursive structure of dominant representations of HIV/AIDS.[10] To begin with, like many HIV/AIDS narratives, Ramón's has an apocalyptic vision.[11] Written as a race against death, the Cuban's testimony consistently portrays Elisa as a life-threatening menace from which it is impossible to escape. Convinced that the Greek woman "any moment now will come to destroy me" (77; 35), as he writes in the opening paragraph in a statement that reverberates throughout his account (84, 99, 101, 106; 42, 59, 61, 66), Ramón, with a sense of doom, awaits his end. Initially conceived as a hopeful cry for help, Ramón's writing soon becomes an outlet for despair: "Right now, only two days away from my imminent demise, when there is no way out for me, I am telling my story mainly as an act of pure desperation and as my last hope, because nothing else is left for me to do" (101; 61). Since Elisa had repeatedly and mysteriously entered his locked apartment building and, on one occasion, while pursuing him in Grand Central Station, "appeared everywhere" (103), Ramón fears that she will just as easily gain access to his jail cell. Repeating earlier pleas to his prison guards for protection, he writes in the last paragraph of his testimony, "What I need is for Elisa not to get in" (107; 68). Clearly, Ramón's fear extends beyond the certainty that Elisa will penetrate his prison cell; he is terrified that the murderous Elisa will penetrate his body's cells.

Foreign-born, exotic, enigmatic, elusive, invasive, and lethal, Elisa brings together several of the features commonly associated with HIV/AIDS in cultural narratives about the epidemic. The "story" of HIV, as it is often told, presents the virus as a foreign, exotic, indiscriminate, and furtive killer that invades the body, in which it carries out its quiet, destructive, and secret work, the appropriation of the cells of the immune system, the destruction of which inevitably leads to death.[12] Like HIV, Elisa has a foreign provenance; she stealthily infiltrates "cells" in pursuit of her pernicious mission, and she feels no compunction about killing. The exotic Elisa may not hail from Africa or Haiti, the places that the United States media originally linked to HIV/AIDS, but she is from Greece, a gay-identified and exoticized "somewhere else."[13] A villain who has claimed "countless victims" (107; 68), Elisa is, as is generally — and misleadingly — said of HIV/AIDS, invariably fatal.[14]

Like HIV, which may go undetected for a long period of time, Elisa, a ticking bombshell, initially hides her destructiveness from the unsuspecting Ramón. But after masking for a while a monstrous inner self with a deceptively beautiful appearance, she eventually reveals her deadly nature to her curious lover.[15] It is then that Ramón finally realizes that she is "una loca peligrosa" (97). In one sense she is, as Dolores Koch translates this phrase, "a dangerous madwoman" (57). But if one considers the colloquial meaning of *loca*, she is also "a dangerous queen." Elisa is *peligrosa* because she is lethal; lethal because she is, allegorically, *el sida*; and *el sida* because she is, among other things, *loca* and *una loca*. In the homophobic imagination, HIV/AIDS is linked to *locas* (queens); in medical discourse, it is linked to a number of illnesses, including *locura* (dementia), a possible neurological consequence of HIV/AIDS.

After having anal intercourse with Elisa/Leonardo, the *loca peligrosa*, Ramón behaves like a *loco*, roaming the streets for days. He tellingly falls ill: "Temblaba, pero no era sólo por el miedo, sino también por la fiebre. Alguna gripe, o *algo peor*, había pescado" ("I was shaking, not only out of fear but because I was running a fever. Maybe I had caught the flu, or *something worse*, during the time I was out on the streets") (101; 61; emphasis added). Seeking shelter, Ramón goes to his friend Sakuntala, who takes him in and gives him medicine to combat a bout of diarrhea. This cluster of references to Ramón's health is highly suggestive, since it encompasses maladies commonly associated with HIV/AIDS. When considered together with Ramón's diarrhea, his fever, and the flu that he fears he may have caught, the ominous and indeterminate circumlocution *algo peor* (something worse) seems to point to, without actually spelling it out, the unnamable syndrome.[16]

But there is something else that validates reading Elisa as a vector of HIV transmission, as the one responsible for contaminating Ramón with *algo peor*. Early in the narrative, after their first night together, Elisa treats Ramón to a dinner at an expensive restaurant: "Next day was my day off, and at dinnertime she suggested going to Plum's, an elegant restaurant that did not concur with the state of my wallet. I informed her of that fact, and she, looking at me intently but with a bit of mockery, invited me to be her guest. I accepted" (80; 38). This passage is significant not for what it says, but for what it does not say — for what is edited out of the novella's original version. In a handwritten and incomplete first draft of *Mona*, Arenas concludes the paragraph with the following sentence: "Y nos fuimos para el lujoso restaurant del *easy sida*" (And we left for the elegant restaurant of *easy* AIDS) (emphasis added).[17] With these two words, *easy sida*, an English-Spanish combination unusual in Arenas's writings, he explicitly connects Elisa to *el sida*. And it is to these two terrifying words, *el sida*, that Ramón's two foreboding words, *algo peor*, clearly, albeit obliquely, allude. Eating with Elisa at Plum's indeed proves to be expensive — but to Ramón, who ends up paying with his life. Although Arenas leaves out direct references to AIDS in the published version of Ramón's testimony, he leaves the syndrome in. He does this by turning AIDS into the novella's structuring absence.

Supporting this reading is the fact that Elisa has many of the features of the classic femme fatale — the beautiful, seductive, and destructive woman who emerges as an erotic icon in the nineteenth century and who populates artistic, literary, and cinematic productions to this day.[18] With her stunning beauty and seductive charm, the "irresistible" (80; 38) Elisa lures Ramón into a dangerous sexual relationship. A "real pleasure-seeker" (79; 38), she shamelessly tells him that all she wants is to have casual sex with him before returning to her country. Although Ramón, who brags about his way with women, initially accepts her terms, he ends up falling in love with her. Much to the *macho*'s dismay, he soon begins to wonder whether he is satisfying her, and ultimately he has to confront the fact that it is Elisa — and not he — who prevails when their sexual "battles" (88, 90) are brought to an end. The mysterious, alluring, and dominant Elisa reduces the self-proclaimed womanizer to nothing, to a literal absence, as his textual eradication demonstrates, for not only does Ramón die, but his body later disappears, never to be found, from the morgue.

The bewitching and predatory Elisa can be connected to the figure of the femme fatale, "that abstraction of the woman posited as simultaneously most fascinating and most lethal to the male" (Doane 125), not only because of the destructive effects that her behavior has on Ramón, but also because of who she is: Mona Lisa. Admired for three centuries as a portrait of a gentle and cheerful woman painted in a natural style that captured the subject as faithfully as possible, Leonardo's most famous painting began to be interpreted differently in the nineteenth century. Particularly because of her smile, perceived as "unfathomable" by the influential nineteenth-century aesthete Walter Pater, who was undoubtedly inspired by the emerging misogynist trope of the sinister femme fatale, *Mona Lisa* began to be regarded by Pater and others as a "vampire."[19] No longer seen as a representation of gentleness but of trouble, Leonardo's masterpiece has demanded since the nineteenth century "not simply contemplation but deciphering"

(Boas 220). Confounding art historians, the mystery of Leonardo's smiling woman, who has become one of the most popular artistic icons of the menacing femme fatale, remains unsolved: who is the woman in the painting? And, more to the point, what does she represent, and in particular what has inspired her beguiling smile?

Like Leonardo's *Mona Lisa*, Arenas's *Mona* requires deciphering. The Cuban's appropriation and literary elaboration of the Italian portrait place Elisa within a well-established female iconic tradition and makes of her an enthralling enigma. Accordingly, like the critics of *Mona Lisa*, the critics of *Mona* are compelled to ask: who is this woman? What does she represent? And what has inspired her beguiling smile? Because of her allusive name and the circumstances surrounding her intrusion into Ramón's life, Elisa can be viewed as a representation of HIV/AIDS, a reading that is supported by Elisa's characterization as a femme fatale, the embodiment of eros and thanatos.[20] Occupying the position of the destructive and deviant femme fatale, the irresponsible and malignant Elisa engages in casual, promiscuous, and nonprocreative sex with men in a constant search for libidinal pleasures. But things are not, as Elisa tells Ramón, what they seem to be, since she is actually Leonardo da Vinci. One can then substitute the artist's name for "Elisa" in the sentence in which I have encapsulated the femme fatale's sexual behavior, and the message of the statement, given the change of sex, undergoes a substantial and significant transformation. It is no longer a description of the typical conduct of a femme fatale, but a common phobic depiction of the sexual behavior of men who have sex with men, which, especially in the age of AIDS, regards their "lifestyle" as fatal. According to this view, gay sex equals death (Hanson 324). Arenas's deadly femme fatale emerges as the HIV-positive "homosexual," the gay *homme fatal*. Thus, *Mona* participates in the production of what Simon Watney calls a "discourse of fatality" (*Policing Desire* 21), which represents gay men as lethal carriers of a life-threatening virus that they, suicidally and homicidally, are responsible for spreading in multiple communities.

Arenas's portrayal of HIV/AIDS as a femme fatale is consistent with dominant representations of the virus/syndrome. As Sander Gilman has pointed out, the iconography of AIDS activates the iconography of syphilis, which puts a woman's face on the disease — that of a "corrupt" female who pollutes the "innocent" male.[21] Because the gay man is popularly feminized, and because, as Leo Bersani has noted, the homosexual and heterosexual imaginaries confuse fantasies of vaginal sex with fantasies of anal sex, in the mainstream media's representations of HIV/AIDS earlier images of sexually transmitted diseases are recirculated with the gay man in the syphilitic prostitute's role. As Bersani writes, "The realities of syphilis in the nineteenth century and of AIDS today 'legitimate' a fantasy of female sexuality as intrinsically diseased; and promiscuity in this fantasy, far from merely increasing the risk of infection, is the sign of infection. Women and gay men spread their legs with an unquenchable appetite for destruction" (211). The personification of HIV/AIDS, and thus "intrinsically diseased," the promiscuous Elisa (Leonardo in the guise of *Mona Lisa*) literally embodies the common conflation of woman and gay man. In the telling of "her" story, Arenas affirms and perpetuates misogynist discourses, past and present, that represent illness and death as a woman or as a woman-identified gay man.

In an insightful analysis of the narrative systems that have been used to tell the story of HIV/AIDS in films, literary works, mass media, medical reports, and everyday communications, Judith Williamson identifies the Gothic—the horror story—as the favored genre to which writers have consistently turned to dramatize the ravages of the "monstrous" virus/syndrome.[22] Not surprisingly, *Mona*, which focuses on the terror posed by the dreaded Elisa, is a horror story, and more specifically a vampire tale. Aligning himself with the many critics who consider *Mona Lisa* a vampire, Arenas includes vampiric elements in his literary rendition of Leonardo's femme fatale. In so doing, he also joins a tradition that links the figure of the vampire to the "homosexual," a connection that has acquired special significance in the context of the HIV/AIDS crisis. Because of its association with bodily fluids (primarily blood), vampirism is called on as an exceptionally graphic way to perpetuate homophobic representations of "homosexuals" —as life-threatening vampires, as men who "bite" and kill.[23]

Although it is true that Elisa is not, literally, a bloodsucking vampire, she can be regarded as one because she sucks the life out of a weaker person.[24] Furthermore, the double life of Arenas's femme fatale evokes that of a vampire. During the day, Count Dracula, the archetypical vampire, lies in a coffin in his castle's burial grounds and at night he rises from the dead to go cruising, as it were, stalking and attacking his prey.[25] During the day, likewise, Elisa retires, lifeless, to a wooden case (the picture frame) in a nineteenth-century neo-Gothic structure, the Metropolitan Museum of Art, only to come out at night in search of hapless lovers (Ramón and others) whom she can seductively smile — bite — to death.[26] And like vampires, Elisa not only possesses "transcendent powers of seduction" (Dyer 79) but also has the power to vanish into mist.[27] Arenas's *Mona* thus exhibits what Ellis Hanson calls "a late-Victorian vampirism" (324), which is prevalent in phobic cultural constructions of HIV/AIDS. Discussing vampirism and its links to gay sex and HIV/AIDS, Hanson writes:

> Whether by strategy or by error, the media have a commonplace tendency to collapse the category of "gay man" with that of "person with AIDS" within a convenient discourse of "high risk." In this way, myths about gay sex serve to amplify myths about AIDS; and so when I speak of the vampire as the embodiment of evil sexuality, I speak of gay men and people with AIDS in the same breath. I am talking about the irrational fear of PWAS [people with AIDS] and gay men who "bite." I am talking about essentialist representations of gay men as vampiric: as sexually exotic, alien, unnatural, oral, anal, compulsive, violent, protean, polymorphic, polyvocal, polysemous, invisible, soulless, transient, superhumanly mobile, infectious, murderous, suicidal, and a threat to wife, children, home, and phallus.
> (325)

Ramón recalls in his testimony a series of monstrously queer apparitions of his vampiric lady of the night. Once, after making love to Elisa, Ramón turns to her to contemplate her "quiet serenity" (84; 43) and notices, if only fleetingly, that her eyes suddenly "faded away" (84); later, as he admires Elisa standing naked before him, he momentarily discovers that she "lack[s] a head" (85); and on another day, in bed, when he is about to begin making love to Elisa, he briefly sees that his lover "ha[s] no breasts" (90; 49). In addition to having these bizarre visions of Elisa, Ramón experiences equally bizarre tactile sensations when he is with her. On one occasion, while kissing her, Ramón suddenly senses "the thick underlip of some animal" (81; 39); and on another, while caressing Elisa's shoulder, Ramón for a moment feels "a sharp protuberance" (81), as if "the bone were out of joint and in the shape of a hook" (81; 40). These fleeting, and seemingly imaginary, depictions of a deformed Elisa are quickly replaced by images of Elisa's gorgeous — and supposedly "real" — body, images that make Ramón forget, as he tells us, "the eccentricities . . . , imperfections, defects, anomalies . . . that at certain moments I detected in her" (93; 52).

These instances of Elisa's bodily disfigurations narratologically have a proleptic function, since they prefigure Elisa's subsequent transformation into the grotesquely disfigured Leonardo. One early vision in particular, which occurs on the first Monday that Ramón and Elisa spend together, most distinctly foreshadows the novella's climactic scene. On their way to an unnamed city in western New York state where Elisa wishes to spend the day, Ramón takes pleasure in seeing the woman's reflection in his motorcycle's rearview mirror.[28] But there is a moment when, instead of Elisa's face, Ramón sees that of "a horrible old man" (82; 41). Visually framed, as in a portrait, within the rearview mirror, this old man's appearance, in the sense of both his unexpected narrative entrance and his unsightly physical looks, prefigures Leonardo's appearance later in the tale. In a scene that brings to life and amplifies the motorcycle "mirror" scene, Elisa indeed turns into a horrible old man before her lover's incredulous eyes. It happens when, after disclosing her true identity to Ramón, Elisa decides to murder him by either stabbing him to death or drowning him in a lake to which she has lured him. Before attempting to commit the homicide, Elisa forces herself sexually on Ramón one last time, and it is while they are having sex that she metamorphoses into the disgusting Leonardo:

> I couldn't stop crying, but I came closer. Still holding the dagger, she
> placed her hand behind my head, quickly aligning her naked body
> with mine. She did this with such speed, professionalism, and vio-
> lence that I realized it would be very difficult for me to come out of
> that embrace alive. I am sure that in all my long erotic experience,
> never has my performance been so lustful and tender, so skillful and
> passionate, because in all truth, even knowing she intended to kill
> me, I still lusted for her. By her third orgasm, while she was still pant-
> ing and uttering the most obscene words, Elisa had not only forgot-
> ten the dagger but become oblivious of herself. I noticed she
> apparently was losing the "concentration and energy" that, as she
> said, enabled her to become a real woman. Her eyes were becoming
> opaque, her face was losing its color, her cheekbones were melting
> away. Suddenly her luscious hair dropped from her head, and I
> found myself in the arms of a very old, bald man, toothless and foul-
> smelling, who kept whimpering while stroking my penis. Quickly he
> sat on it, riding it as if he were a true demon. I quickly put him on all

fours and, in spite of my revulsion, tried to give him as much pleasure as I could, hoping he would be so exhausted he would let me go.
Since I had never practiced sodomy, I wanted to keep the illusion,
even remotely, that this horrible thing, this sack of bones with the
ugliest of beards, was still Elisa. (99; 59)

Immediately before writing about his exposure to Leonardo's repulsive
body, Ramón nostalgically remembers how carefree and happy his days had
been prior to, as he puts it here and in an earlier passage, "la llegada de Elisa"
("the arrival of Elisa") (84; 99). Or, as the reader is invited to read instead,
"la llegada *del sida*" (the arrival of *AIDS*)—an ominous phrase that one can
anagrammatically hear reverberating in Ramón's four words.[29] It is in this
very scene, in which Elisa reveals her shocking news, murderous intent, and
repugnant male body, that a terrified Ramón first realizes that his "end was
near" (98; 58).

Some days later, obsessed with Elisa's threat, Ramón has a nightmare
that harks back to the climactic scene. Evoking the *Mona Lisa*'s landscape,
as was also the case with the horrific scene on the lake, Ramón's nightmare
dramatizes the fulfillment of the fatal (wo)man's wish:

Finally, after so many nights of insomnia, I fell asleep. I dreamed, of
course, of Elisa. Her cold eyes were looking at me from a corner of
the room. Suddenly that corner became the strange landscape with
the promontories of greenish rocks around a swamp. By the swamp,
Elisa was waiting for me. Her eyes were fixed on mine, her hands ele-
gantly entwined below her chest. She kept looking at me with de-
tached perversity, and her look was a command to get closer and
embrace her right at the edge of the swamp. I dragged myself there.
She placed her hands on my head and pulled me down close to her.
As I possessed her, I sensed that I was penetrating not even an old
man but a mound of mud. The enormous and pestiferous mass
slowly engulfed me while it kept expanding, splattering heavily and
becoming more foul-smelling. I screamed as this viscous thing swal-
lowed me, but my screams only produced a dull gurgling sound. I
felt my skin and my bones being sucked away by the mass of mud,
and once inside it, I became mud, finally sinking into the swamp.
(101–2; 62)

Consistent with an interpretation of Leonardo's picture that argues for a figurative link between the enigmatic female figure and the eerie landscape, Ramón's dream literalizes the connection.[30] Elisa fuses with her surroundings, which, in Ramón's oneiric revamping of the painting's background, become a macabre place. The femme fatale, Arenas's creature of the night, turns into a "viscous thing," a "swamp," that "sucks" Ramón to his death. Bearing in mind that Elisa is *Mona Lisa*, and viewing her through Walter Pater's lens, one can see in the sucking "mound of mud" into which she is transformed a vampire's mouth of sorts—an image in a network of symbolic resonances that includes two other equally terrifying orifices with teeth: a *vagina dentata* and an *anus dentatus*. Evocative of the fantasy of a castrating female sexuality, the language of this passage, with its insistence on foul-smelling and repulsive matter, is also redolent of anality. If earlier, in the climactic scene, when forced to anally penetrate Elisa-turned-Leonardo, Ramón describes the opening into which he inserts his penis as a "pestiferous mound" (100; 60), he now describes Elisa in analogous terms, as a "pestiferous mass" (102; 62). These scatalogically inflected linguistic echoes compel the reader to smell in the pestiferous and swallowing swamp into which Elisa has been turned a malodorous and engulfing *anus dentatus*, which, according to Hanson, may stand not just for the gay man's asshole but for all of his bodily holes. They are all construed, in the age of HIV/AIDS, as having deadly vampiric teeth.[31] This being the case, Ramón's demise in his dream, which can be read as a figuration of a death from AIDS, tellingly occurs when his body, coming into contact with dangerous fluids, is sucked in—"vampirized," as it were—by Leonardo's swamp, his *pantano*, a term that in Spanish evokes his *ano*, his anus.

Ramón's testimony concludes with these desperate final words: "Please, help me! Or else I will soon become another of her countless victims, those buried under that greenish swamp [*pantano verdoso*] that you can see in the background of her famous painting, from which she is still watching, with those eyes without lashes, while she keeps smiling" (107; 68). Ramón succumbs to Elisa and death as his dream foretells. The mysterious disappearance of his body without a trace suggests that Ramón ends up in the *pantano verdoso*—the lake in the painting, in the dream, and in the novella's unnamed city in western New York State to which Elisa takes him twice and where Leonardo "comes out" and forces him to have anal sex.

If Mona is an allegory of HIV/AIDS, what is the meaning and significance of the allegory? Following the lead of commentators who find an explanation for *Mona Lisa*'s mystery in Leonardo da Vinci's biography, I argue that readers of *Mona* may turn to Arenas's biography for interpreting the enigma of the novella. More specifically, like *Mona Lisa*, *Mona* can be regarded as a self-portrait of the artist.[32] To pursue this argument, I return to the climactic scene of the novella at the moment when Elisa is transformed from female to male and demands to be anally penetrated by Ramón, who still calls her Elisa:

> So while I possessed him, I kept calling him by that name. But he, in the middle of his paroxysm, turned and looked at me; his eyes two empty reddish sockets.
>
> "Call me Leonardo, damn it! Call me Leonardo!" he shouted, while writhing and groaning with such pleasure as I have never seen in a human being.
>
> "Leonardo!" I began repeating, then, while I possessed him. "Leonardo!" I repeated as I kept penetrating that pestiferous mound. "Leonardo," I kept whispering tenderly, while with a quick jump I got hold of the dagger; then, flailing my arms, I escaped as fast as I could through the yellow esplanade. "Leonardo! Leonardo!" I was still shouting when I jumped onto my motorcycle and dashed away at full speed. "Leonardo! Leonardo! Leonardo!" I think I kept saying, still in a panic, all the way back to New York, as if repeating the name might serve as an incantation to appease that lecherous old man still writhing at the edge of the swamp he himself had painted. (99–100; 59–60)

Calling attention to the act of naming with Ramón's multiple utterances of "Leonardo," this incantatory passage serves a dual purpose. On the one hand, it affirms the true identity of Ramón's sexual partner (Elisa is Leonardo). On the other, in its insistent invocation of the appellation "Leonardo," it conjures up another name: "Reinaldo." Sharing a sequence of vowels (*e, a, o*) and the same four consonants (*l, n, r, d*), "Leonardo" and "Reinaldo" invoke one another. The secrets are out: Ramón is told that Elisa is Leonardo and the reader is told that Leonardo is Reinaldo. In the same way that Leonardo has been read as projecting onto *Mona Lisa* an image of himself, so Reinaldo can be read as projecting an image of himself onto *Mona*. In Arenas's case, that image (Elisa) masks behind an attractive figure an unattractive self, which, after a series of partial apparitions, comes to light and life as a decrepit Leonardo. A handsome man who was proud of his fit body, Reinaldo, feeling ill in 1986, envisioned, by way of the painter's revolting old body, an image of himself that he thought he would eventually have to confront.

In *Antes que anochezca*, referring to the state of his health during the writing of *El portero* (*The Doorman*), a period that extended from April 1984 to December 1986, Arenas admits, "I was already beginning to feel ill" (9; *Before Night Falls* x). And writing, also in his memoirs, about his friend Jorge Ronet's AIDS-related death on 15 April 1985, Arenas says, "The plague that, until then, had been for me nothing but a distant though persistent rumor, now had become something real, palpable, obvious; the body of my friend was proof that, very soon, I could be in the same condition" (334; 310). One can surmise from these comments that Arenas began to experience AIDS symptoms perhaps as early as 1984 or 1985 but definitely in 1986, the year he wrote *Mona*. According to his friend Roberto Valero ("Los últimos tiempos de Reinaldo Arenas" 5A), Arenas was not officially diagnosed until December 1987. In a moving and revealing reminiscence, María Elena Badías, Valero's wife, writes:

> In the summer of 1987, Reinaldo knew that he was ill. I knew it, but I could not even say it to Roberto. I had noticed that Rey had stomach troubles similar to those of a friend who had been infected for a long while. Rey would not admit it even to himself. He was a proud man. It pained him to admit that he would be defeated, that his wonderful body was going to disintegrate. I thought that I could be wrong and that, if in fact Rey was ill, I did not want to be the first to tell him. The first thing that became apparent was the change in his personality. His enormous sadness, previously so ably kept in check by his humor, was no longer possible to contain. In the winter of 1987, he began to disappear for long periods of time, to invent trips, to lie. At the beginning of 1988 he told us, finally, that he was ill. He had to face reality because he was hospitalized with pneumonia. There is no point in going into detail here about the deterioration he suffered; one knows quite well how AIDS proceeds. (24–25)

In *Mona*'s Leonardo, a "sack of bones" (99; 59) with a hideous and ca-daverous visage, Reinaldo stereotypically prefigures his AIDS-ravaged fig-ure — the bodily deterioration of which Badías speaks. In keeping with the common practice in visual representations of people with AIDS, especially in the early years of the epidemic, of juxtaposing before and after photo-graphic images of "bodies" and "anti-bodies," *Mona*'s linear narrative es-tablishes a contrast between Elisa ("before") and Leonardo ("after"), thus bringing into view for Arenas (and his readers) a variation of what Simon Watney has called "the spectacle of AIDS."[33]

By having a portrait as its central motif and by showcasing multiple images of Elisa/Leonardo, *Mona* spotlights the act of seeing — of contem-plation. Ramón's fleeting visions of Elisa's bodily disfigurations and his witnessing, toward the end of the tale, of Elisa's grotesque metamorphosis into Leonardo are "novel" ways in which Arenas allegorically contemplates the stages of his own deterioration: what he takes to be the imminent trans-formation of his body from healthy and seductive to sick and repulsive. The proleptic "mirror" scene on the highway, in which Ramón has a portrait-like glimpse of Elisa's brief transfiguration into a horrible old man, can be read as an emblem of the novella's foregrounding of visual, as well as mental, reflec-tions. As Arenas sees himself reflected in Elisa's menacing and escalating monstrosity, he reflects on the "monstrosity" that he fears may be lurking within — and which will eventually destroy — his body. Writing the shock-ing story of Elisa-turned-Leonardo, Arenas prospectively imagines the AIDS-wasted body of Reinaldo.

Pertinent to this biographical reading of *Mona* is what Elisa says to Ramón, in Italian (which Sakuntala translates in a footnote), in reaction to his obsession with her: "The poison of knowledge is one of the many calamities humans suffer. The poison of knowledge, or, at least, that of curiosity" (95–96; 55). Responding to Ramón's bewilderment, Elisa offers additional enigmatic comments, such as "I have never killed anybody with-out first telling him why" (96; 56) and "They want to know who I am, no matter what the cost; they want to know everything. And in the end, I have to eliminate them" (97; 57). Curiosity and knowledge equal death. The revelation that Elisa makes to Ramón is the revelation that Arenas fears ELISA would make to him: the death sentence that he believes is assured in a positive test result. The personification, in this scene, of the HIV test, and the embodiment, throughout the story, of the syndrome a positive test result would predict, Elisa is the means by which Arenas dramatizes his inner struggles, in 1986, about whether to know or not to know. Whether Reinaldo will become — or not become — Leonardo.

Narrated from the frightened perspective of a heterosexual man, Ramón's testimony reproduces homophobic, transphobic, and AIDS-phobic clichés and stereotypes: that gay men are insatiable sexual predators; that HIV/AIDS and gay male sex are integrally linked; that "promiscuous" seropositive gay men are responsible for spreading the virus among "innocent" "victims" in the so-called general population; that transpeople are murderous villains; that all people with AIDS are bodily (and morally) disfigured; and that AIDS inevitably leads to death. Anyone who has read Arenas's works, and particularly his gay-affirming autobiography, in which he revels in his sexually active life with multiple male partners, would find it difficult to understand the existence, in the Cuban's literary corpus, of a text as profoundly phobic as *Mona*. Especially one that, conflating sex, disease, fear, and death, condemns the erotic pleasures of anal intercourse. Why does Arenas choose to tell the story from the point of view of a homophobic Ramón, who voices his revulsion, unchallenged in the text, for the sexual act that has been most associated with male same-sex sex and the practice of which was central to the Cuban writer's sexual life?[34]

If one keeps in mind the state of knowledge about HIV/AIDS and the alarmist dissemination of that knowledge in 1986 (the year Arenas wrote *Mona*); if one takes into account that life-prolonging anti-HIV drugs were not yet available; and if one also considers Arenas's non-involvement with the gay community and its politics, which prevented him from being exposed to gay-positive HIV/AIDS discourses and to discussions on how to have sex in an epidemic, then one can understand how the general panic surrounding HIV/AIDS could have affected the Cuban author. At the moment he is most vulnerable, when he begins to feel ill and suspect that he has the syndrome, Arenas writes a novella in which he sees himself the way heterosexist society would see him: as what Robert Padgug would call a "gay villain." That he should write, more specifically, a novella about a straight man (Ramón) who is deceived by a gay man with *el sida* (Elisa) is not surprising given "the big news" of 1986: "the grave danger of AIDS to heterosexuals" (Treichler 39). A gay man who openly acknowledged his preference for *hombres de verdad* like Ramón, Arenas adopts in this novella the perspective of those who would consider "homosexuals" a major threat to their lives. Instead of undermining dominant HIV/AIDS-phobic discourses, Arenas writes from within that system of representation. *Mona* is not a text of resistance, but one of complicity and despair. A mea culpa for what Arenas may have perceived — temporarily one hopes — as the error of his ways, Reinaldo's *Mona* remains, like Leonardo's *Mona Lisa*, profoundly disturbing.

Clara C'est Moi

Like *Mona*'s Ramón, who writes his testimony in a rush because he fears that Elisa will prevent him from finishing it, Arenas, fearful that complications from *el sida* will prevent him from finishing his *pentagonía*, rushes in 1987 to write *El color del verano*, the fourth of the five novels in the cycle and the last one he needs to write to finish his magnum opus.[35] Despite his determination, Arenas feels discouraged at times and talks instead about limiting the cycle to the tetralogy already produced.[36] But in the end, like Ramón, who completes his testimony before succumbing to Elisa, Arenas completes his *pentagonía* just before taking his own life during the last stages of his sufferings from *el sida*. One can link Ramón's testimony and Arenas's last novel not only because of the analogous circumstances in which they were written (a writer's race against death), but also because of the world of art that they share. My reading of *El color del verano*, which pays particular attention to Clara Mortera, a painter in the novel, echoes my reading of *Mona* as an HIV/AIDS allegory.

A hodgepodge of vignettes, anecdotes, letters, tongue twisters, prayers, aphorisms, and lectures, *El color del verano* tells the story of the celebration, in 1999, of the fortieth anniversary of Fifo's dictatorship (though Fifo arrogantly prefers to call it the fiftieth). A series of related events takes place, including resurrections of famous people who participate in the festivities; an architectural tour of Old Havana led by Alejo Sholejov;[37] an "oneirical-theological-political-philosophical-satirical conference" (383; *The Color of Summer* 351); a "crucifuckingfixion" (214; 196); and an exclusive reception in Fifo's underground palace. All of these "rare and edifying spectacles" (176; 161) culminate in a carnival parade presided over by Fifo riding a huge red balloon. Friends and foes, Cubans and non-Cubans, make up the motley group of revelers. In the midst of this revelry, Fifo's subjects, dissatisfied with their double lives (publicly praising the dictator but privately denouncing him), take turns absenting themselves from the celebration to gnaw away at the base of the island, release it from its foundation, and thus free it and themselves from the tyrant's control. Although the "rodents" (124; 113) succeed in separating the island from its platform, they violently disagree, while adrift, on the selection of a new place to moor the floating land. The novel ends with the island sinking into the sea.

As we are told in the novel's prologue, which is found halfway through the text, *El color del verano* has an unconventional structure:

> I leave to the sagacity of critics the deciphering of the structure of this novel, but I would like to note that it is not a linear work, but circular, and therefore cyclonic, with a vortex or eye — the Carnival — toward which all the vectors whirl. So, given its cyclical nature, the novel never really begins or ends at any particular place; readers can begin it anywhere and read until they come back to their starting point. Yes, dear reader, you hold in your hand what is perhaps the first round novel to date. (249; 228)

Given that the prologue is embedded in the middle of the narrative, one may ask: who writes it and to what novel does it actually refer? It so happens that, among the multitude of characters in the novel, there is one named Reinaldo, a writer who is working on a novel titled *El color del verano* in which he appears as a character who is writing about Fifo's celebration of his purported fifty years in power. *El color del verano*, the novel we have in our hands, is thus a self-begetting novel that tells two stories: the story of Cuba under a totalitarian regime, in which the island's thriving underground gay world figures prominently, and the story of the novel's telling. Having had his manuscript-in-progress confiscated, destroyed, or lost countless times, Reinaldo is seen beginning the writing of his tale again and again. Eventually, in the penultimate chapter, having completed the manuscript and secured it in sealed bottles, Reinaldo dives into the sea in an attempt to save himself and his novel. But his plan fails, since hungry sharks swallow him and the bottles. While Reinaldo is being devoured, he starts again, in the last chapter, the writing of his novel. The final words of Reinaldo's last text, the account of the sinking of the island, are the final words of the novel we are reading.

The prologue is indeed authored by Reinaldo (both the character and the extratextual writer), and it belongs to both novels titled *El color del verano* (the "fictional" and the "real"). Arenas's inscription of himself play-fully flaunts the autobiographical nature of his vast literary project, which the author, in the guise of the Tétrica Mofeta, affirms in a revealing ventrilo-quizing moment in *El color del verano*: "All the things I've done — poems, stories, novels, plays, and essays — are linked in a series of historical, auto-biographical, and agonic cycles" (345; 315). As this statement suggests, Are-nas (the author) would not want to be distanced from his fictional world, but neither would he want to have his novels read as "truthful" accounts of his life or the lives of countless relatives, friends, foes, and acquaintances whom he has transformed into fictional characters. Responding to friends' reactions to the manuscript of *El color del verano*, a veritable *roman à clef*, Arenas reminded them that his was a book of fiction, not history, and explained that although real people may have inspired him, he did not reproduce their "portraits" but rather transformed them into "metaphors" (Letters to Liliane Hasson, 25 May 1990). And anticipating that *El color del verano* would be read, contrary to his avowed intent, as a "portrait of real-ity," Arenas felt it necessary to begin the novel with a campy statement addressed "Al juez" ("To the Judge"), which in part reads:

> Whoa, girl, just hold it right there. Before you start going through these pages looking for things to have me thrown in jail for, I want you to try to remember that you're reading a work of fiction here, so the characters in it are made up — they're concoctions, denizens of the world of imagination (literary figures, parodies, metaphors — you know), not real-life people. (9; vii)

Arenas's insistence on the novel's primarily imaginative dimension not-withstanding, he undeniably inserted himself — his *retrato*, or portrait — in *El color del verano*. He is recognizably present in this autofiction, and not only in the figure of Reinaldo.[38] Arenas also made his way into the novel in the figure of the painter and prostitute Clara Mortera. Through Clara's art and body, Arenas obliquely reflects on his own art and body.

Clara is featured in more of the novel's segments than any other character except for Reinaldo, and one of those segments, "El hueco de Clara," not only is the longest segment in the novel but also has the added distinction of having been committed to memory by Arenas when he first conceived it in Cuba in the early 1970s.[39] Moreover, if one considers the demands that the novel's complexity and its parade of characters place on its readers, it is significant that Clara's episodes are strategically positioned in the narrative. Clara appears in segments closer to the beginning and the end of the novel, thereby ensuring her noticeability.[40] As if all this were not enough to high-light Clara's centrality, "El despepite," the segment on the unmooring of the island, ends with a sentence giving prominence to Clara. Referring to the preceding segment, "Clara en llamas," in which the painter sets herself on fire after discovering that Fifo's thugs destroyed her paintings, this episode comes to a close with an unforgettable vision of Clara and her island: "And meanwhile, the Island, with Clara in flames, continued drifting away" (439; 405). In light of this, the burning question is: Why does Clara receive so much attention? With Clara in flames, the text sheds light on not one but two tales of a body in pain. Clara can be seen as an illuminating guide, not only to *El color del verano* but also to *Mona*. Written within one year of each other, these novels metaphorically use artists and their art to tell Arenas's HIV/AIDS story.

"I will paint plants with their roots upside down, seeking their nutrients in the sky" (74; 67). So begins "Pintando," the sixth segment of *El color del verano* and the one in which Clara first appears. The passage continues with the painter enumerating in a series of anaphoric statements ("I will paint . . .") the compositional details of a projected painting. A "huge moan of the tropics" (75; 67), Clara's work will feature, among other things: a carnival; citizens gnawing away at their island's foundation; hungry sharks; gays and their underground subculture; Reinaldo, his novel, and the agony over its multiple rewritings; and Clara herself. "Nothing will escape me" (76; 69), Clara says, at the end of her promiscuous catalogue of the painting's ele-ments. And she adds, "That will be my painting. I will paint all that, and right now, right this minute, I am going to start. In an ecstasy of rage and fury I will paint it, all of it, before the Carnival begins" (77; 69). Not revealed until later in the narrative, the title Clara chooses for her painting is *El color del verano o Nuevo jardín de las delicias*. Clara picks up her brush and Reinaldo (author/character) picks up his pen, and they produce, in their respective artistic media, specular works. A *mise en abyme*, prospective in nature be-cause it reflects what is to come later in the novel, Clara's apocalyptic paint-ing shares not only the novel's title, subtitle, and thematic content but also its transgressive spirit. Clara's first sentence, with its reference to "plants with their roots *upside down*" (emphasis added), reveals the carnival topos of the *mundus inversus*, which both mirrored and mirroring texts deploy. Like their model, Hieronymus Bosch's famous triptych (the title of which, *The Garden of Earthly Delights*, is echoed in their subtitles), Clara's painting and Reinaldo's novel are satires that rely on the liberating aesthetics of carnival.

Clara's painting clearly reveals itself to be a pictorial metonym of the novel that contains it. But the novel's concern with self-reflection goes beyond textual mirroring; it extends to the artist's own figuration — the artist's self-reflection. A specular image of Reinaldo's *El color del verano*, Clara's painting is also a mirror in which the painter herself is reflected. Clara, she insists, will be represented on her canvas: "I will paint a heap of bones — me — rotting in a field overrun with weeds" (74; 67); "I will paint the cracked and peeling walls of my body" (74; 67); "and [I will paint] my fallen breasts, and all the consequences thereof" (75; 68); "I will paint all that and much more, because I will also paint the Carnival . . . and me at that Carnival wearing my big falsies and flaunting my forbidden Carnival costumes" (76; 68–69); "and in the third section of the triptych, the final explosion, you will see everyone, myself included, bursting — and to think, after we'd lived through all those horrors!" (76; 69). In the elaborate plan for her painting, Clara also states that, in addition to including easily recognizable self-portraits, the painting will also represent her by means of a double:

> My painting will splatter the entire Island with horror, and on that canvas, the viewer will see, crouched down among the leaves and thorns, or behind a crumbling column, me — *myself or my double* — the whore in hiding, looking at my six-year-old son begging a quarter from a sailor and making signs to him that he knows a woman (me) that the sailor can sleep with, and it'll only cost him five pesos. (75; 68; emphasis added)

The multiple self-representations of the artist on her canvas have their analogues in the multiple self-representations of the embedding narrative's protagonist. For each of his multiple identities, he uses a different name: Gabriel (devoted son), Reinaldo (closeted writer), and Tétrica Mofeta (flaming queen). Like the painter, the novel's writer-protagonist not only has his image replicated in plural self-portraits, but also admits, as does Clara, to having a double — and one who happens to be none other than Clara. Explaining toward the end of the narrative that he is not bothered by the fact that the painter, whom he earlier called "my double" (305), used the title of his novel for the title of her painting, Reinaldo declares that "Clara and he were a single person and that their works therefore complemented one another" (380; 348). Why does *El color del verano* insist on self-consciously foregrounding self-portraiture? Why does the text insist on doubling—more specifically, on the identification of Reinaldo with Clara and on the identification of their autobiographically inflected works with each other?

Known for her artistic talent and promiscuous sexuality, Clara, in her *hueco* (hole), produces with equal ease a series of monumental canvases and a collection of equally striking offspring.[41] As proud of her body as she is of her art, she eventually has to confront publicly, in the climactic scene of her story, what to her is tragic news. Summoning relatives and friends to an emergency meeting in her apartment, Clara, after delivering a passionate defense of a life in prostitution, which has allowed her to support her enormous family and work on her paintings, makes a surprising revelation: "Pero ahora, algo terrible me ha sucedido. Se me han caído las tetas. ¡Miren!" ("But now, something terrible has happened to me. My breasts have fallen. Look!") (363; 333). Standing up, she rips open her long white dress and reveals "her dry, shriveled, discolored tits, which hung like worms or leeches down below her waist" (363; 333). Like Clara's audience, the readers of the novel cannot help but "look" with shock at her fallen breasts. Guided by an insight formulated by Reinaldo, who is among the viewers of the spectacle, the readers are made to see a connection between the artist's infirm body and her body of art. Titled "Retrato de Luisa Pérez de Zambrana," this segment of the novel concludes with Reinaldo's epiphany:

> Then Skunk in a Funk [Tétrica Mofeta], stepping over the sorrowful heads, walked up to the tall, tragic figure and looked at her fixedly. And seeing her standing there—svelte, her gown ripped open, her breasts shriveled, her eyes vacant and staring into space—Reinaldo realized that for a long time Clara had known that her tits had fallen and had suffered because of that, and realized too that this moment of confession was the most painful moment in her life, because she was making her defeat public. And Skunk in a Funk realized something else: she realized that the portrait of the mourning, afflicted, maternal, despairing, patient, enigmatic, and brilliant poetess Luisa Pérez de Zambrana was the self-portrait of Clara Mortera. (364; 333)

The portrait to which this passage alludes is, among Clara's paintings, the one before which Reinaldo, when he first saw it, "fell into a state of ecstasy"

(362). Ostensibly the portrait of Luisa Pérez de Zambrana (1835–1922), Cuba's elegiac Romantic poet who died in her late eighties, alone and practically forgotten, Clara's artistic rendition depicts a young woman, sitting under a tree, with a book in her hands.[42] The work, we are told, "emanated a mystery so total" (362; 332), "was touched with an infinite grief" (362; 332), "was the sum of all misfortunes" (363; 332). And finally:

> That woman, that painting, was not a painting; it was a spell, an awesome and unrepeatable force that could have been born only out of an ecstasy of genius and madness. It was enigma and consolation; it was faith in the belief that come what may, life does still have meaning; and it was absolute despair. It was concentrated diabolism and goodness that struck the person who looked upon it dumb — and then made him weep. (363; 332)

A comparison to what is arguably the most famous portrait in Western art serves as a coda to the description of Clara's portrait of Luisa Pérez de Zambrana: "Perhaps no painting but the *Mona Lisa* itself could compare with that portrait hanging in a dim corner of Clara's stifling hovel" (363; 332).

The reference to Leonardo's *Mona Lisa* is an invitation to read Clara's story intertextually with Arenas's *Mona*, a reading that would explain the inclusion and discussion in *El color del verano* of another enigmatic painting from Clara's collection that also catches Reinaldo's attention. Untitled, this painting is identified by its subject matter, "the enchanted forest," and is described as a hallucinatory place in which every flower "blossomed into a strange pair of scissors endlessly opening and closing" (362; 331). If the painting is somewhat puzzling, so is Reinaldo's response to it. Studying "with great devotion that masterpiece" (362), Reinaldo makes sure not to touch or get too close to it, since he is aware of reports that some viewers had been injured by it and of allegations that a viewer had become HIV-positive from a "prick" (362; 331) of another of Clara's paintings. Might the unidentified, virus-transmitting painting be the *Mona Lisa*–like *Homenaje a Luisa Pérez de Zambrana*? Although the text questions the veracity of the connection between Clara's art and AIDS, it goes on to say that "it was true that Clara received a small commission or a government pardon every time she transmitted AIDS to someone in the general population" (362; 331). What is one to make of the presence of an HIV/AIDS discourse surrounding Clara and her paintings? Does Clara spread the virus through her body or through her body of work? Is the text pointing to the impossibility of separating the artist from her art?

At the time that Arenas wrote this passage about Clara and her paintings, he may have had in mind the story he told in *Mona*, where art and artist not only are one and the same but also the allegorical embodiment of HIV/AIDS. Like Arenas's version of Leonardo's *Mona Lisa*, Clara's paintings are linked to the virus/syndrome. And Clara's *Homenaje a Luisa Pérez de Zambrana*, which is as enigmatic as the famous sixteenth-century portrait to which it is compared, can be explained if one approaches it biographically, an approach that is in line with biographical interpretations of Leonardo's *Mona Lisa*, with my own reading of Arenas's *Mona*, and with Reinaldo's own advice. Like *Mona*'s fatal portrait, the painting of Luisa Pérez de Zambrana is, in essence, a self-portrait of the artist.

In keeping with the connections made throughout the narrative between Reinaldo and Clara, the text of *El color del verano*, by way of Reinaldo's interpretation of Clara's portrait of Luisa Pérez de Zambrana, encourages us to perform an analogous biographical reading of the painter's story. We are invited to see in the life of the artist a narrative portrait of the woman-identified Reinaldo Arenas, Clara's creator, who, like his creation, had to suffer the humiliating experience of having to live through the deterioration of his body. Writing Clara's story, the AIDS-stricken Arenas allegorically confronts, as does Clara when she paints the doleful figure of Luiza Pérez de Zambrana, his own "sum of all misfortunes."[43] "It pained him to admit that he would be defeated, that his wonderful body was going to disintegrate" (24), wrote María Elena Badías of her ailing friend, words that resonate in Arenas's account of Clara's pain, and which is worth quoting again: "For a long time Clara had known that her tits had fallen and had suffered because of that, and . . . this moment of confession was the most painful moment in her life, because she was making her defeat public" (364; 333).

Emblematic of the collapsing AIDS-ravaged body, Clara's fallen breasts put an end to a productive life, a life in which Reinaldo sees his own life reflected.[44] No longer possessing a youthful and attractive body, Clara mournfully laments, "Yo ya no soy yo" ("I am no longer I") (366; 335), a lament that finds its echoes in Arenas's nonfiction. In the introduction to *Antes que anochezca*, written in August 1990, just four months before committing suicide, Arenas, recalling a recent incident in a public toilet in which he was made to feel undesirable, nostalgically and woefully writes, "Yo ya no existía" ("I no longer existed") (9; *Before Night Falls* ix). In a heartrending letter to his friend Armando Álvarez Bravo, also from 1990, where he writes about his illness and the cruelties of a life in exile, Arenas reveals that he now rarely rereads his favorite classics because doing so invariably and painfully fills him with nostalgia for that reader — a young and healthy person — "que ya no soy" ("that I no longer am").[45] It is not difficult to imagine the dying writer uttering to himself his character's words, "Yo ya no soy yo," as he, only months away from his death, rushes to finish Clara's story — his own — in what will turn out to be his last, and according to him his best, novel.

Mami Dearest

The Department of Rare Books and Special Collections of Princeton University Library houses the Reinaldo Arenas Papers. In one of the twenty-eight boxes that contain typescripts and manuscripts, miscellaneous printed material, and correspondence, there is a folder with photocopies of five of the letters that Arenas wrote from abroad to his mother in Cuba. With the salutation "Dear mommy" or "My dear mommy" and signed "Reinaldo" or "Raine" (as his close relatives called him), these short handwritten letters, which range from one to two pages in length, were written in Miami or New York and are dated 26 May 1980, 8 November 1984, 17 July 1988, 28 August 1988, and 14 February 1989. The first letter was written twenty days after Arenas's arrival in the United States; the last letter, twenty-two months before his suicide. Despite their scant number, these letters, especially if read along with the ones Arenas's mother wrote to her son, further reveal Arenas's confrontation with the realities of AIDS.[46]

"I hope that you're well when you receive this letter. I'm well." So begins Arenas's first letter, from 1980, and also, with a slight variation, the second letter, from 1984. The third letter, from 1988, departs from the two previous letters in not indicating that he is well: "I've just received your letter of June 19. I'm happy that you're well." The fourth letter, also from 1988, similarly begins by alluding to the mother's recent correspondence ("I've received all your letters") and later refers to Oneida's health ("Every night I pray God for your health and peace"). The fifth letter, from 1989, starts differently from the others: "I'm spending some quiet days in Miami. The days are beautiful and I think about you so much. I long to see you."

In the opening lines of the first two letters, Arenas avails himself of a commonplace. Following good epistolary etiquette, he inquires after the well-being of his addressee and, in anticipation of a reciprocal concern, goes on to reveal the state of his own health. In Arenas's case, this is not necessarily formulaic, since he means what he writes about himself; he indeed wants his mother to know that he is well. In fact, in the first letter, he writes about having a physical examination and getting a clean bill of health; in the second letter, he tells his mother, "I'm happy," an unlikely affirmation if he had not been well. That Arenas became HIV-positive in the years between the second letter (1984) and the third (1988) may account for the exordial change — the gradual elimination of references to his health — in the last three letters, which also, in contrast with the first two, have a profoundly despairing tone. As Arenas's health deteriorates, so do his epistolary habits, as it were. Although one can read these short letters as constituting a chronicle, albeit skeletal, of the state of Arenas's health, they can also be read as texts that, like *Mona* and *El color del verano*, engage in a rhetoric of indirection, the only way in which Arenas can speak of a pain that he cannot bring himself to express directly in words, even — or perhaps especially — when addressing his mother.[47]

Reading Oneida Fuentes's letters, one learns that her son was not fully forthcoming about his health despite her constant entreaties. In a letter of 5 March 1988, Oneida refers to two letters from Reinaldo that are not archived at Princeton:

> I pray to God that you are well because I'm desperate because I've just received your letter of 9 February where you tell me that you are sick but you don't tell me what you have and I think about so many things since I received your letter of 24 November I haven't had a moment's peace because I knew that you were sick and now I know that you are very sick.[48]

Arenas's February letter, where he writes that he is "sick," confirms for his mother what she has feared since his November letter to her — that he is "very sick." Reprimanding her son for not telling her what disease he has, Oneida writes to him, "I think about so many things."[49] If Arenas is reticent in his letters to his mother to the point that she, in a letter of 19 September 1988, questions the veracity of what he writes — "I fear for your health because I still don't know how you are because I don't know if you're telling me the truth" — Oneida is equally reluctant to express openly what she suspects.

CHAPTER FIVE

· 144 ·

What are the "many things" that occupy her thoughts? Principal among them is clearly AIDS, which Oneida seems to find difficult to name. For instance, in a letter of 15 May 1986, resorting to a circumlocution, she warns Reinaldo to protect himself from "strange diseases." And in a letter of 25 October 1987, she names for the first and last time that which in subsequent letters is to remain unnamed. Referring to her sister's recent surgery in Miami, Oneida tells Reinaldo: "Ozaida writes to me frequently she says she is feeling quite well I'm happy that's so because I've been so worried about her because one's health is all in life and there are so many diseases AIDS is a scourge in the world." Is Oneida speaking about her sister? Or is she obliquely —and perhaps unconsciously—speaking about her son, about whom she also worries constantly, fearing that he will succumb to AIDS? In a letter written on 28 July 1987, Oneida had commented on her son's physical appearance: "We received the photos that Ozaida sent. You look so strange [*raro*] in one of them that I had to be told it was you." Constantly asking Reinaldo to send her photographs of him and repeatedly expressing her desire to speak with him more often on the telephone, Oneida searches for visual and aural proof that her son is not *raro* and that he is well.

In all her letters, Oneida basically writes about the same things: the weather; the difficulties of making ends meet, which are alleviated by relatives' remittances from abroad; news about her extended family; and her suffering from living away from Reinaldo. Most of all, these letters, which in their repetitiveness movingly capture the mundane, trace the pain of a mother who suspects the worst about her son's health. But the extent of her overt communication with Reinaldo about his health is limited to repeated pleas to let her know how he is (e.g., on 19 June 1988, she writes, "I hope you'll write to me and tell me how you are above all about your health which is the most important thing"); expressions of her fear that she might outlive her son (e.g., on 27 December 1987, she writes, "I've prayed to God that I die before you do"); and maternal advice to look after himself (e.g., on 17 February 1988, she writes, "Take good care of your health and of everything so many things happen in the world that one is better off not listening to the radio to avoid learning more about them"; on 5 March 1988, she writes, "Take good care of yourself my son that I don't want to think the worst. I feel so sad always thinking about you"). Although AIDS is kept off the pages of the correspondence between mother and son, it is indirectly there. I propose, furthermore, that Oneida and Reinaldo obliquely speak about AIDS through the unidentified illness of someone else, Vidal, a man who is dear to their hearts.

Married to Ofelia, one of Arenas's aunts, Vidal is first mentioned in a letter that Oneida wrote on 28 July 1985: "Vidal is so-so he is very depressed let's see how far he can go." Six months later, on 19 January 1986, Oneida writes, "Vidal is better let's see how much [his life] stretches out." Oneida's narrative of Vidal's illness, like her brother-in-law's life, "stretches out" until 1989, and in the course of twenty-three letters she keeps her reader — Reinaldo — abreast of the sick man's ups and downs. In 1988 Vidal's illness takes a turn for the worse, which Oneida describes in three letters: "Vidal is doing badly. . . . I don't think he has much left to live" (27 July 1988); "We are fine except for Vidal who gets worse by the day we already know that it is the end" (30 August 1988); "As for us you know we are sad seeing Vidal so gravely ill poor man it breaks our hearts to see him dying slowly. It seems that he is in the final phase" (4 November 1988). On 4 May 1989, referring to Vidal's death, Oneida writes of his widow, "Ofelia is still very sad imagine it's not easy the separation from someone whom you've made a life with and he was so good."

"Imagine," Oneida writes to her son. And imagine he probably did, but not just in that specific instance in which she asks him to empathize with Vidal's grieving widow. Arenas indeed may have put himself in his aunt's place and felt her pain, but I contend that he had been imagining all along. His mother's running account of Vidal's illness and long, slow death sets Arenas's imagination in motion, leading him to put himself in someone else's place — not in Ofelia's but in Vidal's. I imagine the AIDS-suffering Arenas reading his mother's letters and imagining his own protracted and agonizing death. I can only conjecture, of course, but Arenas's correspondence lends credence to the speculation. On 28 August 1988, not mentioning Vidal by name but alluding to him by referring to his son's depression on account of his father's impending death, Arenas writes, "I would not wish too long of a life if it would mean prolonging one's suffering and loneliness." On 14 February 1989, reacting to Vidal's passing, he writes, "Give Ofelia my most sincere condolences. I always loved Vidal and will not forget how good he always was to me. Death is a relief and one has to resign oneself to it. Nobody knows how long we'll be in this world and the important thing is to live in peace and love." Having ended an earlier letter to his mother with a cryptic statement, "I have lived my life" (17 July 1988), Arenas obliquely asks Oneida in these two letters to do some imagining herself: to imagine him in her brother-in-law's place, which she may have been doing all along. Just as readers of *Mona* and *El color del verano* are invited to link allegorically the novels' author to Leonardo and Clara Mortera, the reader of Arenas's letters — Oneida Fuentes — is now prompted by her son to link his *vida* to Vidal's. Only in coded language can a dying Reinaldo Arenas communicate to his mother the fateful news she has feared: that she will outlive her only child.

After Night Falls

....

Reinaldo Arenas is the most
inconvenient corpse in Cuban literature.
NORGE ESPINOSA MENDOZA,
"¿Otro color para una Cuba rosa?"

In the essay "Los dichosos sesenta" (1989), Reinaldo Arenas addresses how
he came to write a lecture, to be delivered at a university, about one of Latin
American literature's most important developments: the novel of the sixties. As he explains, he wrote the lecture while riding on a train, which was
traveling through the boring North American landscape. Not distracted by
anything he saw through his window, Arenas quickly made a list of some of
the most important novels of the 1960s: Alejo Carpentier's *El siglo de las luces*
(*Explosion in a Cathedral*), Julio Cortázar's *Rayuela* (*Hopscotch*), Mario Vargas Llosa's *La ciudad y los perros* (*The Time of the Hero*), José Lezama Lima's
Paradiso (*Paradiso*), Guillermo Cabrera Infante's *Tres tristes tigres* (*Three
Trapped Tigers*), Gabriel García Márquez's *Cien años de soledad* (*One Hundred Years of Solitude*), and José Donoso's *El obsceno pájaro de la noche* (*The
Obscene Bird of Night*). Arenas then "plunged" himself into the "fabulous"
sixties to find an explanation for the nearly simultaneous publication of so
many novels that became "classics" of the so-called Latin American Boom.[1]

In a series of anaphoric — and even euphoric — sentences that reference
the title of the essay, Arenas captures the excitement of the decade:

> Fabulous sixties because the world had been shaken by a sexual revo-
> lution and all prejudices had been swept away in one way or another.
> . . . Fabulous sixties because also a musical revolution had invaded
> the world and the inimitable songs of the Beatles had broken all the
> barriers of incommunication, and all political obstacles, as well as

those of prudishness and affectation, had to give way to poetry. . . .
Fabulous sixties because the young proclaimed that power should be
in the hands of the imagination. ("Los dichosos sesenta" 26–27)

At the end of his catalogue of "fabulous" transformations, Arenas refers to a
watershed in the political landscape around which so many Latin American
writers had coalesced: "Cuba also had had a revolution and a dictatorship
had been overthrown" (27).

Arenas then turns again to the literary scene, affirming that the vitality of
the sixties "impregnated" many writers who, as he puts it, "were committed
almost entirely to freedom and creativity" (28). But an unexpected change
in the view outside the window of the train brought Arenas back to the
present. What he suddenly saw, interrupting ubiquitous fast-food restau-
rants, endless gas stations, and identical trees neatly lined up along the path
of the train, was simultaneously exhilarating and painful:

Suddenly, the train goes by a sports arena. In the light of dusk, I see
carefree and agile young men jumping and throwing a ball in a bas-
ket. And that vision is a flash that cannot but take me back to the
present. And I see myself, as I am, a product of the sixties, at the
threshold of the unfortunate nineties. Someone who cannot identify,
mingle, blend — even if I wanted to, and I wanted to — with those
young men who so freely can throw a ball up in the air and give
themselves over to that act because they are not obsessed with a frustrated dream. (29)

Not one to miss an opportunity to comment on Castro's revolution and its
impact on the Cuban people, Arenas goes on to generalize about the situation of Cuban exiles:

Never . . . will Cuban exiles . . . be able to throw a ball so freely up in
the air — even if we wanted to, even if we desperately tried. Over each
of our gestures, over each of our words hover the inexpressible experience, the frustration, and the unbearable weight of having been witnesses and actors of the glorious sixties . . . , of having dreamt about a
future that instead of moving forward took on a regressive character,
[in] a revolution that devoured us and then spit us out . . . onto this
intolerable hell hole or onto a frozen tundra lashed by all kinds of
winds. (29–30)[2]

Conflating the dynamics of exile with the process of aging, Arenas is nostalgic about the decade that happened to correspond to his youth. Although he asserts, referring to himself and his compatriots in exile, that "an angry frustration encourages and incites us" (30–31), Arenas surprisingly ends his essay on a hopeful note, though one that is also critical of Latino literary traditions: "Perhaps, out of all this, somehow, someone will be able to produce good literature in Spanish in the United States. After all, our literary tradition is one of forlornness [*desamparo*]" (31). Still, unable to erase from his mind the image of the attractive, carefree, young male bodies he had seen playing basketball, Arenas turns to them again to conclude his essay: "But what I am sure of is that I never will we be able to throw a ball up in the air with the cockiness, with the joyful indifference, with the innocence of those young men whom I fleetingly saw as the train relentlessly took me to the place where I had to give my lecture" (31).

I begin by looking more closely, as Arenas himself did, at the basketball players who disrupted his journey back to the sixties. What did Arenas see in these young men as he pondered his inability to identify and mingle with them? Nostalgically contemplating his younger and more vital self as he momentarily saw himself reflected in these young men, an older and AIDS-afflicted Arenas performs here an act of self-exclusion that echoes a related act of self-exclusion earlier in his text: his own omission from the list of writers who, according to Arenas, carried themselves in the 1960s with as much "cockiness" (28) as the basketball players who appeared beyond his train window in the late 1980s. If age, gender, experience, illness, and nationality separated Arenas from the basketball players, what led Arenas to separate himself from the likes of Cabrera Infante, Carpentier, Cortázar, Donoso, García Márquez, Lezama Lima, and Vargas Llosa? Whatever the reasons (and modesty may have been one of them), Arenas ironically replicates what was done to him in his native Cuba during the sixties, which for him were anything but *dichosos*. Despite the fact, for instance, that *El mundo alucinante* (*The Ill-Fated Peregrinations of Fray Servando*) became an instant success abroad, Arenas did not get to enjoy his critical acclaim in the 1960s and 1970s. As in the case of his encounter with the basketball players, he was separated by circumstance from the writers he so admired, a harsh reality that eventually transformed his wish for recognition into a "frustrated dream." In both instances, Arenas leaves a trace of a fantasy of belonging, imagining himself as a player on the basketball court of the eighties and the literary field of the sixties.

For each of the novels he mentions, Arenas offers a description and a critical assessment. He begins with Carpentier's *El siglo de las luces*, in whose depiction of the failure of the French Revolution Arenas reads an allegory of the failure of the Cuban Revolution. He then adds that this novel, in his view Carpentier's "masterpiece" ("Los dichosos sesenta" 24), was published in French first and afterward in Mexico before it appeared in Cuba, in 1963. Although some may quibble with Arenas's inclusion of *El siglo de las luces* on his list, what intrigues me is the fact that Arenas places *El siglo de las luces* at the beginning of his chronology of novels, especially since the year this novel appeared, 1962, also saw the publication of *La muerte de Artemio Cruz* (*The Death of Artemio Cruz*), the first major novel by Carlos Fuentes, the only one of the "Big Four" Boom writers whom Arenas excludes from his inventory. (The other three were Julio Cortázar, Gabriel García Márquez, and Mario Vargas Llosa.) Arenas has made public his dislike of Fuentes (*Antes que anochezca* 326; *Before Night Falls* 305), but personal animosity alone may not be the reason for the Mexican's absence from the Cuban's essay. Although Arenas simply may have wanted to highlight *El siglo de las luces*, his choice is more than a statement about this novel's importance. As he expresses his admiration for *El siglo de las luces*, Arenas simultaneously shifts our attention away from Carpentier and refocuses it on another Cuban writer who also authored in the sixties a novel that can be (and has been) read as an allegory of the Cuban Revolution. I am referring, of course, to Arenas himself and to *El mundo alucinante*, which is his own "masterpiece." Like *El siglo de las luces*, *El mundo alucinante* first appeared in France, before its original Spanish version was published in Mexico, but unlike *El siglo de las luces*, Arenas's novel was never published in Cuba, and its author was the object not of respect and approbation but of scorn and ostracism in his own country. Between the lines of Arenas's brief telling of the story of Carpentier and his novel, one may be able to read Arenas's own story of his initial aspirations and eventual disappointments. Arenas ends his list of Boom authors by exclaiming:

> The fabulous sixties! They are perhaps the reason that during this
> time Latin American writers (among whom there were at least three
> Cubans) published excellent novels. *La dicha* [good fortune] is a state
> of grace, of confidence, of faith, of enthusiasm, of abandon, of desire,
> of play, of invention, of rebellion, of incessant curiosity. *La dicha*,

great *dicha*, is a state of hopeful anticipation and collective intoxication. ("Los dichosos sesenta" 26)

"At least three Cubans," he suggestively says in a parenthetical aside, are
among the Latin American writers who published excellent novels in the
sixties: Carpentier, Cabrera Infante, and Lezama Lima. Arenas's formulation hints that there may be other Cubans who deserve to be included on
the list of the decade's notable Latin American novelists. Arenas's readers
are prompted to add the name of *el desdichado* Arenas, who was kept from
experiencing the "collective intoxication" of the literary sixties.[3]

Writing in 1989, Gerald Martin commented:

> Had he been born outside of Cuba, Arenas would probably have be-
> come one of the most successful Latin American exponents of the
> Magical Realist mode, but fate decreed that he was to live in a coun-
> try where the Socialist Realist . . . mode would dominate, and little
> by little he found this and other restrictions on his personal freedom
> not only unacceptable but quite literally intolerable. (327–28)

Despite his troubles with the Cuban authorities, Arenas wrote incessantly,
having to rewrite some works several times after the manuscripts mysteriously disappeared or were destroyed by "friends" to whom he had entrusted them. A committed and disciplined writer, Arenas would not give
up in Cuba or in exile, where he faced different troubles. But regardless of
his efforts to see his work in print, several novels that he wrote in the 1960s
did not see the light of day until much later, in the 1980s, when the Boom
was long past. "What if?," Arenas asks in "Los dichosos sesenta," echoing
Gerald Martin. In his case, however, he does not hypothesize an alternative
birthplace; instead, his ruminations on the sixties invite his readers to imagine what might have happened to his place in the literary history of the
sixties had his hopes and aspirations not been dashed by the collapse of a
hopeful revolutionary struggle in his country.

But Arenas not only looks back. He also looks forward, ending his essay
with the hope that "someone," following a long-established tradition of
having *desamparo* (forlornness) as *his* muse, will write "good" literature in
Spanish in the United States. I say "his" muse because that "someone" is
arguably none other than Arenas himself. In a self-serving gesture, he is
obliquely making a plea for recognition of the work he published while
living away from his country. Anxious to secure a prominent place in literary

history, Arenas realizes that he is in a precarious situation in the 1980s in the United States. He faces the complicated reality of being a writer in exile and writing in a language that is not the main language of his new home; he also faces the complication of being in exile from a country with a totalitarian regime that, in the 1980s, still enjoyed substantial political currency abroad. Geographically situated in the United States, emotionally anchored in Cuba, and writing exclusively in Spanish, Arenas risked positioning himself in a limited community of writers and readers, mostly his Cuban compatriots outside the island. He had little affinity — linguistic, cultural, or political — with most Chicano, Nuyorican, and other U.S. Latino writers, whom he clearly denigrates when he posits the absence of "good" literature in Spanish in the United States.[4] Ironically, this comment and others that were equally critical may have alienated many of Arenas's potential readers, critics, and publishers and thus put in jeopardy his literary legacy. Arenas may have been "lenguaraz," as fellow Cuban José Prats Sariol has described him ("La voz de *Guanabo Gay*"), but since his pen was at least as active as his *lengua*, or tongue, Arenas died with the satisfaction of having completed a literary project on which he had been working for almost thirty years. Nonetheless, the recognition that he so desperately wanted still eluded him when — poor, marginalized, and suffering from AIDS — he took his own life in 1990.

While living in Cuba, Arenas had to smuggle his manuscripts out of the island, hoping that they would reach someone who would be interested in publishing them. While living in the United States, especially toward the end of his life, Arenas still had to struggle to see his work in print. Having completed *El color del verano* (*The Color of Summer*) and *El asalto* (*The Assault*), the last two novels of his *pentagonía*, Arenas sent copies of the manuscripts to a number of people, including me. A short, handwritten letter, dated 1 September 1990, came with the package:

> Dear Jorge:
> Here are the fourth and fifth novels of the *pentagonía*. I hope you
> have fun reading them. You have my permission to quote from them
> and even to do a critical edition of both. With a big hug from your
> grateful friend
> Reinaldo Arenas

Who among the earlier admirers of Arenas would have imagined that the author of *El mundo alucinante*, a novel that in 1969 secured him a place among the prominent writers of the Boom, would twenty years later, not long before his death, be "peddling" his novels to those of us who had continued to read his work? A year later, in 1991, Ediciones Universal, a modest publishing company in Miami that caters to Cuban exiles and that had released some of Arenas's earlier works, published his last two novels.

But then . . . boom! With the posthumous 1992 publication in Spain of *Antes que anochezca* (*Before Night Falls*) and of its 1993 translation into English, Arenas belatedly became something of a literary superstar.[5] While the stars of the Boom writers were beginning to fade, Arenas's began to rise. By then it was acceptable to see him and his work in a positive light, even among those who earlier had shunned Arenas for his political and sexual views. Although the story of the persecuted dissident writer captivated many readers, it was the story of the sexual outlaw that earned Arenas's autobiography a distinctive place in the Latin American canon.[6] Capturing the hearts and minds of readers everywhere, even in his native Cuba, Arenas has become, in the words of Philip Swanson, "something of a cult figure" (110) — much of it arguably due to Julian Schnabel's highly acclaimed film adaptation of his autobiography, which appeared in 2000. Arenas indeed would have been pleased with the buzz around him and his work, but one has to wonder how he would have reacted to seeing the photograph of Javier Bardem, not his own, on the cover of the paperback edition of *Before Night Falls*. Would he have regarded this as an "erasure," reminiscent of his many years in Cuba as a *no-persona*? Or as a validation and a vindication, reveling in the "commodification" of Reinaldo Arenas that the photograph of the handsome actor who plays him in Schnabel's *Before Night Falls* has helped to promote?[7]

Arenas certainly would have found interesting if not disturbing that, following his death in the United States and primarily after the publication of *Antes que anochezca* in 1992, he has found his way back to Cuba, becoming the object of considerable attention on his beloved island. Although the autobiography has not been readily available because books critical of Castro's government can not circulate freely in Cuba, it has been widely read. As Abilio Estévez, writing in 1994, remembered, "The book has passed from hand to hand. The copies of the carefully produced Tusquets edition of scarcely two years ago are falling to pieces, covers torn off, pages crumpled from use. It has been much discussed" (861). Referring to books by Arenas and other exiled writers whom he has read in Cuba, Yomar González Domínguez speaks of "under-the-table barter," explaining that "chain-lending" (*el presta-presta*) is the best way to have these books circulate (19). According to Amir Valle, Arenas's memoirs also made the rounds via e-mail.[8] Making possible Arenas's return to Cuba, *Antes que anochezca* inspired its readers to set in motion a process by which Arenas began to be given in his native country a newly prominent place in the history of twentieth-century Cuban literature.

In 2002, in an imaginary conversation with his compatriot Ambrosio Fornet, an influential literary critic on the island, Arturo Arango assessed the Arenas phenomenon:

> Perhaps the most difficult question in this conversation would be: what should we do with Reinaldo Arenas? There is no doubt in my mind that for a good number of readers and other persons associated with the library at the UNEAC, the most important literary event so far this decade has been reading Arenas's last novels. I am referring to *El portero, El asalto, Antes que anochezca*, which he calls an autobiography although it contains as much fiction as *El color del verano*, which is indeed the most important, the greatest of all. . . . Now, until today it has been claimed, and correctly, that a great novel against the Cuban Revolution has not been written in exile, and accustomed as we are to thinking in dualistic terms, many will find it difficult to say "*El color del verano* is counterrevolutionary and at the same time a great novel." And if the former is undeniable . . . , the latter seems to me to be equally true. . . . How will we read *El color del verano* a century from now, when the passions surrounding it have been placated? As a former teacher of mine likes to say, few admirers of the *Divine Comedy* remember whether Dante was a Guelph or a Ghibelline or, in the last analysis, on which side were reason and justice. ("En una conversación [imaginaria] con Ambrosio Fornet sobre la novela cubana de los 90" 125–26)

An intellectual "within" the Revolution, Arango can read and appreciate Arenas's literary works despite, as he puts it, the writer's "total incomprehension of this social project" (126).[9] Much has changed since 1971, when it was proclaimed in the Primer Congreso Nacional de Educación y Cultura that the only viable artistic expression was that which served the Revolution. But political passions in Cuba are deeply entrenched, as Arango notes, and some still find it difficult to see beyond Arenas's politics, as was made especially clear in the wake of Schnabel's *Before Night Falls*.[10]

Schnabel's film, shown in Havana only to a select audience, immediately mobilized Cuba's political and cultural elites into damage control to counteract the "danger" it posed to the Revolution. *Before Night Falls* was dissected and attacked in high-level meetings, after which the electronic cultural journal *La jiribilla* appeared, devoting its inaugural issue to Reinaldo Arenas.[11] Pedro de la Hoz, who had co-presided at a meeting of journalists called by the Ministerio de Cultura and the Comité Central del Partido Comunista to discuss the film, authored the lead article, which attacks Schnabel's *Before Night Falls*, reducing it to a libelous *panfleto* that uses Arenas's "delirious" memoirs to mount a "defamatory campaign" against human rights on the island (*"Antes que anochezca*: ¿Arte o panfleto?"). Similarly, Enrique Ubieta Gómez claims that *Antes que anochezca*, "a book written out of hate," describes a Cuba that is totally false ("Arenas y la noche"). And the Los Angeles–based trade unionist and political activist Jon Hillson, offering a passionate defense of Cuba's achievements since 1959, denounces Arenas's memoirs and Schnabel's film as counterrevolutionary "diatribes" ("La política sexual de Reinaldo Arenas"). This trio of articles is followed by essays on the poet Delfín Prats and on a literary prize in Holguín named after Arenas's novel *Celestino antes del alba* (*Singing from the Well*), as well as a piece by Arenas himself, where he writes about his life in exile, and his short story "El Cometa Halley" ("Halley's Comet"). The issue also includes a section titled "El gran zoo," in which material by and about Arenas published abroad is reprinted. Two other contributions — an article on the writer and journalist Amir Valle and an interview with the sociologist and religious studies scholar Aurelio Alonso — close the first issue of *La jiribilla*. How is one to read this compilation of apparently disparate texts?

The point of the three opening articles, the core of the issue, is obvious, which is to excoriate *Antes que anochezca* and its film adaptation in *Before Night Falls* because of their "untruthfulness." Curiously, of the three, one is by a U.S. American, a strategic inclusion, for Hillson's article, published in Spanish and in its original English version, validates what the Cubans (de la Hoz and Ubieta Gómez) denounce in theirs.[12] The editors' use of a corroborating "voice" from the outside to mount their "case" is not limited to Hillson's. Arenas's own voice is also heard — and used against him — insofar as *La jiribilla* appropriates some of the writer's own texts from exile.[13] In one of them, "Adiós a Manhattan," Arenas portrays New York as "an unin-habitable place" — violent, dirty, heartless — where only the wealthy can thrive, which is a depiction of the iconic United States city that pro-Castro Cubans are quite happy to publicize. Five months before his death, the man who once had been dazzled by New York concludes his essay by ruefully lamenting: "Tal vez para un desterrado . . . no haya sitio en la tierra" (Per-haps for an exile . . . there is no place on earth). This portrait of an exiled Arenas in existential turmoil is followed by Eugenio Marrón's "Un poeta que abre las constelaciones," a rosy portrait of the *holguinero* Delfín Prats, the hometown friend and cruising buddy of Arenas's youth, who remained in Cuba after Arenas left. The message that these two contrasting pieces are meant to convey does not escape readers: if the *desterrado* Arenas finds living in New York unbearable, Prats prospers in his *tierra*, where, accord-ing to Marrón, he is "admired and revered by all." Had Arenas not turned his back on Holguín (and, by extension, Cuba), he would have found, as Prats has, a nurturing *sitio* in which to live and write.

Cuba is presented as a place that, as Dean Luis Reyes's "Páginas de Celestino" illustrates, encourages artistic creation and takes pride in its writers, which is exemplified by the annual literary prize that bears the name of the protagonist of the first novel published by Holguín's famous (or infamous) son, Reinaldo Arenas.[14] The overall picture presented in *La jiri-billa* is that the ungrateful, lying, obsessed, misguided, and vengeful Arenas is alone to blame for his troubles, for he chose a path that took him away from Cuba and into a life of hatred in the Cuban exile community. This unattractive image of Arenas is offered as the "portrait that the film owes us," the closing words of Cuban exile Vicente Echerri's venomous depiction of Arenas in an article published abroad on Schnabel's *Before Night Falls*, which the editors of *La jiribilla* not only chose to include but also craftily placed last in their composite "portrait" of Reinaldo Arenas.[15]

It is meaningful that Vicente Echerri has the last word in *La jiribilla*'s "exposé" of Arenas. In Cuba Arenas befriended Echerri but eventually he came to distrust and dislike him so much that he ridiculed him in his works. The editors maliciously used the judgment of Arenas's former "friend," who felt he had been unjustly maligned, to malign Arenas; from the editors' perspective, furthemore, the fact that Echerri is a fellow Cuban exile makes his characterization of Arenas even more compelling than the ones offered by de la Hoz, Ubieta Gómez, and Hillson. Not surprisingly, the other texts that accompany Echerri's in "El gran zoo" also serve to discredit Arenas. One is by Arenas himself, a short excerpt of *Antes que anochezca*, in which he comes across as sarcastic and pugnacious in his denunciation of Cuban exiles who insist on promoting a dialogue with Castro. Another is an article by Fernando Villaverde, which appeared in 1983 in Miami's *El nuevo herald*, that discussed the conflicts between Arenas and Belkis Cuza Malé, the exiled Cuban poet and editor of *Linden Lane* magazine. (Arenas's association with the magazine came to an ugly end within a year of its founding because of his editorial differences with Cuza Malé.) And another is a fragment that the editors incorrectly claim to have taken from "Reinaldo y yo," a touching reminiscence by Cuza Malé that had appeared in *El nuevo herald* in 2001. The fragment, which is actually from Villaverde's 1983 article, refers to Cuza Malé's version of the *Linden Lane* magazine episode and quotes her as saying: "Reinaldo Arenas no ha renunciado. Yo lo he botado a patadas" (Reinaldo Arenas has not resigned. I have kicked him out). Clearly, the editors of *La jiribilla* took great delight in reproducing these words twice in the same issue, insidiously suggesting, by misrepresenting the fragment's provenance, that in 2001 Cuza Malé still held a grudge against Arenas, which was not the case.[16]

The closing two pieces in the issue relate indirectly to *La jiribilla*'s portrait of Arenas. "Neutralidad culposa" defends Amir Valle against attacks by Cuban exiles for advancing in the independent electronic bulletin *Letras en Cuba* a position respectful of all literature written by Cubans, whether they are on or off the island, regardless of the authors' political persuasions. Cuban exiles reacted the way they did, the article argues, because they could not tolerate "the maturity of Cuba's cultural politics," which has the "capacity to evaluate with depth and balance the totality of Cuba's literary patrimony." (Ironically, Valle eventually became a victim of Cuba's "mature" cultural politics: the Ministerio de Cultura did not allow him to continue publishing *Letras en Cuba* after its thirtieth issue; and in 2005 he was denied permission to return to Cuba from Europe, where he had been promoting his works, because of "official" dissatisfaction with the publication, in Spain, of his book on prostitution in Cuba.) In the other piece, "Grandezas y miserias," Aurelio Alonso denounces the "counterrevolutionary" Cuban scholars who attended the Latin American Studies Association Conference in 2000 and the Cubans who picketed the Miami hotel where the conference was held. Although these two contributions are not specifically about

Arenas, their aim is to paint an unfavorable image of Cuban exiles, a group to which Arenas belonged during the last decade of his life and in whose "gritería anticubana" (anti-Cuban shouting), as it is described in "Neutralidad culposa," he participated; in fact, Arenas was among the loudest *gritones*.

Political and cultural ideologues targeted Arenas when he lived in Cuba because of his "counterrevolutionary" stance, his openly gay sexuality, and his experimental and denunciatory fiction. Cuba's view of Arenas in the last two decades has gone through a substantial transformation, due primarily to three critical changes in Cuban society. First, the collapse of the Soviet Union (Cuba's longtime patron) and the changing nature of the global political order have resulted in some liberalization in Cuban governance and economics. Second, the cultural politics of Castro's Cuba are no longer what they were during the heyday of socialist realism; there is more interest in diverse and alternative themes, styles, and forms. Third, in the context of reforms to Cuba's penal code, which are part of a project of "transformism" that involves the incorporation of the gay body into the body politic, the nature of antihomosexual repression has substantially changed.[17]

In the new millenium the "anxieties" about Arenas still exist in Cuba, but with varying degrees of intensity. If during his lifetime Arenas was ostracized in his native country on all three grounds, there are now divergent responses to Arenas's anti-Castro politics, his homosexuality, and his literary production. This tension runs through the inaugural issue of *La jiribilla* insofar as it denounces the strident critic of the Revolution and finds the impudent homosexual disconcerting, but acknowledges the talented writer. For instance, Jon Hillson, obviously not a fan of Arenas's politics and by his own admission not a reader of the writer's entire oeuvre, harshly censures *Antes que anochezca*, but incorporates into his essay's conclusion what a Cuban poet once told him: "You know, one cannot understand Cuban contemporary literature without reading Reinaldo Arenas." Likewise, Enrique Ubieta Gómez ends his essay, in which he condemns the author of *Antes que anochezca* for not having understood "the greatness of *his* Revolution," with an unexpected statement: "Arenas will transcend because of that zone of his literature that hatred could not contaminate. And that is enough to secure him an honorable place in the history of Cuban literature." Ubieta Gómez can appreciate Arenas's work but, by distinguishing between "zones" within Arenas's corpus, he is among those who, in Arturo Arango's view ("En una conversación [imaginaria] con Ambrosio Fornet sobre la novela cubana de los 90"), cannot fully appreciate Arenas's literary production.

"El Cometa Halley," Arenas's parodic continuation of Federico García Lorca's *La casa de Bernarda Alba*, seems to be in the "zone" that is safe for the readers of *La jiribilla* to enter, since anti-Castro politics does not play a role in Arenas's short story — or so seem to think the editors of the journal (a view that my reading of "El Cometa Halley" challenges). The short story's postmodern playfulness and the fact that the author of Arenas's intertext was a famous gay man (who also happens to have a cameo role in "El Cometa Halley," lusting after Pepe el Romano) appear not to be a concern. This short story by Arenas may have been a safe choice, but its presence in *La jiribilla* is certainly provocative, for García Lorca's homosexuality and homicide, which the text of "El Cometa Halley" evokes, prompt one to notice a meaningful gap in Eugenio Marrón's telling of Delfín Prats's story. "Un poeta que abre las constelaciones" neglects to mention the widely known fact that the Cuban poet is gay and that he, like the gay Spanish poet, suffered at the hands of the authorities. This story is as well known to Cubans as is García Lorca's. It is true that Prats was not murdered, as was García Lorca (Castro's Cuba did not go to that extreme in its treatment of homosexuals), but for years he was silenced — reduced to a *no-persona*, as Arenas would say — and lived under the watchful eyes of ideological and cultural extremists.[18] One can only conjecture why Marrón chose not to discuss Prats's homosexuality and the impact that it had on his life as a man and as a writer. Whatever the reasons, Marrón obliquely suggests that gay poets like Delfín Prats may have been victimized in the earlier years of the Revolution, but in present-day Cuba they can peacefully live and write. Had Reinaldo been more like his buddy Delfín, he might still be alive and in Holguín. That is the story that *La jiribilla* seems to want its readers to believe.

In 2001, the same year that *La jiribilla* was launched with the issue on Arenas, Lourdes Arencibia Rodríguez published *Reinaldo Arenas entre eros y tánatos*, the only book-length study of Arenas by a Cuban living on the island. As Arencibia Rodríguez explains, this was possible because Cubans had reached the maturity to evaluate Arenas's oeuvre without needing to have others tell them that Arenas is an important figure in Cuban and Latin American letters. Unlike Arenas scholars outside Cuba, who, she claims, have dealt primarily with the political aspects of his work, Arencibia Rodríguez chooses to pay attention to "the indisputable qualities of his literature" (11). She thus counterposes the literary and the political, a spurious dichotomy on which the book is based. "I'm interested in discussing literature" (11), she declares, as if a political text were ipso facto nonliterary. Written with the explicit goal of contributing to "the recuperation of the figure of Arenas" (47), Arencibia Rodríguez's book was oddly enough published not in Cuba but in Colombia, despite the fact that in 1999 the jury of the Concurso de Ensayo Alejo Carpentier had selected its manuscript as a finalist and recommended its publication.

Reinaldo Arenas entre eros y tánatos had its official presentation in Havana in June 2002 at the Instituto Cubano del Libro. Rafael Acosta de Arriba, one of the presenters, expressed regret that the book had not been published in Cuba, and then went on to praise Arencibia Rodríguez for privileging a literary, and not a political, approach to her subject. According to Acosta de Arriba, although Arenas was a key author in twentieth-century Cuban narrative, politics and ideology interfered with his literary talents, "ruining the extraordinary re-creator of Fray Servando Teresa de Mier" ("Para conocer las voces del agua"). In *Reinaldo Arenas entre eros y tánatos*, he explains, Arencibia Rodríguez rightly sets aside "the mythical image" manipulated by those who are against the Revolution and offers instead a study of her compatriot's "rich and unique literary oeuvre" ("Para conocer las voces del agua").[19] Like Arencibia Rodríguez, Acosta de Arriba reclaims a "literary" Arenas while denouncing his politics.

Arencibia Rodríguez's book is not the sustained and rigorous literary analysis of the works of Arenas that it purports to be or that Acosta de Arriba applauds. Essentially a catalogue of the writer's works, *Reinaldo Arenas entre eros y tánatos* is more descriptive than analytical. Despite its limitations, however, the book would have been a useful introduction to a writer not easily accessible in Cuba were it not for the fact that Arencibia Rodríguez, hiding behind the literary to avoid the political, offers incomplete and, for the most part, distorted views of Arenas's works. For instance, in a cursory treatment of *El color del verano* and *El asalto* (she devotes five and two pages, respectively, to these major works), she does not refer to Fifo or Reprimerísimo, central characters who are satirical and grotesque representations of Fidel Castro. In her analysis of *Arturo, la estrella más brillante* (*The Brightest Star*), she does not mention the UMAP camps, the indispensable context by which to understand and appreciate the novella. And in the two pages that she writes on *Necesidad de libertad*, Arenas's collection of political and literary essays, she says practically nothing. Moreover, *Antes que anochezca*, of which Arencibia Rodríguez says that "it is part autobiography, part street sociology, and part political manifesto" (*Reinaldo Arenas entre eros y tánatos* 97), merits only two pages. It is as if Arenas's autobiography had no literary value, making it undeserving of Arencibia Rodríguez's attention. How is one to read a book on Arenas that, among other flaws, excludes from its discussion the writer's most famous work?

Lourdes Arencibia Rodríguez fits the mold of the island Cuban reader to whom Arturo Arango refers ("En una conversación [imaginaria] con Ambrosio Fornet sobre la novela cubana de los 90"), one who is incapable of approaching Arenas's oeuvre without prejudice. As Arencibia Rodríguez has admitted, "I don't like all of Arenas either," explaining that he takes positions "that I reject, that make me dizzy, that I simply cannot digest" ("En las arenas de Reinaldo"). She makes Arenas's works "digestible" by suppressing the political writer and turning him instead into someone who, by transcending the political, "takes his conclusions to a universal plane" (*Reinaldo Arenas entre eros y tánatos* 134). With this interpretive — and obviously political — move, Arencibia Rodríguez diminishes a writer who, in her book, becomes "Arenas apenas" (Barely Arenas) — if I may borrow the apt title of a critical review of *Reinaldo Arenas entre eros y tánatos* published in *La gaceta de Cuba*, one of Cuba's leading literary journals (edited by none other than Arturo Arango).[20] And, significantly, this effort to recuperate a "literary" Arenas, despite the author's political and ideological accomodations, was not published in Cuba.

Between 1992, when *Antes que anocheza* was first published, and 2001, when the inaugural issue of *La jiribilla* appeared and Arencibia Rodríguez's book came out in Colombia, Arenas's name was favorably or neutrally invoked with some regularity in Cuban cultural and literary publications.[21] But island readers of Arenas who during this period wrote extensively and seriously on his works had to turn to publishers in other countries.[22] In 2001 *La jiribilla* published a long interview with Tomás Fernández Robaina that focused entirely on Arenas ("Las arenas movedizas"). The following year, in 2002, a scholarly article on Arenas appeared in Cuba, the first to my knowledge; this was Arencibia Rodríguez's "En busca de un tiempo de fábulas," which was published in *Temas*, a highly regarded cultural journal.[23] Drawn from *Reinaldo Arenas entre eros y tánatos*, Arencibia Rodríguez's article, not surprisingly, erases the political dimension of Arenas's works. In 2004 Alberto Garrandés published two articles on Arenas, one on *Celestino antes del alba* ("El castillo de tierra roja") and the other on *El mundo alucinante* ("Fray Servando"), electronic publications in *CubaLiteraria* that Garrandés later included in his 2008 book on Cuban narrative of the 1960s, *El concierto de las fábulas: Discursos, historia e imaginación en la narrativa cubana de los años sesenta* (133–38, 253–59). To Garrandés's credit, in one of the articles he references the complicated publishing history of *El mundo alucinante*, which, he explains, contributed to the "anomalous" and "irregular" reception of this novel in Cuba, a reception "made worse . . . by the stigmatization of Arenas and of some of his books that became known after he had established residence in the United Sates" ("Fray Servando" and *El concierto de las fábulas* 253). It is now "safe" to write about two novels by Arenas that were deemed problematic when they were published in the 1960s; it is acceptable as well to write about "El Cometa Halley," which Arenas authored in exile, since this short story does not openly engage in anti-Castro politics. In her book-length study of incest in literature, published in 2008, Leidy Vidal devotes four pages to "El Cometa Halley" but opts not to discuss the incest-themed *Viaje a La Habana*, a politically charged novella to which Vidal only makes a passing reference.

I have found three other pieces in Cuban publications that relate to Arenas: an interview, in 2003, with Oneida Fuentes, Arenas's mother, in *El caimán barbudo* ("Donde las arenas son más diáfanas"); another interview with Fernández Robaina, published in *La gaceta de Cuba* in 2010, which is also devoted to Arenas ("Rei-surrección"); and an excerpt in *La isla en peso* of Fernández Robaina's then unpublished "Misa para un ángel," a book about Arenas that combines fact and fiction. The editors of *La isla en peso*, in their introduction, refer to Arenas as "unforgettable and always present" (see "Inicio"). Fernández Robaina's *novela-testimonio*, as it has been publicized, appeared in 2010. It is significant that *Misa para un ángel* was published by UNEAC and that this institution, which in the 1970s had ostracized Arenas, hosted a public presentation of the book (on 17 September 2010). Carlos Velazco, the book's presenter, claimed in his remarks ("Cópula con Reinaldo Arenas") that although Arenas's oeuvre had been "discarded or barely discussed in his country," it has always been a "cornerstone" of Cuban literature.[24]

Arenas's exilic production clearly has a readership in Cuba, as attested by references in influential island journals to *Antes que anochezca*; *Arturo, la estrella más brillante*; *El asalto*; *El color del verano*; *La Loma del Ángel*; *Otra vez el mar*; *El palacio de las blanquísimas mofetas*; *El portero*; and *Viaje a La Habana*. It is quite telling, however, that these multiple and repeated references to Arenas and his works have not translated into serious, full-fledged studies of the writer's oeuvre. Even Arturo Arango, who is on record extolling the merits of *El color del verano*, has devoted only three paragraphs to what he considers a great novel, which he discusses in an essay on the role of history in Cuban fiction ("La historia por los cuernos" 37).[25]

The award-winning novelist Ernesto Pérez Castillo has recently expressed a sentiment shared by many in Cuba:

> No matter how upsetting it may be for some people, Reinaldo Arenas is a Cuban writer and his novel *El color del verano* is one of the possible keys to which anyone interested in exploring our identity and understanding what it means to be Cuban must turn. . . . Like him, many other writers who produced and are producing their work on the other side of the puddle are and will be part of the national literary corpus. (5)

Raúl Aguiar, in 2001, commented on young writers in Cuba and the "underground" literature they were reading:

> I in particular and the group with which I associate do not differentiate between the literary quality of Guillermo Cabrera Infante, Reinaldo Arenas, or Severo Sarduy, on the one hand, and that of those in Cuba, Lezama Lima, Virgilio Piñera or Alejo Carpentier, on the other hand. They are all towering figures in Cuban literature. (García Ronda et al. 180)

In 2008, in a panel discussion on young Cuban literature and its relation to the national canon, one of the participants, Norge Espinosa Mendoza, explained:

> Today we don't read [Nicolás] Guillén as much, today we don't read [Alejo] Carpentier as much, today we do not know exactly who was, for instance, Antonio Benítez Rojo, but we are asking ourselves who is Enrique Labrador Ruiz, and so forth. What we are talking about, therefore, is that it is very difficult to establish exactly how to relate to

this canon, in which also writers who are not being published in Cuba have increasing prominence; let's give as an example Reynaldo [*sic*] Arenas. (See "Joven literatura cubana" 2)

Even Ambrosio Fornet, who has found it difficult to objectively evaluate novels that condemn the Cuban Revolution, can bring himself to admit that "Arenas's novels are novels of a writer . . . and what a writer, and what novels," adding, "I may agree with them or not, some are better than others, but all of them have a level of artistic elaboration that compels me to treat them as authentic literature" ("Un visión crítica"). And Miguel Barnet, one of Cuba's most acclaimed writers, can now publicly say that Arenas, "a treasure of Cuban culture," belongs to "our spiritual patrimony" ("Lo que se sabe no se pregunta"). Notwithstanding the significance of these statements, the recuperation in Cuba of this "treasure" has been, at best, slow and selective, and, at worst, motivated by Cuba's revolutionary ideology.

When Cuban writers die in exile, they go through in their country what Rafael Rojas calls a "recovery ceremony," a process that mutilates their intellectual biographies because of Cubans' selective views about what is "recoverable" (*El estante vacío* 203–4). Accordingly, Reinaldo Arenas is now included in the pantheon of national literary figures, but his membership in this select group has been limited to a "dismembered" Arenas. He is remembered primarily as the author of *Celestino antes del alba* and *El mundo alucinante*, novels that he wrote in the 1960s and that do not openly condemn the Cuban Revolution and its leaders. (As if suffering from historical amnesia, island Cubans today seem to have forgotten how these novels were read in the sixties and seventies and how their author was ostracized as a result.) Despite Arenas's recent inclusion in the national literary canon, not much written by him has been published on the island since his "recovery" began. "El Cometa Halley" has been made available in two cultural journals, *La jiribilla* and *El caimán barbudo*, and in two anthologies, *Aire de luz: Cuentos cubanos del siglo XX* and *La ínsula fabulante: El cuento cubano en la Revolución, 1959–2008*.[26] Arenas's essay "Adiós a Manhattan" and a long excerpt of a chapter in *Antes que anochezca* ("El exilio") appeared in *La jiribilla*.[27] And a fragment of *Celestino antes del alba* is included in *CubaLiteraria*'s electronic publication *La literatura cubana en la Revolución: Literatura escrita en la década de los 60 y primeros años de los 70*.[28] That there has not been a Cuban edition of *El mundo alucinante*, regarded by most critics as Arenas's most important novel, is blamed on the writer's heirs, who, respecting his wishes, have not granted Cuba permission to publish his works.[29] Copyright laws, certainly, have not deterred island Cubans from publishing Arenas (albeit short pieces). Rogelio Riverón, editor of Editorial Letras Cubanas, has explained that it was possible to include Arenas and other exiled writers in *La ínsula fabulante* because the Centro Nacional de Derecho de Autor, following Cuban legislation and recognizing that the 2008 anthology was a "commemorative project," gave the publishers permission to do so.[30] According to Riverón, the works that are included are there because of "a right of a cultural nature" ("Ruptura y tradición"). Riverón is referring to Ley 14, which in 1977 codified Cuban copyright laws, which had been suspended since the mid-1960s. Although the law grants rights to authors, these rights are subordinated to the "superior interest" of the State in matters regarding the development and dissemination of science, technology, education, and culture. More specifically, Article 41 allows Cuba to declare "national patrimony" the works of deceased Cuban writers if the copyrights of those works are held by persons with permanent residence abroad, as is the case with Arenas.[31] How would Riverón explain Cuba's decision to publish some of Arenas's works and not others? Why publish multiple times "El Cometa Halley" and not, for instance, *El color del verano*, a great novel in the judgment of many in Cuba?

"El Cometa Halley" has become the "proof" that it is not true that Arenas's works are not allowed to be published in Cuba. This is illustrated by *La jiribilla*'s peculiar response to the Chilean novelist Roberto Ampuero's admonition to President Michelle Bachelet for attending the 2009 International Book Fair held in Cuba, a country where, Ampuero explains, the works of many writers, including Arenas, are forbidden. In the section "Noticias de Pueblo Mocho," having first quoted the section of Ampuero's open letter to President Bachelet in which he states that there is censorship in Cuba, the editors of *La jiribilla* simply — and categorically — state, "P.S., Roberto Ampuero is lying." They go on to substantiate their claim by offering the table of contents of two recent Cuban anthologies in which works by some of the "forbidden" writers mentioned by Ampuero are published. One of them, *La ínsula fabulante*, includes "El Cometa Halley" (see Ampuero and "Noticias de Pueblo Mocho"). What is left unsaid in *La jiribilla* is that most of Arenas's works, even if the writer's heirs were to allow their publication in Cuba, would not be published on the island under the current regime unless there were a revocation of chapter 5, article 39, section ch, of the Cuban Constitution, which states, "There is freedom of artistic expression as long as its content does not go against the Revolution" (see *Constitución Política de la República de Cuba*).

Pro-Castro Cubans want to promote a "safe" Arenas, not the author of politically volatile works. This is not the writer whom Arenas's heirs, honoring his wishes, are committed to promoting. Cuba has the right to claim Arenas as one of its own, just as Arenas's heirs have the right not to give permission to have his works published in Cuba. Both parties, engaging in ideological warfare, find themselves at an impasse with no end in sight. "What should we do with Reinaldo Arenas?," asked Arturo Arango in 2002, as he pondered the position Cuba should take vis-à-vis a native son who was a brilliant writer and an outspoken critic of the Revolution. A decade later, there is still no satisfactory response to Arango's important question. Island Cuban readers, in the meantime, await the return of Reinaldo Arenas to the island he loved so much.

However one may view what is happening with Arenas in Cuba today, the undeniable fact remains that the once unnameable Reinaldo Arenas can now be named in Cuba, and not necessarily for denunciation. Arenas's name not only regularly graces the pages of Cuban literary and cultural publications, but is also placed alongside those of Cuba's literary giants in official presentations at national events in which high-level political dignitaries are in attendance.[32] Arenas's name is also remembered — and honored — by others not in the literary establishment, as it is, for instance, by the national queer organization named after him, the Fundación LGBT Reinaldo Arenas.[33]

Arenas's oeuvre may be scarcely available in Cuba; readers may have to use ingenious methods to get their hands on his work; and serious scholarship on Arenas by island Cubans may be lacking. Nevertheless, Arenas has become entrenched in the Cuban literary imagination, figuring in the texts of writers on the island who, in some instances, openly acknowledge their appreciation for Arenas by dedicating their works to him.[34] In addition to having influenced a younger generation of writers, Arenas is also a presence in the imaginative literature of admiring compatriots who, paying homage to him, incorporate Arenas into their fictions through direct or indirect references to the writer or his work.[35] One of these admirers is Ronaldo

Menéndez, author of *El derecho al pataleo de los ahorcados*, winner of the Premio de Cuento Casa de las Américas in 1997.

In "Money," one of the short stories in Menéndez's collection, Arenas's *Antes que anochezca* has a significant role. The story's main characters, an unnamed married couple in Havana, realize that they have lost thirty dollars of the $1,100 they have saved to emigrate to Mexico. Ten days before, the husband had taken a fifty-dollar bill to buy a pair of jeans and, not having a wallet, he had placed the money inside a book in his backpack; he now suspects that after paying twenty dollars for the pants, he may have put the change inside the book and forgotten about it. When his wife inquires about which book it was, the husband responds that it's the only one that they have carried lately from place to place, Reinaldo Arenas's, which, as they recall, they had lent to a writer friend. (That the book is Arenas's autobiography is indirectly suggested in a turn of phrase that the narrator uses to refer to the couple's reaction when they realize that they have lost the money: "They completely resign themselves before night falls to be able to sleep" [68].) Does the couple's friend have the thirty dollars or, having been robbed recently of his savings, did he make use of his friends' money? Or, as the husband also speculates, did his lover take the money from him during a sexual tryst that occurred immediately after his purchase of the jeans? In his lover's house, the husband later finds three ten-dollar bills on her night-stand, takes them, and guiltily leaves after his lover casually lets it drop in conversation that her older brother had given her some money to buy new clothes. The husband and wife then visit their writer friend, whom they do not question about the missing thirty dollars and from whom they retrieve the book, only to discover that there is no money inside. The husband, who needs an explanation for the money that he has taken from his lover, then tells his inconsolable wife that he has found a buyer for the book, "a best-seller for which I can get the thirty dollars" (75). He goes to the *malecón*, gazes at Havana's contaminated harbor into which the sewage of Havana hotels flow, and proceeds with his plan:

> Finally, he takes out Reinaldo Arenas's book, turns its pages as if he were handling a stack of dollar bills, and throws it into the ocean: a gigantic, blue, open and seemingly democratic ocean for the crazies on rafts who throw themselves into the water leaving behind the palm trees. The book quickly sinks with the inertia of the fall, disap-

pears for a few minutes, then attempts to float, but soon becomes invisible under the gray of the sewage. (75)

The lying and cheating husband returns home to his wife to share with her the good news that he has sold the book, only to be surprised by the presence there of his lover, who tells him that she knows perfectly well where the thirty dollars came from. His scheme having failed, the husband opts for silence and "abandons himself to the image of the book," which, as we are immediately told again, in the last lines of the story, sinks with the inertia of the fall and then disappears into the harbor.

Although the husband's lover may claim that she knows where the money came from, the other two characters — as well as the reader — cannot be so sure. It is true that the husband took three ten-dollar bills from his lover's nightstand, but is this the money that the lover's brother had given her, as she has alleged? Or is it the married couple's money, which the lover stole from the cheating husband? In this story of deception, the reader can be certain of only two things: the centrality of money and sex to its plot and, more intriguingly, the importance of the book in which the two converge — a book likened to a stack of dollar bills before it is thrown into the harbor and the image of which, vanishing from sight in Cuba's contaminated waters, brings the tale to an end.

The inclusion of *Antes que anochezca* in "Money" and that of money within the covers of Arenas's autobiogaphy encourages a specular reading. Arenas's memoirs and Menéndez's short story mirror each other in that both focus on Cuba and sex. More specifically, *Antes que anochezca* and "Money" are about infidelity, if we take the term to reference unfaithfulness to Fidel. Menéndez's main characters, a husband and wife caught up in a drama of domestic infidelity while they plot their emigration, are, in the eyes of loyal revolutionaries on the island, unfaithful Cuban citizens. They are as determined to leave Castro's Cuba in 1994 as the *infidelis* Arenas had been years before, which he managed to do in 1980 and wrote about in *Antes que anochezca*. What is inscribed on the pages of Arenas's autobiography and what is hidden within those pages animate and facilitate the characters' pursuit of expatriation. In the end, however, their aspirations for freedom are temporarily dashed, and they are left without enough money to carry out their plan and without the inspiring book, which is last seen literally sinking under the weight of shit. If Menéndez, who left Cuba in

1997, invites one to read "Money" as a text about political disaffection, he wants his reader to take note of the role that *Antes que anochezca* plays in the lives and dreams of his characters. In the conclusion, Arenas's autobiography may be submerged in excrement (a metaphorical representation of official Cuba's "dumping" on what they regard as a counterrevolutionary book), but the final image with which we are left, that of a calm and reflective man mentally holding on to *Antes que anochezca*, conveys a message of hope: Arenas's autobiography may sink in the murky waters of Havana's contaminated harbor, but its ideas and dreams live on.

The book in the story, which is talked about but kept mostly out of sight until it becomes "invisible" in the sewage in Havana's harbor, symbolically speaks volumes about the situation of Arenas's oeuvre in his country. For Arenas's books, which circulate among readers in the murky currents of Cuban politics and culture today, experience analogous problems of visibility. Like the story's coveted book, Arenas's works are "appreciated" on the island but remain practically unpublished in Cuba. In spite of this, however, the once "worthless" Arenas now has substantial "currency," as intimated in "Money" by the pecuniary metaphor that turns the autobiography into dollars. Arenas's works circulate in a community of readers who, like the characters in Menéndez story, claim the right to pocket the "money" — that is, claim Arenas as theirs. Arenas's "value" is indeed high in the current Cuban literary marketplace, and the writer and his works are emerging from the turbid waters of clashing ideologies.[36]

Outside Cuba, Arenas has posthumously emerged triumphant, achieving after death the kind of international recognition of which he only had glimpses in life. Not only are Arenas's works now widely distributed in their orginal Spanish and in translations, but also his life and oeuvre have inspired writers, poets, artists, choreographers, dramatists, filmmakers, and composers.[37] A recent and notable case in point is the Cuban American composer Jorge Martín, whose opera based on the Cuban's memoirs had its world premiere on 29 May 2010. Martín's rendition of Arenas's life, a full-length opera in two acts performed by the Fort Worth Opera, was enthusiastically received by admiring opera critics and fans.[38] As the performers bowed at the end to an appreciative audience, *Antes que anochezca* floated not in a sea of sewage, as in Menéndez's story, but in an ocean of resounding applause at the Bass Performance Hall.

My partner and I flew from our home in Maine to Fort Worth, Texas, for the opening of the opera—a queer finale for my many years of work on Reinaldo Arenas. Not an opera connoisseur, I was there to celebrate a writer whom the composer and I admired—and to revel in the irony of it all. As I enjoyed the performance, I wondered how Arenas, a Cuban gay writer of humble origins who died impoverished in exile, would have reacted to seeing his story come to life on an opera stage. He indeed would have been honored, but I think he would have been amused as well. For Arenas, known for his unpretentiousness, would have been tickled to see himself—a *guajiro*—as the protagonist of what arguably would be for him a stuffy art form.[39] I suspect that Arenas would have been pleased with Martín's score, which blends different kinds of musical material, but especially with his libretto, which faithfully captures Arenas's complicated family romance, active erotic life, passionate commitment to writing, and relentless condemnation of Castro's government. He also probably would have been delighted with the casting of Wes Mason, who embodied him on stage with charisma, confidence, and vigor. (I can hear the irreverent Arenas making libidinous remarks about the hunky baritone.) When I imagine Arenas sitting in the audience, I see him appreciating Martín's opera, alternately feeling nostalgia for his beloved island, satisfaction about having completed his literary oeuvre, and sadness for having to die in a place other than Cuba. Despite the applause and ovation Martín's *Before Night Falls* received from the audience, I don't think that Arenas would have been moved to join in the jubilation. Because for Arenas, nothing, not even having entered the grand and spectacular world of opera (or of cinema), could compensate for the loss of Cuba.

In the last scene of the opera, after Arenas commits suicide and Lázaro casts his friend's ashes on the ocean, the Muses sing:

> Reinaldo, your fire will never die. Your works will send their light
> into the darkness of endless night. The sea receives your ashes like
> seeds on a meadow, sending forth your life through the world. Perhaps one day you will kiss the shore of your native island, your lost,
> beloved homeland.

Martín's opera ends on a hopeful note: Arenas's ashes potentially reaching the shores of his unforgettable Cuba, a reunion sealed with a kiss between the son and his fatherland. I can certainly imagine the remains of Arenas's body circulating one day in crystalline Cuban waters and frolicking, as Arenas hoped to do, with young male swimmers in reckless abandon, just as I can also envision a day when Arenas's body of works will circulate freely in Cuba. This would indeed be a happy ending.

·NOTES·

Prologue

1 On the "new" biographical criticism, see William Epstein; and Hoffmann.

1.

I Scream, Therefore I Am

1 On the honorable mention that Arenas received in 1965 and 1966 for *Celestino antes del alba* and *El mundo alucinante*, respectively, see "Notas de la UNEAC" and "Premio UNEAC de Novela Cirilo Villaverde." In 1968 Arenas submitted *Con los ojos cerrados* to the Premio Casa de las Américas (not to the literary competition sponsored by UNEAC as the *Diccionario de la literatura cubana* incorrectly claims), but it did not receive an honorable mention. One juror, the Chilean Jorge Edwards, publicly expressed admiration for *La vieja Rosa*, a short novel that was included in Arenas's collection. The Uruguayan literary critic Ángel Rama, who contrary to Arenas's claim was not among the jurors, smuggled a copy of the manuscript of *Con los ojos cerrados* out of Cuba and published it in Montevideo in 1972. Another copy of the manuscript, which Arenas gave to José Yglesias, an author and journalist from the United States who in the late 1960s spent time on the island doing research for a book on Cuba, is now in the Hispanic Caribbean Manuscripts collection of the University of Notre Dame. See Arenas, "Conversación con Reinaldo Arenas" 56; Arenas, "Memorias de un exiliado" 47–48; "Casa 68"; and Edwards.

2 On Castro's Cuba and homosexuality, see Espinosa Mendoza, "Historiar en el vacío"; Espinosa Mendoza, "¿Otro color para una Cuba rosa?"; Fernández Robaina, "Los homosexuales y la Revolución"; Guerra; Leiner; Lumsden; Morales, Vives, and Hernández; Salas 150–77; Sierra Madero; Young; and Zayas. For an insightful account of homosexuality in Cuban literature, see Bejel.

3 On the "new man," see Guevara; Salomón-Beckford; and Sorensen 24–42.

4 If in Cuba, as in other communist countries, a conflation was made between homosexuality and capitalism, in the United States in the 1950s a conflation

was made between homosexuality and communism. As Brad Epps succinctly puts it, "For the United States as for Cuba, homosexuality is the political other" (241).

5   For Castro's views on homosexuality, see also Fidel Castro, "Discurso pronunciado por el Comandante Fidel Castro Ruz"; Fidel Castro, *My Life* 222–25; Fidel Castro, "No cayó en el vacío el sacrificio de los mártires"; Fidel Castro, "Speech to the Fighting People"; Castro and Borge 139–41; and Conde 127–31.

6   This is a striking appropriation of "Work will make you free," the slogan placed at the entrance of Nazi concentration camps.

7   In the "Mesa Redonda Sobre Homosexualismo" that took place in February 1971, the attorney Magali Casell López refers to the "scientific treatments" to which homosexuals were subjected as one of a number of measures that were taken in Cuba for the prevention and repression of homosexuality (*Mesa redonda sobre homosexualismo* 11).

8   In January 1965 the U.S. poet Allen Ginsberg, on an official visit to Cuba to serve as a juror in a literary contest sponsored by Casa de las Américas, was quickly expelled from the island for speaking out against official policies, including Cuba's treatment of homosexuals, who — the outspoken Ginsberg soon discovered — were being subjected to police harassment, raids, and *depuraciones* (purges) at educational institutions. In an interview some years later Ginsberg mischievously recalled, "The worst thing I said was that I'd heard, by rumor, that Raúl Castro was gay. And the second worst thing I said was that Che Guevara was cute" (7). José Mario, a young gay poet whom Ginsberg befriended in Havana, was among the writers sent to the UMAP camps, an experience from which Arenas was spared. Mario was the founder of El Puente (1961–65), a publishing house around which a group of young writers coalesced and which was accused, among other things, of promoting homosexuality and "decadent" literature. See Mario, "Allen Ginsberg en La Habana"; Mario, "La verídica historia de ediciones El Puente"; and Miskulin 37–53, 89–109.

9   On the UMAP camps, see Llovio-Menéndez 140–74; Otero 110–12; Ronet; and Ros.

10 Prieto Morales's article is an example of the homophobia widespread in the press and other venues in Cuba. See Castellanos for an analysis of the homophobic discourse in several Cuban publications but especially in the weekly *Mella*, the official organ of the Unión de Jóvenes Comunistas (until 1966), which Castellanos takes as illustrative of the ways in which multiple sectors of Cuban society viewed homosexuality.

11 On homosexuality, Freud, and psychiatry in Cuba in the 1960s and 1970s, see,

in addition to Crain; González Martín, "Algunas consideraciones críticas sobre la teoría freudiana"; González Martín, "Desarrollo de las ideas neurofisiológicas en Cuba en el curso del proceso revolucionario"; Leiner 33–43;
Marqués de Armas; *Mesa redonda sobre homosexualismo*; Pérez Villar et al.; and
Salas 162–65.

12   On the "Padilla Affair," see *El caso Padilla*; Díaz Martínez; Padilla, *Fuera del juego*; and Padilla, *Self-Portrait of the Other* 128–66, 178–89.

13   See Reynaldo González 226–40; Heras León and Navarro; López, "Defender
todo lo defendible, que es mucho" 30–31; Rama, "Una nueva política cultural
en Cuba"; and Rojas, *Tumbas sin sosiego* 449–50. In 2007, in reaction to a
Cuban television program that featured Luis Pavón Tamayo without mentioning his role during the repressive Quinquenio Gris (also known as the
Pavonato), Cubans on and off the island electronically engaged in a "virtual"
debate about Cuba's cultural politics. For a compilation of these e-mails, see
"*Consenso* en la polémica intelectual." See also Ponte, *Villa Marista en plata*
49–173.

14   See Arenas, "Contra la integridad y estabilidad de la nación"; Castellanos;
Raúl Castro; "Declaration by the First National Congress on Education and
Culture" 5; Duanel Díaz 119–64; García Galló, *El diversionismo ideológico*; Ley
1262; and *Tesis y resoluciones* 223–26.

15   On changes in Cuba's cultural politics beginning in the mid-1980s, see Black;
Duanel Díaz 165–98; and Rojas, *El estante vacío* 78–79, 154–61.

16   Contrary to what Castro said, Mariel was not "open"; the Cuban government
controlled the exodus, using it to Cuba's advantage. Cuban officials made
Cuban Americans take on their boats those whom the government deemed
"undesirables," including common criminals who were released from prison,
people with mental illnesses, and homosexuals; at times, they even forced
boat captains to take these people instead of the family members they had
planned to transport. On the Peruvian embassy and Mariel, see García 46–
80; and Pedraza 151–76. On the Mariel Generation, see Barquet, "La generación del Mariel." On Cuba's perspective on the Peruvian embassy incident
and the Mariel exodus, see Fidel Castro, "Speech to the Fighting People."

17   For this section, I draw not just on Arenas's *Antes que anochezca*, but also on
his shorter autobiographical texts ("Adiós a Manhattan," "Aquí estamos,"
"Cronología," "Exhortaciones para leer a Juan Abreu," "Grito, luego existo,"
and "Un largo viaje de Mariel a Nueva York") and interviews with him (see
Valero, Hasson, and Ette 199–202). I also rely on reminiscences by Arenas's
friends and acquaintances: Abreu, *A la sombra del mar*; Abreu, "Presencia de
Arenas"; Nicolás Abreu Felippe; Alberto, "Reinaldo Arenas"; Álvarez Bravo,
"Reinaldo Arenas"; Anhalt; Badías; Barquet, "Rebeldía e irreverencia de Rei-

naldo Arenas"; Cárdenas; Conte; Cuza Malé; Eliseo Diego, "El silencio de los elogios"; Estévez; Fernández Robaina, "Las arenas movedizas"; Fernández Robaina, "Rei-surrección"; Gómez Carriles; Manrique, "After Night Falls"; Manrique, "The Last Days of Reinaldo Arenas"; Santiago; Valero, "La tétrica mofeta en su palacio blanquísimo"; Valero, "Los últimos tiempos de Reinaldo Arenas"; and Victoria, "La catarata." In addition, I draw on Arenas's correspondence. See Arenas, *Cartas a Margarita y Jorge Camacho*; and Arenas, Correspondence. For useful biographical accounts, see Hasson; Ocasio, *Cuba's Political and Sexual Outlaw*; Ocasio, *A Gay Cuban Activist in Exile*; and Santí, "The Life and Times of Reinaldo Arenas."

18 Arenas lost his copy of the story, but Eliseo Diego kept his. It was published in 1999 in *Encuentro de la cultura cubana*.

19 For enthusiastic appraisals of *Celestino antes del alba*, see Barnet, "Celestino antes y después del alba"; Eliseo Diego, "Sobre *Celestino antes del alba*"; Henríquez Ureña 231–32; Lezama Lima 159; and Rodríguez Feo 136. There was even a theatrical representation of the novel on Cuban television, which Arenas thought was horrendous.

20 *Le Puits*, the French translation of *Celestino antes del alba*, did not appear until 1973.

21 Arenas dedicated *El mundo alucinante* to Camila Henríquez Ureña and Virgilio Piñera, "for their intellectual honesty" (7; *The Ill-Fated Peregrinations of Fray Servando* v). See Carballo (535–45) for a detailed account of the negotiations involved in the publication of *El mundo alucinante* in Mexico.

22 In one of his letters to Carballo, Arenas dared to say that the manuscript of *El mundo alucinante* and those of works by other Cuban writers "lay dormant here under the implacable suspicion of the inquisitor of the moment" (qtd. in Carballo 540).

23 The novelist Lisandro Otero is a good contrast to Arenas. A fervent defender of the Revolution, Otero first published *Pasión de Urbino* in Buenos Aires in 1966; the novel's Cuban edition appeared in 1967.

24 On the controversy surrounding *Mundo nuevo*, see Mudrovcic.

25 *No-persona* is a term that Arenas repeatedly used to describe himself in Cuba in the 1970s. See, for example, "Grito, luego existo" 20.

26 For Arenas's initial celebration of New York City, when he first arrived there and felt so much at home, and his subsequent condemnation of it for having turned into a nightmare, see "Un largo viaje de Mariel a Nueva York" and "Adiós a Manhattan."

27 See Arenas and Camacho, *Un plebiscito a Fidel Castro*, which includes the open letter and related documents.

28 See Ortega; and Rama, "La riesgosa navegación del escritor exiliado."

29 It is curious that the issue following the controversial one on exile includes an article (not on the topic of exile) by the Cuban exile Octavio Armand and an interview with Lydia Cabrera, also a Cuban exile, whose groundbreaking anthropological work was banned in Cuba at the time. See Armand, "Reading Reading"; and Cabrera.

30 On Arenas and Rama and their dispute, see by Arenas: *Antes que anochezca* 143, 308–9; *Before Night Falls* 119, 287–88; "Don Miguel Riera"; "Reinaldo Arenas responde a Ángel Rama"; and "Una rama entre la delincuencia y el cinismo." See by Rama: *Diario* 74, 111, 130, 131, 158–59; Letters to Reinaldo Arenas; "Las malandanzas de Reinaldo Arenas"; *Novísimos narradores hispanoamericanos en marcha* 19, 155–71; "Política y naturaleza de los exilios latinoamericanos"; and "Reinaldo Arenas al ostracismo." See also Corral; and Ocasio, *A Gay Cuban Activist in Exile* 57–64.

31 On Arenas and Sarduy's relationship, see Gallo. See by Arenas: "Adorada Chelo"; *Antes que anochezca* 142–43, 306–7, 309; *Before Night Falls* 118, 286–87, 288; *Cartas a Margarita y Jorge Camacho* 36, 39, 92, 94, 96, 99, 101, 104, 113, 116, 117–18, 119, 121, 122, 132, 139, 159, 163, 166, 170, 181, 189, 190, 193, 230, 250, 252, 261, 279, 298, 301, 312, 315, 409–10; *El color del verano* (*The Color of Summer*); *Encore une fois la mer*; Letter to Michael Chodkiewicz; Letter to Editions du Seuil; Letters to Tony Cartano, 22 June 1990; Letters to Thomas Colchie, 19 November 1985; Letters to Liliane Hasson, 25 May 1990; Letters to Severo Sarduy; and "Severo Sarduy." See by Sarduy: "Diario de la peste" 34; "Escrito sobre Arenas"; Letters to Reinaldo Arenas; and Telegram to Reinaldo Arenas. See also Anhalt 1; and Coste.

32 See Arenas, "Cortázar: ¿Senil o pueril?"; and Arenas, "Gabriel García Márquez: ¿Esbirro o es burro?" In his letter of 30 November 1981, Rama tells Arenas that he categorically disapproves of these two articles and points out that their tone and language diminish the effectiveness of his arguments. Although the published version of the Cortázar article (in *Necesidad de libertad*) is dated January 1983, it was written in 1980, as attested by typescripts of the article. See Reinaldo Arenas Papers, box 17, folder 10. Arenas must have sent Rama a copy of the unpublished Cortázar article along with a copy of the García Márquez article, which he wrote in 1980 and 1981, the year it appeared in print. See Reinaldo Arenas Papers, box 18, folder 9.

33 Arenas elaborates on the connection between the erotic and the literary in a description of his daily routine in Havana: "In the afternoons I would lock myself in my little room in Miramar, and sometimes write until late into the night. But during the day I roamed all the beaches, barefoot, and enjoyed unusual adventures with wonderful guys in the bushes, with ten, eleven, twelve of them sometimes; at other times with only one, who would be so extraordi-

nary he would satisfy me as much as twelve" (*Antes que anochezca* 127–28; *Before Night Falls* 101–2).

34 The *pentagonía* is a five-novel cycle that delineates the portrait of a gay artist and also tells what Arenas called a secret history of Cuba. It consists of *Celestino antes del alba* (1967; republished in 1982 as *Cantando en el pozo*), *El palacio de las blanquísimas mofetas* (1980), *Otra vez el mar* (1982), *El color del verano* (1991), and *El asalto* (1991). On the *pentagonía*, see Soto, *Reinaldo Arenas: The Pentagonía*. Arenas's correspondence with Jorge and Margarita Camacho movingly captures the determination of an AIDS-stricken Arenas to finish the cycle. The love and support of these two dear friends, who for Arenas were more like a brother and a sister, gave him the strength to fight against his ailing body in order to bring his oeuvre to completion. See *Cartas a Margarita y Jorge Camacho*. Among Arenas's published books are novels, including the *pentagonía*, *El mundo alucinante* (1969), *La Loma del Ángel* (1987), and *El portero* (1989); novellas, including *La vieja Rosa* (1980), *Arturo, la estrella más brillante* (1984), and *Viaje a La Habana* (1990); short stories, including *Con los ojos cerrados* (1972; republished in 1981, with an additional story, as *Termina el desfile*), *Adiós a mamá* (1995), and *Sobre los astros* (2006); poetry, including *El central* (1981), *Voluntad de vivir manifestándose* (1989), *Leprosorio* (1990), and *Inferno* (2001); a volume of five short theatrical pieces, *Persecución* (1986); essays, collected in *Necesidad de libertad* (1986); a miscellany of short stories and essays collected in *Final de un cuento* (1991); and his autobiography, *Antes que anochezca* (1992). See Valero, Hasson, and Ette, "Bibliografía areniana," which includes books and other publications.

35 According to Valero ("La tétrica mofeta en su palacio blanquísimo" 48), Arenas's ashes are in the possession of Lázaro Gómez Carriles, who, following his friend's wishes, will scatter them in "free" Cuban waters. See also Hasson 174, 178. Arenas's Last Will and Testament states only a desire that his "ashes be disbursed at sea."

2.
Climbing the Family Tree

1 The second, and longest, part of this tripartite novel is titled "Hablan las criaturas de queja" ("The Creatures Utter Their Complaints") (23; 17). *Agonía*, or agony, is the term used to name six sections of the novel.

2 Within the narrative, there is only one reference to the title. The dead Esther, alluding to her family, says to Fortunato, "We go higher and higher, until we realize how high we are, and then we fall—like always, right into the Palace of the White Skunks, where all of them, lined up in the Great Hall holding long spears, are waiting for us. We fall into the arms of the beasts, that is to

say, and since they had thought we were lost forever, they almost start to have a little affection for us" (*El palacio de las blanquísimas mofetas* 257–58; *The Palace of the White Skunks* 229). In an interview, Arenas says of the title, "Well, that is totally ironic, aggressive, and humorous. Because there is no palace and because there aren't extremely white skunks" ("Conversación con Reinaldo Arenas" 64). For an analysis of the novel's ludic spirit and its assimilation to the carnival topos of the *mundus inversus*, see Olivares.

3 My conversation with Arenas about Pérez Galdós and *Fortunata y Jacinta* took place in Miami, Florida, on 20 November 1980.

4 In *Antes que anochezca* Arenas explains that he named his protagonist Fortunato as a tribute to Fortunato Córdoba, a former lover of his who was a medical student at the University of Havana and who later enlisted as a guerrilla fighter in his native Colombia, where Arenas fears that he eventually may have been killed (129–30; *Before Night Falls* 103–4). Although this may be true, when Arenas and I discussed in 1980 the possible connection between his novel and *Fortunata and Jacinta*, he did not offer this explanation.

5 Although Arenas models Fortunato's grandfather after his own maternal grandfather, a shopkeeper who would go for days without talking to anyone, this should not detract from the quite telling contrast that can be established between the two fictional shopkeepers.

6 Polo laments his fate as the father of only daughters: "Has anybody ever seen such a family as this one I brought into the world for having bad luck? Of the four daughters I had, two of them were abandoned [*dejadas*], one fit for nothing, the other one a widow and crazy to boot, and really abandoned [*dejada*], because the man died after he foisted her off on me" (*El palacio de las blanquísimas mofetas* 126; *The Palace of the White Skunks* 111). Polo's account of his family excludes, as does the narrative, a fifth daughter known as "the Hated One" (15, 294) who, unlike her four sisters, does not reside in their parents' house and is mentioned only occasionally in the text.

7 The excerpt quoted here, which is taken from the version of the essay in *Necesidad de libertad*, does not appear in the essay's earlier version, published in *La gaceta de Cuba*, "El reino de la imagen," in which sections about creative freedom and the poet's need to be alert so as not to become an instrument of the state were censored (see Arenas, "Conversation with Reinaldo Arenas" 137–38). The polemics in the 1960s were possible because it was not until 1971, with the pronouncements of the Primer Congreso Nacional de Educación y Cultura, that the Stalinization of Cuban culture was officially institutionalized.

8 For useful accounts of the development of Cuba's cultural politics in the 1960s and 1970s, and especially of the polemics surrounding literary realism,

see Menton 123–56; Quintero Herencia 445–68; Rama, "Una nueva política cultural en Cuba"; and Rojas, *Tumbas sin sosiego* 173–74, 196–98, 298, 449–50. See Aguirre, García Buchaca, and Portuondo, who were among the promoters of socialist realism in Revolutionary Cuba. See also Pogolotti, *Polémicas culturales de los 60*.

9   On Arenas's views on literary realism, see also his "Benítez entra en el juego"; "Charlemos con Reinaldo Arenas" 38; "*Cien años de soledad* en la ciudad de los espejismos"; "Conversación con Reinaldo Arenas" 62–63; and "El páramo en llamas."

10   I am only concerned here with the novel's primary story line involving Juanito Santa Cruz and the two female protagonists. Admitting to Jacinta that he is the father of Fortunata's child, Juanito tries to assure his wife that he will love him as though he had been born to her. But one cannot believe the words of a man known to be a habitual liar and who, early in the novel, when told that Fortunata was carrying his child, made no serious attempt to find his pregnant lover, whom he had abandoned to marry Jacinta. Fortunata and Juanito's first son died shortly after he was born.

11   Arenas was especially fond of the anonymous sixteenth-century picaresque novel *Lazarillo de Tormes* and José Lezama Lima's *Paradiso*, both of which have fatherless sons as protagonists. Arenas not only wrote eloquently about Lezama and his works, but also wrote a synopsis for a film adaptation of the Cuban's novel. He also authored an abridged and modernized version of *Lazarillo de Tormes* for high-school students. See Arenas, *Lazarillo de Tormes*; and Arenas, "Sinopsis de un film sobre *Paradiso*." See also Hasson 75, 150.

12   This scene is autobiographical, as is evident from Arenas's memoirs and interviews, where he describes with some wistful relish his only encounter with his father. I say more about this in chapter 3.

13   In chapter 3, in my analysis of Arenas's autobiography, I take up again the discussion of the song.

14   In "Comienza el desfile," which Arenas wrote in 1965, the narrator tells some women whom he meets on his way to Velazco, where he hopes to be able to join the rebel forces, "My father lives there" (14).

15   On the affinity between literary practice (reading and writing) and masturbation, see Bennett and Rosario; Cohen; Laqueur 247–358; and Schehr 109–47.

16   In *Celestino antes del alba*, the young protagonist's writing is referred to by others as "filth" (*puercadas, cochinadas*) (171; *Singing from the Well* 156) and "faggotry" (*mariconería*) (16).

17   In "A la sombra de la mata de almendras," Arenas symbolically links a tree, the focal point of the story, to a penis, which produces, in Andrew Bush's words, "ejaculatory leaves" (395).

18 On masturbation and the "olfactory imaginaire," see Looby.

19 Let us not forget that the "popular" *roman-feuilleton* played a significant role in the development of the "serious" nineteenth-century realistic novel. On the traces in Pérez Galdós of the formulaic and melodramatic serial novel (to which is akin the twentieth-century radio soap opera after which Fortunato models his novels), see Romero Tobar 162–98; and Yndurain.

20 According to Arenas, he wrote four novels during his adolescence: "¡Qué dura es la vida!," "Adiós, mundo cruel," "El caníbal," and "Trágame tierra." "¡Qué dura es la vida!" is part of the Reinaldo Arenas Papers at Princeton University Library. The other three novels were either lost or remained in the possession of Arenas's mother in Cuba (Oneida Fuentes died in Havana in 2010).

21 In chapter 3, I elaborate further on the relationship between money and the father figure.

22 On Fortunato's "everyday resistance," see Kushigian 170–76.

23 Arenas wrote *El palacio de las blanquísimas mofetas* between 1966 and 1969, as he indicates in the typescript of the novel. See Reinaldo Arenas Papers, box 10, folders 1–4. On "Morir en junio y con la lengua afuera," see Bordao, *La sátira, la ironía y el carnaval literario en "Leprosorio (Trilogía poética)" de Reinaldo Arenas* 78–96; and Soto, *Reinaldo Arenas* 137–42.

24 Arenas is not alone in recognizing the centrality of the mother and father in Perceval's story. See Bloch (198–227) for what is perhaps the best analysis to date of Perceval's romance as a "quest for the father." Unlike Arenas, Bloch does not consider that Perceval's quest is motivated by a need to "surpass" his father, but rather by a desire to achieve the knightly status that his father had attained. On fathers and mothers in Perceval's story, see Baron; Debora B. Schwartz; and Wolfgang.

25 For homoerotic readings of Perceval's story, see Burgwinkle 89–137; and Roberts.

26 For a notable exception, see Eduardo González.

27 I should note here that *Cecilia Valdés* is also about absent fathers. As is well known, Villaverde's novel opens with an unidentified man from the white Spanish elite (later identified as Cándido Gamboa), who, secretly assuming financial responsibility for Cecilia Valdés, his illegitimate mulatto daughter, tells the infant's black grandmother that he cannot give Cecilia his name. It will take two decades before the name of her father is revealed to Cecilia, who by then has suffered the tragic consequences of the secret of her genealogy. As her father had done to her mother when Cecilia was born, Cecilia's white lover — who unbeknownst to her is her half brother — abandons her shortly after she gives birth to his child. Harking back to its beginning, the novel

ends with another fatherless daughter who, as Arenas imagines it, will begin the tale anew ("La literatura cubana dentro y fuera de Cuba" 7). For an excellent reading of the role that the concealment of the name of the father plays in *Cecilia Valdés*, see Méndez Rodenas, "Identity and Incest in *Cecilia Valdés*."

28 I have made extensive use of Alfred J. MacAdam's translation, but have made substantial changes to it to make it conform more closely to the Spanish original.

29 Of the novel's thirty-four chapters, five are titled "Del amor," in which three of the characters (Cecilia, Leonardo, and José Dolores) take turns expressing their views on the subject of love.

3.
In Search of the Father(land)

1 The Cuban authorities confiscated the first version of his memoirs when he was arrested. Arenas did not resume writing them until 1987, when he was living in exile and had been diagnosed with AIDS: "I did not have the strength to sit at my typewriter, so I started dictating the story of my life into a tape recorder. I would speak for a while, take a rest, and then continue. I had already started my autobiography in Cuba, which I had titled *Before Night Falls*. Being a fugitive living in the woods at the time, I had to write before it got dark. Now darkness was approaching again, only more insidiously. It was the dark night of death. I really had to finish my memoirs before nightfall. I took it as a challenge. And so I continued working on them. After filling a cassette, I would give it to a friend, Antonio Valle, for typing" (*Antes que anochezca* 11; *Before Night Falls* xii).

2 Critics have called attention to lies and exaggerations in *Antes que anochezca* either to demonstrate the narrative's falsehoods or to show the roles that these lies and exaggerations play in the rhetorical strategies of the autobiography. Delfín Prats, Arenas's partner in sexual escapades in Cuba, says of his friend and his memoirs, "The adventures that he attributed to me were terrible. . . . As testimony, his writing fails; as fiction, it does not" ("Yo tengo un mal karma" 26). Arenas's use of hyperbole, particularly in the telling of his sexual life, may be partly explained by the fact that exaggerations are a common practice in erotic memoirs. Moreover, one must not forget that *Antes que anochezca*, like all autobiographies, does not have to be "historically accurate" but rather "metaphorically authentic" (Adams ix).

3 In *Misa para un ángel*, a text about Reinaldo Arenas that combines fact and fiction, Tomás Fernández Robaina, one of Arenas's friends during his Havana years, briefly writes about Arenas's mother, his father, and the scene on the riverbank. This section features the mother's "voice" telling her interlocutor, among other things, that Arenas reproached her for not letting him meet his

father, that he always brought this up when they quarreled, and that he could never forgive her for it (91–94). On Arenas's father, see also 95, 98, 107–10.

4 As Freud theorizes it, the "complete" form of the male Oedipus complex includes, in varying degrees, its "positive" form (a rivalry between the boy and his father for the mother's affection) as well as its "negative" form (a rivalry between the boy and his mother for the father's affection). The resolution of the positive (heterosexual) form occurs with the boy's identification with the father; the resolution of the negative (homosexual) form occurs with the boy's identification with the mother. On the Oedipus complex as expounded by Freud, who, as is well known, does not offer a systematic exposition of it in his writings, see Laplanche and Pontalis, *The Language of Psychoanalysis* 282–87; and Simon and Blass. Although one must be wary of Freud's universalizing claims, I find support for my reading of *Antes que anochezca* in Arenas himself, who explains in oedipal terms his life history and also the history of Castro's Cuba.

5 The text makes clear that the child's initial erotic connection with his mother evolves into an identification with her and with her object-choice. For example, referring to his first same-sex experience, at the age of eight, with a male cousin four years his senior, Arenas recalls, "While Orlando was sticking it into me, I was thinking of my mother, and of all the things that during all those years she never did with a man, which I was doing right there in the bushes within earshot of her voice, already calling me for dinner" (29; 12). Some pages later, Arenas describes a sexual coupling between a mare, on which he and his mother had been riding, and a stallion: "We had to jump off and allow them, right in front of us, to complete their copulation, a sexual encounter that was both powerful and violent and really so beautiful that it would have aroused anybody. After the battle, my mother and I rode in silence. . . . Probably she, as well as I, would have liked to be the mare, who now trotted so lightheartedly over Arcadio Reyes's land" (42; 21).

6 On money and anality, see Abraham; Ferenczi; Freud, "Character and Anal Erotism"; Freud, "On Transformations of Instinct as Exemplified in Anal Erotism"; and Laplanche and Pontalis, *The Language of Psychoanalysis* 35–36.

7 In the documentary *Havana*, reminiscing about his only meeting with his father, Arenas says, "I did not see him again; I just have the image of the two pesos."

8 Referring to his friend's love of swimming, which Arenas consistently describes in erotic terms, Juan Abreu associates it with Arenas's desire to connect with an understanding mother and his absent father: "By the ocean, Reinaldo would undergo a transformation; he would stretch, seemingly getting rid of everything that soiled him, of the loneliness that finally killed him,

and he would throw himself into the water as if into the arms of a loving mother who at last accepted him unconditionally, without recriminations, *as if into the arms of a protective father who has reappeared*" ("Presencia de Arenas" 15; emphasis added).

9   On primal fantasies (primal scene, castration, and seduction), see Laplanche and Pontalis, *The Language of Psychoanalysis* 331–33.

10 In the psychoanalytic paradigm, some gay men have an incestuous paternal longing, which may result in the presence of a "phantom father" in their relationships. According to Charles Silverstein, "The phantom father is an internal person who lives within the son and is sometimes projected onto the son's lover. He is an idealized father whose image was formed in the early years of the boy's life. . . . He is the father who was desired then and is demanded now. This phantom father is impervious to time and experience; his image is rigid, and even when the gay man becomes an adult he continues to view his father through his childhood eyes. . . . For a significant number of gay men, the father (whether real or phantom) is a potential sex object — and perhaps their first fantasy lover" (26). See also Isay 31–44; Sadownick, "My Father, My Self"; Sadownick, *Sex Between Men* 162–63; and Saslow.

11 This dream brings to mind the novelist Manuel Pereira's visits to Lezama. According to Arenas, Lezama used to tell Piñera that Pereira "would visit him and sit on his lap, sometimes bringing on a powerful erection" (112; 87). In his dream Arenas takes Pereira's place and transforms his own visits to Lezama into something more than the mischievously sexual conversations in which he normally "turned Lezama into an accomplice, sharing my adventures with him" (128).

12 Lezama's sexual preferences may explain the suggestive connection made in Arenas's dream between him — and not Piñera — and Arenas's father. Unlike the effeminate Piñera, who favored the passive position in his sexual encounters with tough men, the corpulent and macho-appearing Lezama preferred the active role in his sexual encounters with younger men. Lezama's marriage in 1964 to María Luisa Bautista, a friend of the family, was his mother's last wish before she died that year. See Arenas, *Antes que anochezca* 105–13; Arenas, *Before Night Falls* 79–87; and Cabrera Infante, "Two Wrote Together." Like Arenas, Lezama attempts through his work to fill the void left by his absent father, who died when he was a child. See Cruz-Malavé 70–116.

13 On automourning in the Homeric poem, Henry Staten explains, "Mourning in the *Iliad* is represented as a structure of self-reflection in which the death of the other arouses automourning in the onlooker" (40).

14 On Achilles's automourning, Staten writes: "Akhilleus sees in Priam's grief for dead Hektor the grief of his own father, Peleus, for Akhilleus's expected

death. Akhilleus imagines his father weeping inconsolable tears for him, then weeps for his poor father weeping for him and in this way affects himself deeply with the pathos of his own disappearance. Akhilleus's grief for his own death thus arises here in a double reflection as he sees Peleus's grief reflected in Priam's and then in the mirror of Peleus's mirrored grief finds the magnified representation of his own grief for himself" (40). Achilles also experiences automourning with the death of Patroclus, who emerges in the poem as Achilles's *therápon*, his alter ego (see Nagy 33, 292–93; and Staten 43). Arenas laments his impending death when some of his friends die of AIDS-related complications. For instance, writing about Guillermo Hernández, Arenas, already diagnosed with the syndrome, says, "Because in short it is not for the dead person for whom we cry but for ourselves" ("La dignidad de Guillermo Hernández"). See also *Antes que anochezca* 334; *Before Night Falls* 310.

15 On Arenas and the *Iliad*, see also his "Elogio de las furias."

16 *Viaje a La Habana* is the eponymous novella in a collection that includes two other novellas, *Que trine Eva* and *Mona*. *Viaje a La Habana* and *Mona* were conceived and written in exile. Six months before committing suicide, Arenas wrote to Liliane Hasson and told her that her French translation of *Viaje a La Habana* moved him "enormously," adding, "I cried when I read it." See Arenas, Letters to Liliane Hasson, 17 June 1990.

17 Arenas uses italics throughout the narrative when Ismael, in the most tense and intimate moments, interrupts the omniscient narrator's account and speaks in the first person. See Arenas, Letters to Tony Cartano, 14 June 1990.

18 According to Laplanche and Pontalis, "Freud always held the model fantasy to be the reverie, that form of novelette, both stereotyped and infinitely variable, which the subject composes and relates to himself in a waking state" ("Fantasy and the Origins of Sexuality" 13).

19 Ismael is oblivious (as is the reader) to the multiple clues disseminated throughout the novella that suggest that Carlos knew all along that Ismael was his father.

20 Benigno Sánchez-Eppler has written about the possible intertextual relationship between *Viaje a La Habana* and *Ismaelillo* (1882), Jose Martí's book of poems about and for his young son, which Sánchez-Eppler reads "as the expression of a father's grief for not having a *patria*, a fatherland, in which to live together with his son" ("Call My Son Ismael" 70). Arenas's novella, according to Sánchez-Eppler, "provides a provocative recasting of the *Ismaelillo* which turns Martí's hyper-sensuous exilic re-memorations of paternal and filial love into an explicitly incestuous and homoerotic narrative with a frank counter-homophobic and counter-revolutionary political agenda" (70). Curiously, in a letter to Charles Dana, José Martí wrote about *Ismaelillo*, "I have

just published a little book, not to profit from it, but to give it as a present to those I love, on behalf of my son, who is my master: it's the story of my love affair with my son: one tires of reading so many stories of love affairs with women" (253).

21 In *Seres extravagantes*, the filmmaker Manuel Zayas documents his search for Arenas's father, whom he finds with the help of Carlos Fuentes, one of Arenas's maternal uncles. José Antonio Arenas ("Toto") does not say much in the documentary other than to admit to womanizing and to express admiration for Oneida Fuentes, whom he calls an "honorable" woman. Carlos Fuentes remembers José Antonio Arenas as having been "tall, strong, handsome" in his youth.

22 I further discuss the connection between Castro and the castrating mother in chapter 4.

23 The aura of fantasy in *Viaje a La Habana* has its echo in *Antes que anochezca*, where Arenas's father, as if phantasmagorically and seemingly unscathed by the stones hurled at him by the boy's mother, moves unswervingly toward his bewildered son.

24 It is as if Arenas, through his fiction, were vindicating his mother, since in *Viaje a La Habana* it is the mother figure who brokers the meeting between father and son, something to which, in real life, Arenas's mother had been steadfastly opposed. I further explore the vindication of the mother in chapter 4.

25 An unabridged translation into Spanish, *La Habana*, was not published until 1981. Roberto Ignacio Díaz calls *La Havane*, a compilaton of thirty-six letters, a "hybrid text" ("Merlin's Foreign House" 58), since it incorporates multiple modes of representation, such as travelogue, romantic novella, sketch of manners, and autobiography. The abridged Spanish version, *Viaje a La Habana*, includes only ten letters.

26 The letter from which Arenas takes the epigraph for his novella is the third in Countess Merlin's *Viaje a La Habana* and the fifteenth in *La Havane*. More precisely, Arenas uses Merlin's *La Habana* (the 1981 unabridged Spanish translation) as his source, but he underscores his homage to Merlin by titling his novella *Viaje a La Habana*, since this is the title by which Merlin's account of her voyage to Havana is widely known.

27 Merlin occupied a marginal position because, in addition to residing outside of Cuba, she was a woman writer — and one, moreover, who wrote in French — at a moment when writing was a masculine privilege. See Roberto Ignacio Díaz, "Merlin's Foreign House"; Roberto Ignacio Díaz, "Paratextual Snow"; and Méndez Rodenas, *Gender and Nationalism in Colonial Cuba*.

4.
All About Mother

1 Written in Miami Beach in 1986, "El Cometa Halley" was first published in a Venezuelan magazine, *Exceso*, in 1989 and was subsequently included in *Final de un cuento*, a posthumous miscellany of essays and stories, and in *Adiós a mamá*, a posthumous collection of stories. I quote from the latter.

2 First identified in 1682 by Edmond Halley, the comet returns to Earth every seventy-six years. Capturing the human imagination, it has been associated with the overthrow of despotic rulers and the end of terrestrial life. The return of the comet in 1910 in particular produced mass hysteria. Curiously, despite the belief that it would bring the end of the world, many people welcomed it with outrageous "comet parties," of which the Alba sisters' orgy in Arenas's story is an imaginative re-creation. The phallic connotations of the comet's tail were common in the popular imagination of 1910. For example, a Cuban *guaracha* of that year, about a jealous wife who cuts off her unfaithful husband's penis, includes the following lyrics: "No te apures, Enriqueta / que el mundo ya no termina / porque ayer la Mallorquina / le cortó el rabo al cometa" (Enriqueta, don't you fret / the world is not going to end / because yesterday the Mallorquina / cut the tail off the comet) (qtd. in Fernández Soneira). On Halley's Comet, see Calder; Etter and Schneider; and Gropman.

3 On carnivalesque "casting-down," see Bakhtin, *Rabelais and His World* 19, 21, 370; Morson and Emerson 443; and Stallybrass and White 9, 23, 183. In my use of the carnivalesque as an analytic category, I mainly follow Peter Stallybrass and Allon White. Distancing themselves from those who see carnival in the strict Bakhtinian sense as a licensed — hence, ineffectual — revolt, Stallybrass and White place it in broader categories of symbolic inversion and transgression, which allow us to see carnival as a site of struggle that may lead to change.

4 If in *La casa de Bernarda Alba* there are only two ways of escaping — namely, insanity or suicide (Ozimek-Maier 84) — "El Cometa Halley" explores a third way: escape by way of the sea. Arenas, whose passion for the ocean is well known, may have been inspired by La Poncia, who says, "I wish I could go across the sea away from this battleground of a house" (García Lorca, *La casa de Bernarda Alba* 189; *The House of Bernarda Alba* 164).

5 According to Julia Kristeva, "It is . . . not lack of cleanliness or health that causes abjection but what disturbs identity, system, order. What does not respect borders, positions, rules" (4).

6 The typescript of this draft is part of the Reinaldo Arenas Papers, box 14, folder 5.

7 The translation into English does not fully render the etymology of *fachada*;

the Spanish noun, like *façade*, can refer to the visible face of a building and to the deceptive or illusory appearance of something or someone.

8   See Rosen for a balanced historical view of prostitution.

9   On transvestite poetics, see Savran 115–20. On women as homosexual men in García Lorca, see Binding 212–16; and Urrea. Not surprisingly, in *El color del verano* (*The Color of Summer*) (198; 181), Arenas connects a gay character in his novel with García Lorca's Adela.

10   "Adiós a mamá" was first published in *Novísimos narradores hispanoamericanos en marcha, 1964–1980*, an anthology edited by Ángel Rama in 1981. I quote from Arenas's collection.

11   The striking parallel between the author's household, which is fictionalized in his novels, and the Alba household has not escaped critics. See, for example, Wood 21. In *Adiós a mamá* Arenas seems to arrange the stories thematically, not chronologically.

12   Written in Havana in 1974 and revised in New York in 1988, *El asalto* was published posthumously in 1991.

13   On Castro's evocative surname, see Epps 262–63.

14   On *El asalto*, see Biron 120–42; and Epps 275–82. Arenas has spoken of "an entire gallery of mothers" in *Otra vez el mar* (*Farewell to the Sea*), the third novel of the *pentagonía*; among them one finds "the dictator mother," a precursor of the mother in *El asalto* ("Conversation with Reinaldo Arenas" 144). In *Arturo, la estrella más brillante* (*The Brightest Star*), the figure of the mother is also associated with Castro's repressive government. As this novel concludes, the protagonist's mother, dressed in military gear, leads the troop of soldiers who kill her son, one of thousands of homosexuals sent to labor camps because of their sexuality.

15   On Achilles and Patroclus, see Halperin 75–87; and Sergent 250–58.

16   Arenas worked on both texts simultaneously. He began writing *Viaje a La Habana* in 1983 and finished it in 1987. He wrote "El Cometa Halley" entirely in 1986. I am not suggesting that Arenas altogether stopped depicting the mother as an oppressive figure, which is how she appears in *Antes que anochezca* and *El color del verano*, the last two works he wrote before his death.

17   On the preoedipal mother, see Sprengnether. Insightfully challenging the mother's "spectral" presence in Freud's treatment of the child's sexual development, Sprengnether underscores the profound importance of maternal power during the two-person phase in infantile life. Unlike Freud, who generally limits the mother's position to object of her son's libidinal urges, Sprengnether argues for the mother's central position as a sexually desiring and aggressive subject. I should note here that portraying José as a child is

congruent with Arenas's view of himself as a child. See, for example, his poem "Viejo niño" and his interview in the documentary *Havana*.

5.

Facing AIDS

1 Direct mentions of AIDS appear on the following pages: *Antes que anochezca* 78, 115, 318, 334, 337–39; *Before Night Falls* 54, 89, 297, 310, 313–16.

2 Reinaldo Arenas Papers, box 3, folder 2.

3 On AIDS and allegory, see Morrison; and Parker.

4 The names of some characters in this novel, as is typical in Arenas's work, are veiled allusions to the author's friends and acquaintances. The circumstances surrounding the publication of Ramón's testimony echo Arenas's own difficulties in dealing with publishers. And like the 1999 edition of Ramón's testimony, some of Arenas's texts were published with countless printing errors, of which Arenas repeatedly complains in his correspondence.

5 Arenas alluded to himself by name in the texts of two earlier novels, *La Loma del Ángel* (*Graveyard of the Angels*) and *El portero* (*The Doorman*). He also appears as a major character in *El color del verano*.

6 Set in the future, the story's plot unfolds after 4 October 1986, when the novel was completed, as indicated at the end of the manuscript. Arenas thus foresees his death from AIDS occurring in the year following the completion of the novel. But Arenas, who was officially diagnosed in 1987, lived until 1990, the year he committed suicide and *Mona* was published.

7 I am thinking of the Greek roots of allegory: *allos* (other) and *agoreuein* (to speak). See "Allegory."

8 Much has been written on what is meant by "transgender." According to Jay Prosser, "The etymological history of the term 'transgender' certainly reveals the threads of transgender connecting to and separating from queerness as much as from transsexuality. 'Transgenderist,' from which 'transgender' derives, was coined in the late 1980s to describe a male subject with a commitment to living as a woman more substantial than that denoted by 'transvestite' or 'cross-dresser.' . . . In contradistinction to the transsexual, the transgenderist crossed the lines of gender but not those of sex; in contradistinction to the drag queen, the transgenderist's feminine gender expression was not intrinsically bound up with a homosexual identity nor could its livedness be made sense of through drag's performativity. . . . What complicates the task of specifying transgender apart from queerness and transsexuality, however, is that the threads of difference between these projects and subjects are rewoven in the second sense in which 'transgender' has come to be used, often (con-

fusingly) concurrently with the first. 'Transgender' now also functions as a container term, one that refers not only to transgenderists but to those subjects from whom it was originally invented to distinguish transgenderists: transsexuals and drag queens, transvestites and cross-dressers, along with butches and intersexuals and any subject who 'trans-es' sex or gender boundaries" (176).

9 On two other occasions, Ramón refers to Elisa as "that thing" (100, 103; 60, 64).

10 Cultural representations of HIV/AIDS frequently deploy the figure of the "monster." John Erni writes: "The fantasy structure of morbidity proliferates paranoiac identification of menace and emotional moribundity, bound by a series of morbid narratives, including most visibly the constructions of HIV as monstrosity, the intensively visual depictions of the disfigurement and wasting of the body, the horrifying statistical projections and death counting, the fantasy of 'gay genocide,' and of course the trauma of AZT" (36). But, as Simon Watney points out, "AIDS commentary does not 'make' gay men into monsters, for homosexuality is, and always has been, constructed as intrinsically monstrous" (*Policing Desire* 42). For a fine discussion of the homosexual as monster, see Benshoff.

11 On AIDS and apocalyptic rhetoric, see Long.

12 On dominant representations of AIDS, see Crimp; Julia Epstein; Erni; Griffin; Landers; Meyer; Treichler; Watney, *Policing Desire*; and Williamson.

13 As Paula A. Treichler explains, "The term *exotic*, sometimes used to describe a virus that appears to have originated 'elsewhere' (but 'elsewhere,' like 'other,' is not a fixed category), is an important theme running through AIDS literature" (46). Greece not only is associated in modern gay sensibility with Ancient Greek same-sex sexual practices among men, but is also a major destination in present-day gay tourist culture.

14 Critiquing the notion that AIDS is "invariably fatal," Simon Watney writes, "One must at once distinguish between approaches to AIDS which proceed from entirely fatalistic assumptions concerning the rate of progression from HIV to AIDS and the life expectancy of people living with AIDS, and other approaches which attempt to question and problematize precisely such fatalism" ("Short-Term Companions" 159–60). See also Erni 37–40.

15 Throughout his account, Ramón underscores how the dangers posed by Elisa are not betrayed by her appearance. For example, in Grand Central Station, where he publicly expresses his fears of Elisa, various people ignore him because the woman they see is "a grand lady, serene, elegant, expertly made up and attired" (104; 64).

16 Especially at the beginning of the HIV/AIDS crisis, many people feared that colds or flu symptoms were possible signs of HIV infection. People with

HIV/AIDS are known to have frequent bouts of diarrhea. At the American Public Health Association Annual Meeting in 1986, the AIDS activist Michael Callen said, "AIDS is about bedpans and respirators. It's about loss of control — control of one's bowels and bladder, one's arms and legs, one's life. . . . It's about swelling and horrible disfigurement, the fear of dementia. It is horror" (162).

17　This version of the novel can be found in the Reinaldo Arenas Papers, box 13, folder 3.

18　On the femme fatale, see Bade; Doane; and Stott. Arenas may have been inspired, partially at least, by *Mona Lisa* (1986), Neil Jordan's acclaimed film noir about a stunning femme fatale named Simone, a call girl who is the Mona Lisa of the story.

19　In an essay on Leonardo da Vinci, included in his influential book *The Renaissance*, Walter Pater refers to *Mona Lisa*'s "unfathomable smile, always with a touch of something sinister in it" (97), adding that "like the vampire, she has been dead many times" (99). On *Mona Lisa* as a femme fatale, see Boas.

20　Like the femme fatale, HIV/AIDS is associated with eros and thanatos. As Judith Williamson notes, "They (sex and death) are also inevitably linked with AIDS: sex as a means of HIV transmission, death as its probable outcome" (70).

21　As Gilman explains, "The appropriation of the iconography of syphilis for the representation of people with AIDS is not random; it is, rather, a result of the perception that the sexual orientation of people with AIDS was determinant, and that these people suffered from a sexually transmitted disease. In addition, the 'taming' of syphilis and other STDs with the introduction of antibiotics in the 1940s left our culture with a series of images of mortally infected and infecting people suffering a morally repugnant disease — without a sufficiently powerful disease to function as the referent of these images. During the 1970s there was an attempt to associate this iconography with genital herpes, but the symptomology of this viral disease was too trivial to warrant such an association over the long run. AIDS appeared then as the perfect referent, even if it was not a 'typical' STD" ("AIDS and Syphilis" 98).

22　Williamson sees the presence of primarily two genres, horror and melodrama, in cultural representations of AIDS. She explains, "Where the stress is on the 'activity' of the viral monster, one might say that AIDS discourse is closest to Gothic horror, and when it is on the 'passive' (non-complaining) suffering of the 'victims' it moves over into Sentimentalism" (75).

23　On homosexuality and vampirism, see Dyer; and Hanson.

24　According to J. Gordon Melton, "Nineteenth-century romantic novelists and occultists suggested that real vampirism involved the loss of psychic energy to the vampire and wrote of vampiric relationships that had little to do with the exchange of blood. . . . The metaphor of psychic vampirism can easily be extended to cover various relationships in which one party steals essential life elements from the other" (xxiii).

25 On vampires, see Bunson; and Melton.

26 Elisa comes out only at night, except for Mondays, when the museum is closed.

27 References to mist and fog throughout Arenas's narrative (81, 85, 91, 95, 100; 39, 43–44, 50, 55, 60) simultaneously evoke vampire tales and the *Mona Lisa*'s "misty atmosphere" (Bramly 366).

28 There is a divergence of opinion among the editors of Ramón's testimony regarding which city Elisa and Ramón visit: Syracuse (Sakuntala), Albany (Lorenzo and Echurre), or Ithaca (2025 editors). This is just one example of several in the text of how Arenas refuses to write an authoritative, nineteenth-century-like tale. Ambiguity and uncertainty prevail throughout.

29 By way of support for this reading, I offer what Arenas has to say, in *Antes que anochezca*, when recalling his early years in New York: "It was really a dream come true and a constant celebration. I was writing a lot then, but New York was never more vital; it will probably never be again as it was then. I have the comfort of having lived those last years, *before the plague arrived* [*antes de que llegara la plaga*], before the curse fell upon this city, as it always falls on all things truly extraordinary" (318; *Before Night Falls* 297; emphasis added).

30 On the relationship between the female figure and the landscape in Leonardo's painting, see Bramly 364–66; and Webster Smith.

31 Critiquing homophobic psychoanalytic myths about male gay sex, Hanson writes, "I mean the psychoanalyst who has defined me in terms of his own repugnance for feminine sexuality, who has made me not so much *vagina dentata* as *anus dentatus*. Rectum, urethra, mouth, tear ducts, a gash in the skin. All my orifices are one and the same, and all my orifices have teeth" (325).

32 On *Mona Lisa* as Leonardo's self-portrait, see Collins 106–7; Pater 77–101; Sassoon 267–68; and Lillian Schwartz. Although the *Mona Lisa* as Leonardo is just a theory and one not widely accepted by art historians, Arenas no doubt was aware of it and used it as the structuring motif of *Mona*. Arenas goes against the historical record when he says that Leonardo was "not graced by beauty" (98; 57), and he clearly approaches *Mona Lisa* from the perspective that sees in Leonardo's famous painting a portrait of an enigmatic and vampiric femme fatale, the view that has prevailed since the nineteenth century. Arenas may have been drawn to Leonardo because of some significant similarities in their biographies: illegitimacy, emotional attachment to their mothers, and passive homosexuality. Given that Arenas uses a passage from Leonardo's *Notebooks* as *Mona*'s epigraph, I would argue that he had

more than a superficial knowledge of the artist's life and work. On Leonardo's biography, see Bramly; Clark; Collins; and Freud, "Leonardo da Vinci and a Memory of His Childhood."

33 According to Watney, "The political unconscious of the visual register of AIDS commentary . . . assumes the form of a diptych. On one panel we are shown the HIV retrovirus . . . made to appear, by means of electron microscopy or reconstructive computer graphics, like a huge technicolor asteroid. On the other panel we witness the 'AIDS victim,' usually hospitalized and physically debilitated, 'withered, wrinkled, and loathsome of visage.' . . . This is the *spectacle* of AIDS, constituted in a regime of massively overdetermined images" ("The Spectacle of AIDS" 78). On "bodies" and "anti-bodies" (healthy bodies vs. ill bodies) in discussions of AIDS representations, see Gilman, *Picturing Health and Illness* 115–72; and Landers. On before and after representations of people with AIDS, see Erni 43–47; and Meyer.

34 On the significance of anal sex to conceptions of male homosexuality, see Bersani; and Miller 134.

35 On *El color del verano*, see Fowler Calzada, "Arenas: Homoerotismo y crítica de la cultura"; Soto, *Reinaldo Arenas* 55–63; and Soto, *Reinaldo Arenas: The Pentagonía*.

36 Personal correspondence with the author (28 June 1988). See also the prologue to the novel (250; 228); and Arenas, *Cartas a Margarita y Jorge Camacho* 197, 203, 205, 242.

37 As he had done in *El mundo alucinante* (*The Ill-Fated Peregrinations of Fray Servando*) (198–99; 222), Arenas satirizes the novelist Alejo Carpentier, connecting him here, unfairly perhaps, to the socialist-realist writer Mikhail Sholokhov. See Loss 66–67. For a fine discussion of Arenas's views on Carpentier, see Santí, "Introducción" 43–52. Arenas included Carpentier's *El siglo de las luces* (*Explosion in a Cathedral*) among the "classics" of the so-called Latin American Boom of the 1960s. In *Antes que anochezca* Arenas asks, "Whatever happened to Alejo Carpentier's work after he completed *El siglo de las luces*? His writing became slipshod, dreadful, impossible to read to the end" (116; *Before Night Falls* 90).

38 On gay autofiction, see White.

39 In the prologue to *El color del verano*, Reinaldo writes, "I memorized a chapter or two (such as the one entitled 'Clara's Hole') and the Thirty Truculent Tongue Twisters (which didn't yet number thirty), so I managed to preserve some of my writing that way" (246; 225). If one excludes the playlet "La fuga de la Avellaneda" with which the novel opens, "El hueco de Clara" is the longest of the 115 segments in the novel. Clara is alluded to, mentioned, or featured in 27 segments; her name appears 173 times.

40 Clara is featured in segments 6, 23, 71, 89, 91, 93, and 112. Despite the author's insistence on the novel's cyclical nature, which would allow its segments to be read in any order, I would argue that most readers (if not all) read the segments in the order in which they appear in the novel.

41 The title of the longest segment in which Clara is featured, "El hueco de Clara," refers to both the painter's living space and her vagina. One of Clara's children, the product of a daisy chain involving Clara, her husband, and a multiethnic and multiracial multitude of men, was "one of the most curious examples in the history of genetics" (186; 171).

42 Arenas based Clara's painting of the poet on one of Pérez de Zambrana's poems, "A mi amigo A. L.," which is a self-portrait.

43 Like the "real" Reinaldo, his fictional double suffers from AIDS.

44 The similarities between Clara Mortera and Reinaldo Arenas are numerous. In addition to the ones already indicated — a life that revolves around sexual activity and artistic productivity, and the grief that results from experiencing bodily deterioration — Clara and Arenas come to the end of their lives in analogous ways. During their final months and days, they concentrate their energies on completing their oeuvre before committing suicide. Like Clara, who finishes her paintings in a "rapture of fury" (77), "in a single fit of creative inspiration" (380; 348), Arenas, blessed with "creative fury," immerses himself in a "furious impulse" to finish his *pentagonía*. See Arenas, *Cartas a Margarita y Jorge Camacho* 265; and Arenas, Letters to Armando Álvarez Bravo, 27 April 1990. Also, Clara's painting of "the enchanted forest" (362; 331) makes the reader think of Arenas's essay "Martí ante el bosque encantado." Clara Mortera is a fictionalization of the Cuban painter Clara Morera, who appears as Clara Romero in *Antes que anochezca* (272–78) and as Blanca Romero in *Before Night Falls* (249–56).

45 See Arenas, Letters to Armando Álvarez Bravo, 27 April 1990.

46 See Arenas, Letters to Oneida Fuentes. Arenas was in the habit of photocopying the letters he wrote before mailing them. I have not been able to determine why there are photocopies of only five letters to his mother at Princeton. This small number should not be read as evidence of minimal contact between mother and son. For Oneida Fuentes's letters to her son, of which there are about fifty and which were written between 1982 and 1989 (some are undated and some are fragments), see Fuentes, Letters to Reinaldo Arenas.

47 In his correspondence with Margarita and Jorge Camacho, however, Arenas was very open about his illness, sharing details about its progress, addressing with resignation what he regarded as his impending death, and making ar-

rangements with them for his literary estate. See Arenas, *Cartas a Margarita y Jorge Camacho*.

48 Oneida's letters reflect the fact that she did not have much schooling.

49 In *Antes que anochezca*, Arenas says that he always kept from his mother his affliction with AIDS, claiming that even as late as 1989, during his mother's second visit to the United States, she did not notice that he was dying (13; *Before Night Falls* xiv). Oneida's letters make it difficult to believe Arenas's assertion that his mother was totally unaware of the state of his health. Moreover, in an interview in 2003, in which she refers to her trip to the United States in 1989, Oneida contends that she asked Arenas then whether he was sick and that he denied it (Fuentes, "Donde las arenas son más diáfanas" 23).

Epilogue

1 On the "Boom," see, for example, Donoso; King; and Rodríguez Monegal.

2 The "hell hole" (*arenal*) refers to Miami, where Arenas read this essay at the ceremony that handed out the III Premios Letras de Oro; the "frozen tundra" (*páramos helados*) refers to New York, where Arenas lived.

3 Arenas would have been pleased to read that, in his native Cuba, Alberto Garrandés has written, "I believe that, because of its caliber, *El mundo alucinante* can only be compared with the forces unleashed by what I've called 'an inexorable triumvirate': *El siglo de las luces*, *Paradiso* and *Tres tristes tigres*" (*El concierto de las fábulas* 254; see also 221–25).

4 For a thoughtful discussion of Arenas's complex relationship with U.S. Latino literature, see Prieto Taboada.

5 Arenas's autobiography was widely reviewed in the mainstream and gay press in the United States. The *New York Times Book Review* not only published a glowing review of *Before Night Falls* with a handsome cover photograph of the author, but also selected the English translation of Arenas's autobiography as an "Editors' Choice." See González Echevarría; and McGrath 599.

6 By most accounts, *Antes que anochezca* is the first openly gay autobiography by a major Latin American writer who unabashedly wrote about his erotic life.

7 For a lucid discussion of the role that Schnabel's *Before Night Falls* has played in the "commodification" of Arenas, see Loss 117–49.

8 Copies of some of Arenas's books and almost a complete run of *Mariel* (the literary magazine that Arenas published in exile with other *marielitos*) can be found today in the libraries of the UNEAC and Casa de las Américas (see Arango, "Una travesía desde los márgenes" 9; Quiroga 22; and Fernández Robaina, "Carta acerca de *Antes que anochezca*" 155). As of 24 July 2010, the

electronic catalogue of the Biblioteca Nacional José Martí (BNJM) included the following titles by Arenas: *Adiós a mamá*; *Antes que anocheza*; *Arturo, la estrella más brillante*; *Celestino antes del alba*; *El color del verano*; *El mundo alucinante*; *Necesidad de libertad*; *Persecución*; and *Voluntad de vivir manifestándose* (e-mail to the author from the reference department at the BNJM, 24 July 2010). Although these books do not circulate, they are available in the Salas de Lectura, according to a reference librarian at the BNJM who kindly responded to my inquiries (e-mail to the author from the reference department at the BNJM, 9 August 2010). Lourdes Arencibia Rodríguez's experience at the BNJM while researching *Reinaldo Arenas entre eros y tánatos*, however, belies the assertion that Arenas's books are easily accessible to the reading public (see Arencibia Rodríguez, "En las arenas de Reinaldo"). Although it may be true that some books by Arenas and other exiled writers are available in public libraries, they are not read by the average reader. The books of exiled writers who are not published in Cuba are primarily read by a limited number of people with access to copies that have made it onto the island and that circulate in what Antonio José Ponte calls a "chain of conspirators" ("Un arte de hacer ruinas" 181).

9 According to Rafael Rojas (*El estante vacío* 138–50), socialist intellectuals in Cuba today who advocate a socialism infused with anti-Stalinist sentiments confront an insurmountable dilemma, since politically and institutionally Cuban socialism has not ceased to be totalitarian. In Rojas's view, despite the recent denunciation of the Quinquenio Gris, cultural matters in Cuba continue to be subordinated to official ideology, regardless of what some island Cuban intellectuals say.

10 That the Cuban cultural establishment reacted more aggressively to Schnabel's film than to the autobiography that inspired it may be explained by the fact that movies may reach a wider audience than books. Cubans arguably felt the need to counteract the "counterrevolutionary" message of an internationally acclaimed film.

11 See Espinosa Mendoza, "¿Otro color para una Cuba rosa?"; and Zayas. See also *La jiribilla*.

12 In 2002, in an issue devoted to homosexuality in Cuban art and literature, *La jiribilla* reprinted Hillson's article on Arenas. It was also published that year as a *cuaderno* (a forty-two-page pamphlet) in an attempt to make it more readily available (in print) to a larger reading public. In 2003, Hillson presented his text on Arenas as a public lecture at the XVI Congreso Internacional de Sexología, which was held in Havana.

13 I use the verb *appropriate* because the editors did not have the right to publish Arenas's works.

14 Holguín's Asociación Hermanos Saíz and its Ediciones "La Luz" instituted in 2000 the Premio Celestino de Cuento, which is open to any writer in Cuba under the age of thirty-five.

15 See Echerri; and "El gran zoo."

16 See Arenas, *Antes que anochezca* 14; Arenas, *Before Night Falls* xv; Cuza Malé; "El gran zoo"; and Villaverde.

17 On Cuba's project of "transformism," in which Mariela Castro Espín (President Raúl Castro's daughter) plays a major role, see Negrón-Muntaner. Although homosexuality is no longer a criminal offense in Cuba, homosexuals are still legally vulnerable, since they can be regarded as "antisocials" with a propensity to be in a "state of dangerousness." See *Código Penal* (Libro I, título XI, capítulo I, artículos 72 and 73); Evenson 158–60; and Lumsden 81–95. Moreover, while homosexuality has been decriminalized, this should not be conflated with full sexual equality. In an interview in 2010, Fidel Castro, claiming not to be a homophobe, expressed regret for the UMAP camps (calling them "a great injustice") and admitted that he had to assume responsibility for their existence. At that time, Castro explained, he was not vigilant about what was happening with homosexuals because he was occupied with matters of utmost importance (e.g., the threat of United States imperialism). Castro's formulation, of course, reproduces the long-standing practice of diminishing the "importance" of sexual politics. See Fidel Castro, "Soy el responsable de la persecución a homosexuales que hubo en Cuba."

18 In 1968 Delfín Prats received UNEAC's Premio David de Poesía for *Lenguaje de mudos*, which was published but immediately destroyed because of its homo-eroticism. Prats remembers: "My book was thrown, as it were, into the black hole of memory. That is to say, it did not circulate, it was not sold, it was not presented, it was not discussed at all" ("Yo tengo un mal karma" 24). After losing his job as a translator at the Academia de las Ciencias in Havana in 1971, Prats returned to Holguín, where he has lived ever since. Unlike Arenas, he did not consider exile as an option. Following a long silence, Prats published in 1987 *Para festejar el ascenso de Ícaro*, in which he included some poems from *Lenguaje de mudos*, which had been published in Madrid in 1970 by José Mario, whom Prats had met in Havana in the 1960s along with other writers associated with El Puente. Prats received the Premio de la Crítica for *Para festejar el ascenso de Ícaro*; since then, other prizes — national and provincial — have been bestowed on him. See Arenas, "¿Rehabilitación o castración?"; Prats, Letter to Roberto *y demás*; Prats, "Yo tengo un mal karma"; and Verity Smith.

19 In a presentation earlier that year of Jon Hillson's *La política sexual de Reinaldo Arenas*, Acosta de Arriba prefaced his laudatory remarks about Hillson's *cuaderno* by stating that Arenas was one of the most important writers of the

last century but that he could not "agree with his anthological mythomania, eccentric affectation, and propensity to mix truths and lies to distort reality" (Acosta de Arriba, "La política sexual de Reinaldo Arenas").

20　See Amiot. The author of the review is a non-Cuban scholar who resides in France.

21　I have surveyed a wide range of major Cuban sources, including journals such as *El caimán barbudo*, *Casa de las Américas*, *La gaceta de Cuba*, *La isla en peso*, *La jiribilla*, *Temas*, *Unión*, and *Vitral*; book-length literary studies published by, among others, Casa de las Américas, Editorial Letras Cubanas, and Ediciones UNIÓN; and the websites CubaLiteraria: Portal de Literatura Cubana and UNEAC: Unión de Escritores y Artistas de Cuba. Between 1992 and 2001, there were substantially more favorable or neutral references to Arenas than critical ones. After the release of Schnabel's *Before Night Falls*, criticism of Arenas became more pronounced, but favorable or neutral references to Arenas also significantly outnumbered critical ones from 2001 to the present. I only found two references to Arenas prior to 1992.

22　See Abreu Arcia; Estévez; Fernández Robaina, "Carta acerca de *Antes que anochezca*"; Fowler Calzada, "Arenas: Homoerotismo y crítica de la cultura"; and Fowler Calzada, "Arenas, el irreverente." In his 1998 book on homosexuality in Cuban literature, *La maldición: Una historia del placer como conquista* (winner of Cuba's Premio de la Crítica), Fowler Calzada mentions Arenas only in passing—admiringly, I should point out (5, 151). It is equally notable that special issues of *La jiribilla* and *La gaceta de Cuba* devoted to homosexuality in Cuban art and literature do not include serious, analytical studies of Arenas's works (see "La vida en rosa" and "La voz homoerótica"). *La jiribilla* reprints Jon Hillson's article, which attacks Arenas, and an article by Marilyn Bobes on homosexuality in Cuban literature, originally published in *Revolución y cultura* in 1993, which refers to "the lamentable case of a writer like Reinaldo Arenas" (18). In *La gaceta de Cuba*, although Arenas is lauded in the brief introduction for having written novels in which the homoerotic voice "reaches an unusual protagonism in our literature" ("La voz homoerótica" 2), his "presence" in the issue is limited to four other brief references ("La voz homoerótica" 17, 20, 22, 24). Pedro Pérez Rivero also excludes Arenas from his studies of homosexuality in Cuban literature, *De Sodoma vino un ángel* and *Del portal hacia dentro*.

23　An earlier version of Arencibia Rodríguez's article appeared in Miami in 2001 in a collection of essays on Arenas that was published electronically (in the journal *Nexos*, which is no longer available online) and in book form. See Arencibia Rodríguez, "Cuando lleguen los grandes aguaceros."

24　On 25 February 2003 and 7 February 2009, I was able to access an entry on

Arenas in *CubaLiteraria*'s electronic *Diccionario de autores cubanos*. It was apparently removed for a while, but I was able to access it again on 7 May 2011. Each time I accessed the entry, it had a different URL (see "Arenas, Reinaldo"). An entry on Arenas appears in the electronic *Diccionario de escritores holguineros* (see "Arenas, Reinaldo [Holguín]").

25 If Arango openly expresses his admiration for Arenas the writer, he also makes sure that it is understood that he does not share Arenas's politics and that his critique of the system, unlike Arenas's, comes from within the Revolution. See Arango, "Una travesía desde los márgenes" 9. In 2007 Ena Lucía Portela, one of the most engaging writers in Cuba today, wrote a piece celebrating *El color del verano*, but it was published in Spain. Its publication, according to Portela, "irritated" a number of people in Cuba. In 2010 Portela's article on Arenas was published in Cuba in an "independent" digital journal. See Portela "El escalofrío y la carcajada"; and Portela, "No me hagas preguntas capciosas."

26 In 1993, six years before "El Cometa Halley" was first published in Cuba, Leonardo Padura (who resides in Cuba) had included Arenas's short story "A la sombra de la mata de almendras" in *El submarino amarillo (Cuento cubano 1966–1991)*, an anthology that appeared in Mexico. In a short note about Arenas, Padura says that the story belongs to *Termina el desfile*, a collection of stories by Arenas that appeared in Spain in 1981, a year after he left Cuba. In a review of Padura's anthology, published in *Unión*, Jorge Domingo criticizes Padura for including a story not written in Cuba and argues that a story from *Con los ojos cerrados*, published in Montevideo in 1972, "when [Arenas] still lived among us," would have been a better choice (90). Domingo's remarks are interesting for two reasons. First, he believes in distinguishing between the Reinaldo Arenas who lived in Cuba and the one who lived in exile. Second, he is not well informed (and neither is Padura) about Arenas's literary production. "A la sombra de la mata de almendras," written in 1967 and originally published in 1969 in *La gaceta de Cuba*, is part of *Con los ojos cerrados*. In exile Arenas republished the 1972 collection as *Termina el desfile*, which includes the original stories and an unpublished one (the eponymous story), which appears at the end of the volume. I point this out as an example of island Cubans' unfamiliarity with Arenas's works in the early 1990s.

27 The editors of *La jiribilla* included "Adiós a Manhattan" in the inaugural issue and used it, among other texts by Arenas and by others, to mount a campaign against Arenas. In the following issue, which is devoted to the city of Miami, the editors included "El exilio," in which Arenas criticizes the materialism and anti-intellectualism of his compatriots in exile, to support *La jiribilla*'s critique of Cubans in Miami.

28 See Arenas, *Celestino antes del alba* (fragment). *Celestino antes del alba* has not been published again in Cuba since 1967, when UNEAC first published it, according to a reference librarian at the Biblioteca Nacional José Martí (e-mail to the author from the reference department at the BNJM, 17 August 2010).

29 See García Santos. In Arenas's Last Will and Testament, one reads: "I direct that none of my works be published or otherwise distributed within the Republic of Cuba until such time as a democratic form of government be instituted to govern said country."

30 On the front cover of Garrandés's *La ínsula fabulante*, below the editor's name, one reads, "50th Anniversary of the Triumph of the Revolution."

31 On copyright laws in Cuba, in addition to Ley 14, see also Hernández-Reguant 15–16; Smorkaloff 111–16; Valdés Díaz, "Acerca de la autoría y la titularidad en el contexto jurídico cubano"; and Valdés Díaz, "Otra perspectiva."

32 Before an audience that included Raúl Castro, the Cuban poet César López, an honoree at the 16th International Book Fair, held in Havana in 2007, spoke in favor of an all-inclusive cultural politics and named writers who had left the island, including Arenas ("Mensajes de César López").

33 The Fundación LGBT Reinaldo Arenas is critical of the "normalizing" work on behalf of Cuban queers that is being carried out by Mariela Castro Espín and the Centro Nacional de Educación Sexual (CENESEX). See Negrón-Muntaner 175–77. On the Centro, see the CENESEX website, http://www .cenesexualidad.sld.cu. One can find on the Web references to activities sponsored by the Fundación LGBT Reinaldo Arenas and the ensuing clashes with the police. See, for example, Janjaque Chivaz. Cuba regards the Fundación as the "brainchild of the United States Interests Section in Cuba and of the Unity Coalition of Florida." See "COLEGAS y sus aliados mercenarios."

34 "To the memory of Reinaldo Arenas" reads the dedication of a short story written in 1992 by Jesús Jambrina, "Con los ojos cerrados," a title that pays homage to a story by Arenas with the same name. Jambrina published his story in Argentina in a collection titled *Perverso cubano*, in 1999, when he was editor of *Revolución y cultura*. José Prats Sariol, Arenas's friend and contemporary, dedicated two of his novels, *Mariel* and *Guanabo Gay*, to him. Censored in Cuba after its author had read the galleys, *Mariel* was eventually published in Mexico, in 1997, while Prats Sariol still lived in Cuba; *Guanabo Gay* appeared in Mexico in 2004, the year Prats Sariol went into exile (see Prats Sariol, "Entrevista con el escritor cubano José Prats Sariol"). Ramón Elías Laffita dedicated to Arenas his poem "La luz, otra vez la luz," which is included in his collection *Palabras hacia la noche* (2005).

35 Pedro de Jesús, Jorge Ángel Pérez, and Guillermo Vidal are among the writers in whose works one can detect the "influence" of Reinaldo Arenas.

See Ichikawa 94; Jambrina, "Hay que ser escritor"; Murrieta 132; and Riverón, "Como quiere que lo vean, se esconde" 61. For literary texts in which Arenas "appears" in direct or indirect references to him or his work, see Aguiar Díaz 53; Arango, "La Habana elegante" 50–51; Curbelo 73, 105; González Herrero 27; Pérez 117; Prats Sariol, *Guanabo Gay* 24, 76, 100, 195, 203, 204, 227, 265, 267; Prats Sariol, *Mariel* 355; and Varona Roque 5. Three of these won national literary prizes: Jesús David Curbelo's *Diario de un poeta recién cazado* (Premio José Soler Puig 1998), Jorge Ángel Pérez's *El paseante Cándido* (Premio UNEAC de Novela 2000), and Mariela Varona Roque's "Anna Lidia Vega Serova lee un cuento erótico en el patio de un museo colonial" (Premio de Cuento *La gaceta de Cuba* 2001). In 2008 the *holguinero* (like Arenas) Alcides Pereda was a finalista in the Premio de Cuento *La gaceta de Cuba* with "El color del verano," a title that echoes that of the fourth novel of Arenas's *pentagonía*. Pereda won in 2009 the Premio Celestino de Cuento (named after Arenas's first novel) with the collection *La lluvia que trajo el viento*. See Infante; and "Premio de Cuento." *El canto del pozo ciego*, the translation of the Cuban American Jorge Ignacio Cortiñas's play *Blind Mouth Singing*, which was inspired by Arenas's first novel and had its world premiere in Chicago in 2006, had its Cuban premiere in Havana on 10 July 2010. See Fulleda.

36   For an insightful reading of "Money" as an allegory of literary production and consumption during the Special Period, see Whitfield 67, 69, 74–79.

37   For writers, dramatists, and poets outside Cuba who pay homage to or have been inspired by Arenas, see Abreu, *Gimnasio*; José Abreu Felippe; Alberto, *Caracol Beach*; Álvarez Bravo, "Anochecer de Reinaldo Arenas"; Bevin; Bolaño; Bordao, "Inaplazable fugitivo"; Cortiñas; Gálvez; Islas; Luz; Ana Menéndez; Navarrete; Olivares Baró; Pau-Llosa; Piñera Arenas; Segarra Báez; Soroa; and Victoria, "La estrella fugaz." Arenas has also been a source of inspiration for artists such as José Luis Cortés, Clara Morera, and Lydia Rubio. See Cotter; "Exposición 'Clara Morera, Reinaldo Arenas y *El color del verano*'"; Rubio; and Strong. The choreographer Johannes Birringer of Alien-Nation, a multimedia arts organization and laboratory for cross-cultural performance, created in 1997 *Before Night Falls*, a performance-installation inspired by Arenas's memoirs that was performed that year in Atlanta, Cleveland, and Dresden. Birringer's 1995–96 mutimedia performance-concert *Lovers Fragments* included texts by Arenas (it had a "film premiere" in Havana, at Casa de las Américas, in December 1995). In 1996 Alan West imagined an opera with Arenas as the central character. In 1998 Arenas's short story "Final de un cuento" was staged, under the direction of Alberto Bokos, at the Artenbrut theater in Barcelona. In 2007 an opera by Chazam based on

Arenas's *El mundo alucinante* was performed at the Théâtre Molière in Bordeaux. In 2010 Tony Mitchell's "Reinaldo Arenas," a flamenco performance, was part of the Elegetebéfest at the Centro Cultural Provincial in Malaga. In 2011 *Reinaldo Arenas (A True Story)*, a short film by Lucas Leyva, appeared. See the AlienNation Company websites http://www.aliennationcompany .com and http://www.ruf.rice.edu/~orpheus/com.html; Birringer 240–66; "Cartelera"; *Le Monde hallucinant/El mundo alucinante*; Pastrana; *Reinaldo Arenas (A True Story)*; West, "Sones peregrinos" 108–9; and West, *Tropics of History* 182–83. In addition to Julian Schnabel's full-length film *Before Night Falls*, a number of documentaries have been made in which either Arenas or his writing is featured. See, for example, *Conducta impropia*, *Dos patrias Cuba y la noche*, *Havana*, and *Seres extravagantes*. Arenas is included in Ira Sachs's elegiac documentary *Last Address*, which commemorates a generation of New York artists who died of AIDS-related causes between 1983 and 2007 using images of the exterior of their "last address."

38   For reviews of the opera and its recording, see the composer's website, http:// www.jorgemartin.com.

39   I should point out that opera plays a role in *El color del verano*, where Arenas humorously re-creates Countess Merlin's 1840 Havana performance of fragments of Bellini's *Norma*. Merlin sings not in an elegant concert hall but in a gigantic public urinal (formerly Merlin's family home) where gay men are engaging in promiscuous sex. For a smart reading of Arenas's incorporation of Merlin in *El color del verano*, see Roberto Ignacio Díaz, "Mercedes Merlin, la ópera y Reinaldo Arenas."

·WORKS CITED·

Abraham, Karl. "Contributions to the Theory of the Anal Character." *Selected Papers of Karl Abraham, M.D*. Trans. Douglas Bryan and Alix Strachey. London: Hogarth, 1927. 370–92.

Abreu, Juan. *A la sombra del mar: Jornadas cubanas con Reinaldo Arenas*. Barcelona: Casiopea, 1998.

———. *Gimnasio: Emanaciones de una rutina*. Barcelona: Poliedro, 2002.

———. "Presencia de Arenas." *Reinaldo Arenas: Recuerdo y presencia*. Ed. Reinaldo Sánchez. Miami: Universal, 1994. 13–20.

Abreu Arcia, Alberto. "Reynaldo [sic] Arenas: El tormento de la escritura." *Crítica: Revista de la Universidad Autónoma de Puebla* 74 (1999): 13–16.

Abreu Felippe, José. "Dos poemas y un breve comentario." *Reinaldo Arenas, aunque anochezca*. Ed. Luis de la Paz. Miami: Universal, 2001. 122–24.

Abreu Felippe, Nicolás. "Mi amigo Reinaldo Arenas." *Reinaldo Arenas, aunque anochezca*. Ed. Luis de la Paz. Miami: Universal, 2001. 184–93.

Acosta de Arriba, Rafael. "Para conocer las voces del agua." *La jiribilla* 59 (June 2002), http://www.lajiribilla.co.cu/2002/n59_junio/1447_59.html, accessed 13 April 2010.

———. "La política sexual de Reinaldo Arenas: Realidad y ficción." *La jiribilla* 50 (April 2002), http://www.lajiribilla.co.cu/2002/n50_abril/1296_50.html, accessed 19 October 2009.

Adams, Timothy Dow. *Telling Lies in Modern American Autobiography*. Chapel Hill: University of North Carolina Press, 1990.

Aguiar Díaz, Jorge Alberto. "Cielo sobre Havana." *Adiós a las almas*. Havana: Letras Cubanas, 2002. 50–61.

Aguirre, Mirta. "Realismo, realismo socialista y la posición cubana." *Estudios literarios*. Havana: Letras Cubanas, 1981. 424–67.

Alberto, Eliseo. *Caracol Beach*. Madrid: Alfaguara, 1998.

———. "Reinaldo Arenas." *Dos Cubalibres*. Barcelona: Ediciones Península, 2004. 240–45.

"Allegory." *The New Princeton Encyclopedia of Poetry and Poetics*. Ed. Alex Preminger
and T. V. F. Brogan. Princeton: Princeton University Press, 1993. 31–36.

Almendros, Néstor, and Orlando Jiménez Leal. *Conducta impropia* (script).
Madrid: Playor, 1984.

Álvarez Bravo, Armando. "Anochecer de Reinaldo Arenas." *El día más memorable*.
Miami: Universal, 1999. 83–91.

———. "Reinaldo Arenas." *Vuelta* 15.171 (1991): 71–73.

Amiot, Julie. "Arenas apenas." *La gaceta de Cuba* 6 (2002): 76–78.

Ampuero, Roberto. "Carta de Roberto Ampuero a la Presidenta Michelle Bachelet." *El mercurio*, 1 February 2009, D7.

Anhalt, Nedda G. de. "Recuerdo a Reinaldo Arenas." *Sábado* (*unomásuno*'s supplement), 15 June 1991, 1, 4–5.

Arango, Arturo. "En una conversación (imaginaria) con Ambrosio Fornet sobre la
novela cubana de los 90: El caso de Reinaldo Arenas." *Segundas reincidencias
(escribir en Cuba ayer)*. Santa Clara: Editorial Capiro, 2002. 125–26.

———. "La Habana elegante." *La Habana elegante*. Havana: Ediciones UNIÓN,
1995. 39–57.

———. "La historia por los cuernos." *La gaceta de Cuba* 6 (2008): 33–38.

———. "Una travesía desde los márgenes." Interview by Elizabeth Mirabal Llorens
and Carlos Velazco Fernández. *Revolución y cultura* 4 (2009): 6–16.

Arenas, Reinaldo. "Adiós a mamá." *Adiós a mamá: De La Habana a Nueva York*.
Barcelona: Altera, 1995. 53–79.

———. "Adiós a Manhattan." *El nuevo herald*, 17 July 1989, 9A. Reprint, *La jiribilla* 1
(May 2001), http://www.lajiribilla.co.cu/2001/nro1mayo2001.html, accessed
19 October 2009.

———. "Adorada Chelo." *Necesidad de libertad*. Mexico City: Kosmos, 1986. 101–2.

———. "A la sombra de la mata de almendras." *Con los ojos cerrados*. Montevideo:
Arca, 1972. 71–76. Reprint, *El submarino amarillo (Cuento cubano 1966–1991):
Breve antología*. Ed. Leonardo Padura. Mexico City: Universidad Nacional
Autónoma de México/Ediciones Coyoacán, 1993. 64–70.

———. *Antes que anochezca*. Barcelona: Tusquets, 1992.

———. "Aquí estamos." *Catálogo de letras* 1 (1994): 8–9.

———. "Arenas disparu?" *Necesidad de libertad*. Mexico City: Kosmos, 1986. 149.

———. *Arturo, la estrella más brillante*. Barcelona: Montesinos, 1984.

———. *El asalto*. Miami: Universal, 1991.

———. *The Assault*. Trans. Andrew Hurley. New York: Viking, 1994.

———. "Autoepitafio." *Voluntad de vivir manifestándose*. Madrid: Betania, 1989. 110.

———. *Before Night Falls*. Trans. Dolores M. Koch. New York: Viking, 1993.

———. "Benítez entra en el juego." *Unión* 7.2 (1968): 146–52.

———. *The Brightest Star. Old Rosa: A Novel in Two Stories*. Trans. Andrew Hurley. New York: Grove, 1989. 45–104.

———. *Cantando en el pozo*. Barcelona: Argos Vergara, 1982.

———. *Cartas a Margarita y Jorge Camacho (1967–1990)*. Ed. Margarita Camacho. Seville: Point de Lunettes, 2010.

———. *Celestino antes del alba*. Havana: UNEAC, 1967.

———. "Celestino antes del alba." *Mundo nuevo* 21 (1968): 33–40.

———. *Celestino antes del alba* (fragment). *La literatura cubana en la Revolución: Literatura escrita en la década de los 60 y primeros años de los 70. CubaLiteraria*, http://www.cubaliteraria.cu/monografia/literatura_revolucion/index.html, accessed 23 July 2010.

———. "Celestino y yo." *Unión* 6.3 (1967): 117–20.

———. *El central*. Barcelona: Seix Barral, 1981.

———. "Charlemos con Reinaldo Arenas." Interview by Ana Roca. *Americas* 33.9 (1981): 36–38.

———. "*Cien años de soledad* en la ciudad de los espejismos." *Casa de las Américas* 8.48 (1968): 134–38.

———. *El color del verano*. Miami: Universal, 1991.

———. *The Color of Summer*. Trans. Andrew Hurley. New York: Viking, 2000.

———. "El Cometa Halley." *Adiós a mamá: De La Habana a Nueva York*. Barcelona: Altera, 1995. 81–107. Reprint, *Aire de luz: Cuentos cubanos del siglo XX*. Ed. Alberto Garrandés. Havana: Letras Cubanas, 1999. 261–73. *La jiribilla* 1 (May 2001), http://www.lajiribilla.co.cu/2001/nro1mayo2001.html, accessed 19 October 2009; *El caimán barbudo* 318 (2003), http://www.caimanbarbudo.cu/caiman318/paginas/reinaldo.htm, accessed 8 December 2003; *La ínsula fabulante: El cuento cubano en la Revolución, 1959–2008*. Ed. Alberto Garrandés. Havana: Letras Cubanas, 2008. 261–75.

———. "Comienza el desfile." *Con los ojos cerrados*. Montevideo: Arca, 1972. 9–22.

———. "Comunicado." *Necesidad de libertad*. Mexico City: Kosmos, 1986. 150–52.

———. *Con los ojos cerrados*. Montevideo: Arca, 1972.

———. "Contra la integridad y estabilidad de la nación: Sentencia contra René Ariza." *Necesidad de libertad*. Mexico City: Kosmos, 1986. 76–78.

———. "Conversación con Reinaldo Arenas." Interview by Jorge Olivares and Nivia Montenegro. *Taller literario* 1.2 (1980): 53–67.

———. "Conversation with Reinaldo Arenas." Interview by Francisco Soto. *Reinaldo Arenas: The Pentagonía*. By Francisco Soto. Gainesville: University Press of Florida, 1994. 137–54.

———. Correspondence. Reinaldo Arenas Papers. Boxes 23–26 and box 28, folder 1.

———. "Cortázar: ¿Senil o pueril?" *Necesidad de libertad*. Mexico City: Kosmos, 1986. 70–74.

———. "Cronología (irónica, pero cierta)." An unnumbered four-page autobiographical sketch distributed by Argos Vergara in 1982 when it published *Otra vez el mar*.

———. "Delfín Prats Pupo." *Necesidad de libertad*. Mexico City: Kosmos, 1986. 81–82.

———. "Los dichosos sesenta." *Final de un cuento*. Huelva: Diputación Provincial de Huelva, 1991. 23–31.

———. "La dignidad de Guillermo Hernández." *El nuevo herald*, 5 December 1988, 7A.

———. "Don Miguel Riera." *Necesidad de libertad*. Mexico City: Kosmos, 1986. 114.

———. "Elogio de las furias." *Necesidad de libertad*. Mexico City: Kosmos, 1986. 253–55.

———. "El encadenamiento del fraile." *La gaceta de Cuba* 5.53 (1966): 6.

———. *Encore une fois la mer*. Reinaldo Arenas Papers. Box 9, folders 1 and 2.

———. "Entrevista: Reinaldo Arenas." Interview by Perla Rozencvaig. *Hispamérica* 10.28 (1981): 41–48.

———. "Entrevista a Reinaldo Arenas: Experimentación y tradición." Interview by Marithelma Costa and Adelaida López. *Studi di letteratura ispano-americana*. Milan: Istituto Editoriale Cisalpino–La Goliardica, 1986. 103–13.

———. "Entrevista exclusiva a Reinaldo Arenas." Interview by Paulo Octaviano Terra. *Linden Lane Magazine* 11.3 (1992): 19–20.

———. "Esa capacidad para soñar: Entrevista con Reinaldo Arenas." Interview by Antonio Prieto Taboada. *Revista interamericana de bibliografía* 44.4 (1994): 683–97.

———. "La escritura como re-escritura, textos y pre-textos." Reinaldo Arenas Papers. Box 18, folder 24.

———. "Estancia en Pamplona." *Casa de las Américas* 7.43 (1967): 87–90.

———. "Exhortaciones para leer a Juan Abreu." *Libro de las exhortaciones al amor*. By Juan Abreu. Madrid: Playor, 1985. 5–12.

———. "El exilio." *La jiribilla* 2 (May 2001), http://www.lajiribilla.co.cu/2001/nro2mayo2001.html, accessed 19 March 2010.

———. *Farewell to the Sea*. Trans. Andrew Hurley. New York: Viking, 1986.

———. *Final de un cuento*. Huelva: Diputación Provincial de Huelva, 1991.

———. "Gabriel García Márquez: ¿Esbirro o es burro?" *Noticias de arte* 6.7–8 (1981): 15. Reprint, *Necesidad de libertad*. Mexico City: Kosmos, 1986. 66–69.

———. "Goodbye Mother." Trans. Jo Labanyi. *The Faber Book of Contemporary Latin American Short Stories*. Ed. Nick Caistor. London: Faber, 1989. 53–66.

———. *Graveyard of the Angels*. Trans. Alfred J. MacAdam. New York: Avon, 1987.

———. "Grito, luego existo." *Necesidad de libertad*. Mexico City: Kosmos, 1986. 14–23.

———. "Halley's Comet." *Mona and Other Tales*. Trans. Dolores M. Koch. New York: Vintage, 2001. 138–56.

———. *The Ill-Fated Peregrinations of Fray Servando*. Trans. Andrew Hurley. New York: Avon, 1987.

———. *Inferno*. Barcelona: Lumen, 2001.

———. Last Will and Testament. Reinaldo Arenas Papers. Box 27, folder 9.

———. *Lazarillo de Tormes*. New York: Regents, 1984.

———. *Leprosorio (Trilogía poética)*. Madrid: Betania, 1990.

———. Letter to Michael Chodkiewicz. Reinaldo Arenas Papers. Box 24, folder 3.

———. Letter to Editions du Seuil. Reinaldo Arenas Papers. Box 9, folder 1.

———. Letters to Armando Álvarez Bravo. Reinaldo Arenas Papers. Box 23, folder 1.

———. Letters to Tony Cartano. Reinaldo Arenas Papers. Box 25, folder 16.

———. Letters to Thomas Colchie. Reinaldo Arenas Papers. Box 26, folder 10.

———. Letters to Oneida Fuentes. Reinaldo Arenas Papers. Box 28, folder 1.

———. Letters to Liliane Hasson. Reinaldo Arenas Papers. Box 24, folder 11.

———. Letters to Severo Sarduy. Reinaldo Arenas Papers. Box 26, folder 7.

———. "Lezama o el reino de la imagen." *Necesidad de libertad*. Mexico City: Kosmos, 1986. 105–13.

———. "La literatura cubana dentro y fuera de Cuba." Reinaldo Arenas Papers. Box 18, folder 26.

———. *La Loma del Ángel*. Malaga: Dador, 1987.

———. "Magia y persecución en José Martí." *La gaceta de Cuba* 6.66 (1968): 13–16.

———. "El mar es siempre el símbolo fundamental de la liberación (conversación con Reinaldo Arenas)." Interview by Jacobo Machover. *La memoria frente al poder: Escritores cubanos del exilio: Guillermo Cabrera Infante, Severo Sarduy, Reinaldo Arenas*. By Jacobo Machover. Valencia: Universitat de Valencia, 2001. 251–70.

———. "Martí ante el bosque encantado." *Necesidad de libertad*. Mexico City: Kosmos, 1986. 56–61.

———. "Memorias de un exiliado." Interview by Liliane Hasson. *La escritura de la memoria: Reinaldo Arenas: Textos, estudios y documentación*. Ed. Ottmar Ette. Frankfurt am Main: Vervuert, 1992. 35–63.

———. *Mona*. *Mona and Other Tales*. Trans. Dolores M. Koch. New York: Vintage, 2001. 30–68.

———. *Mona*. *Viaje a La Habana*. Madrid: Mondadori, 1990. 67–107.

———. "Morir en junio y con la lengua afuera." *Leprosorio (Trilogía poética)*. Madrid: Betania, 1990. 69–99.

———. *El mundo alucinante*. Mexico City: Editorial Diógenes, 1969.

———. *Necesidad de libertad*. Mexico City: Kosmos, 1986.

———. *Otra vez el mar*. Barcelona: Argos Vergara, 1982.

———. *The Palace of the White Skunks*. Trans. Andrew Hurley. New York: Penguin, 1993.

———. *El palacio de las blanquísimas mofetas*. Caracas: Monte Ávila, 1980.

———. "El páramo en llamas." *Recopilación de textos sobre Juan Rulfo*. Ed. Antonio Benítez Rojo. Havana: Casa de las Américas, 1969. 60–63.

———. *Persecución*. Miami: Universal, 1986.

———. *El portero*. Malaga: Dador, 1989.

———. "¡Qué dura es la vida!" Reinaldo Arenas Papers. Box 13A, folders 1–5.

———. "¿Rehabilitación o castración?" *El nuevo herald*, 11 October 1988, 7A.

———. "Reinaldo Arenas: Aquel mar, una vez más." Interview by Nedda G. de Anhalt. *Rojo y naranja sobre rojo*. By Nedda G. de Anhalt. Mexico City: Vuelta, 1991. 133–67.

———. "Reinaldo Arenas: 'Escribir es un acto de irreverencia.'" Interview by Armando Álvarez Bravo. *El nuevo herald*, 21 April 1990, 1D, 5D.

———. Reinaldo Arenas Papers. Literary Papers and Manuscripts Division, Department of Rare Books and Special Collections, Princeton University Library, Princeton, New Jersey.

———. "Reinaldo Arenas responde a Ángel Rama." *El Miami Herald*, 31 December 1982, 5.

———. "El reino de la imagen." *La gaceta de Cuba* 8.88 (1970): 23–26.

———. "La represión (intelectual) en Cuba." *Escandalar* 4.1 (1981): 90–93. Reprint, *Necesidad de libertad*. Mexico City: Kosmos, 1986. 40–49.

———. "Revista *Mundo nuevo*." *La gaceta de Cuba* 6.66 (1968): 16. Reprint, *Necesidad de libertad*. Mexico City: Kosmos, 1986. 34.

———. "Señor Emir Rodríguez Monegal." *Necesidad de libertad*. Mexico City: Kosmos, 1986. 39.

———. "Severo Sarduy." *Necesidad de libertad*. Mexico City: Kosmos, 1986. 167–69.

———. *Singing from the Well*. Trans. Andrew Hurley. New York: Penguin, 1987.

———. "Sinopsis de un film sobre *Paradiso*, novela de José Lezama Lima." Reinaldo Arenas Papers. Box 15, folder 4.

———. *Sobre los astros*. Seville: Point de Lunettes, 2006.

———. *Termina el desfile*. Barcelona: Seix Barral, 1981.

———. "Tres mujeres y el amor." *La gaceta de Cuba* 7.71 (1969): 26–28.

———. "Una rama entre la delincuencia y el cinismo." Reinaldo Arenas Papers. Box 19, folder 26.

———. "Un largo viaje de Mariel a Nueva York." *El Miami Herald*, 25 November 1981, 7. Reprint, *Necesidad de libertad*. Mexico City: Kosmos, 1986. 247–51.

———. *Viaje a La Habana. Viaje a La Habana.* Madrid: Mondadori, 1990. 109–81.

———. "La vida es riesgo o abstinencia: Entrevista con Reinaldo Arenas." Interview by Carlos Espinosa Domínguez. *Quimera* 101 (1990): 54–61.

———. *La vieja Rosa.* Caracas: Librería Cruz del Sur, 1980.

———. "Viejo niño." *Voluntad de vivir manifestándose.* Madrid: Betania, 1989. 96–97.

———. *Voluntad de vivir manifestándose.* Madrid: Betania, 1989.

———. "Los zapatos vacíos." *Encuentro de la cultura cubana* 12–13 (1999): 109.

"Arenas, Reinaldo." Diccionario de autores cubanos. *CubaLiteraria*, http://cubaliteraria.cu/autores/autor.asp?Nombre=Reinaldo&Apellidos=Arenas, accessed 25 February 2003; http://www.cubaliteraria.cu/autor/ficha.php?q=arenas&Id=660, accessed 7 February 2009; http://www.cubaliteraria.cu/autor.php?idautor=1807, accessed 7 May 2011.

"Arenas, Reinaldo (Holguín)." Diccionario de escritores holguineros (1862–2008). Monografías.com, http://www.monografias.com/trabajos68/diccionario-escritores-holguineros/diccionario-escritores-holguineros2.shtml, accessed 27 July 2010.

Arenas, Reinaldo, and Jorge Camacho. *Un plebiscito a Fidel Castro.* Madrid: Betania, 1990.

Arencibia Rodríguez, Lourdes. "Cuando lleguen los grandes aguaceros." *Reinaldo Arenas, aunque anochezca.* Ed. Luis de la Paz. Miami: Universal, 2001. 73–105.

———. "En busca de un tiempo de fábulas." *Temas* 28 (2002): 120–33.

———. "En las arenas de Reinaldo." *La isla en peso* 6, http://www.uneac.org.cu/LaIslaEnPeso/num06/central.htm, accessed 17 April 2010.

———. *Reinaldo Arenas entre eros y tánatos.* Bogotá: Soporte Editorial, 2001.

Armand, Octavio. "Minicurso para borrar al escritor cubano del exilio." *Escandalar* 3.2 (1980): 86–89.

———. "Reading Reading." *Review* 31 (1982): 10–12.

Arrufat, Antón. *Virgilio Piñera: Entre él y yo.* Havana: Ediciones UNIÓN, 1994.

Bade, Patrick. *Femme Fatale: Images of Evil and Fascinating Women.* London: Ash and Grant, 1979.

Badías, María Elena. "Lo que compartimos con Reinaldo Arenas." *Reinaldo Arenas: Recuerdo y presencia.* Ed. Reinaldo Sánchez. Miami: Universal, 1994. 21–26.

Báez, Luis. "Unidades Militares de Ayuda a la Producción (UMAP)." *Granma*, 14 April 1966, 9.

Bakhtin, Mikhail. *Problems of Dostoevsky's Poetics.* Trans. Caryl Emerson. Minneapolis: University of Minnesota Press, 1984.

———. *Rabelais and His World.* Trans. Hélène Iswolsky. Cambridge: Massachusetts Institute of Technology Press, 1968.

Barnet, Miguel. "Celestino antes y después del alba." *La gaceta de Cuba* 6.60 (1967): 21.

———. "Lo que se sabe no se pregunta." Interview by Leandro Estupiñán. *CubaLiteraria*, 17 September 2007, http://www.cubaliteraria.com/articulo.php? idarticulo=10097&idseccion=30, accessed 21 May 2010.

Baron, F. Xavier. "Mother and Son in *Sir Perceval of Galles*." *Papers on Language and Literature* 8.1 (1972): 3–14.

Barquet, Jesús J. "La generación del Mariel." *Encuentro de la cultura cubana* 8–9 (1998): 110–25.

———. "Rebeldía e irreverencia de Reinaldo Arenas." *Reinaldo Arenas: Recuerdo y presencia*. Ed. Reinaldo Sánchez. Miami: Universal, 1994. 27–38.

Before Night Falls. Dir. Julian Schnabel. Fine Line Features, 2000.

Bejel, Emilio. *Gay Cuban Nation*. Chicago: University of Chicago Press, 2001.

Bennett, Paula, and Vernon A. Rosario, eds. *Solitary Pleasures: The Historical, Literary, and Artistic Discourses of Autoeroticism*. New York: Routledge, 1995.

Benshoff, Harry M. *Monsters in the Closet: Homosexuality and the Horror Film*. Manchester: Manchester University Press, 1997.

Bersani, Leo. "Is the Rectum a Grave?" *October* 43 (1987): 197–222.

Bevin, Teresa. *Havana Split*. Houston: Arte Público, 1998.

Binding, Paul. *García Lorca o la imaginación gay*. Barcelona: Laertes, 1987.

Biron, Rebecca E. *Murder and Masculinity: Violent Fictions of Twentieth-Century Latin America*. Nashville: Vanderbilt University Press, 2000.

Birringer, Johannes. *Performance on the Edge: Transformations of Culture*. New York: Continuum, 2000.

Black, Georgina Dopico. "The Limits of Expression: Intellectual Freedom in Postrevolutionary Cuba." *Cuban Studies* 19 (1989): 107–42.

Bloch, R. Howard. *Etymologies and Genealogies: A Literary Anthropology of the French Middle Ages*. Chicago: University of Chicago Press, 1983.

Boas, George. "The *Mona Lisa* in the History of Taste." *Journal of the History of Ideas* 1.2 (1940): 207–24.

Bobes, Marilyn. "El homosexualismo en la literatura cubana." *Revolución y cultura* 32.5 (1993): 16–19. Reprint, *La jiribilla* 37 (January 2002), http://www .lajiribilla.co.cu/2002/nro37enero2002.html, accessed 19 October 2009.

Bolaño, Roberto. *Los detectives salvajes*. Barcelona: Anagrama, 1998.

Bordao, Rafael. "Inaplazable fugitivo." *Reinaldo Arenas, aunque anochezca*. Ed. Luis de la Paz. Miami: Universal, 2001. 116–17.

———. *La sátira, la ironía y el carnaval literario en "Leprosorio (Trilogía poética)" de Reinaldo Arenas*. Lewiston: Edwin Mellen, 2002.

Bramly, Serge. *Leonardo: Discovering the Life of Leonardo da Vinci*. Trans. Sian Reynolds. New York: Edward Burlingame, 1991.

Browning, Richard L. *Childhood and the Nation in Latin American Literature*. New York: Peter Lang, 2001.

Bunson, Matthew. *The Vampire Encyclopedia*. New York: Crown, 1993.

Burgwinkle, William E. *Sodomy, Masculinity, and Law in Medieval Literature: France and England, 1050–1230*. New York: Cambridge University Press, 2004.

Bush, Andrew. "The Riddled Text: Borges and Arenas." *MLN* 103.2 (1988): 374–97.

Cabrera, Lydia. "A Conversation with Lydia Cabrera." Interview by Suzanne Jill Levine. *Review* 31 (1982): 13–15.

Cabrera Infante, Guillermo. "En España han sido en extremo generosos conmigo." *ABC* (Cultura), 24 April 1998, 64–65.

———. "Two Wrote Together." *Mea Cuba*. Trans. Kenneth Hall (with the author). New York: Farrar, Straus and Giroux, 1994. 331–60.

Calder, Nigel. *The Comet Is Coming! The Feverish Legacy of Mr. Halley*. New York: Viking, 1981.

Calinescu, Matei. "Secrecy in Fiction: Textual and Intertextual Secrets in Hawthorne and Updike." *Poetics Today* 15.3 (1994): 443–65.

Callen, Michael. "Surviving and Thriving with AIDS." "PWA Coalition Portfolio." *October* 43 (1987): 161–66.

Carballo, Emmanuel. *Diario público 1966–1968*. Mexico City: Conaculta, 2005.

Cárdenas, Esteban Luis. "Reinaldo Arenas: El brillo de la gloria." *Reinaldo Arenas, aunque anochezca*. Ed. Luis de la Paz. Miami: Universal, 2001. 199–206.

"Cartelera." *La vanguardia*, 4 July 1998, 45.

"Casa 68." *La gaceta de Cuba* 6.63 (1968): 2.

El caso Padilla: Literatura y revolución en Cuba: Documentos. Ed. Lourdes Casal. Miami: Universal, 1971.

Castellanos, Ernesto Juan. "El diversionismo ideológico del rock, la moda y los enfermitos." Lecture presented as part of the series La política cultural del período revolucionario: Memoria y reflexión, Centro Teórico-Cultural Criterios, Havana, 31 October 2008, http://www.criterios.es/pdf/9castellanosdiversion ismo.pdf, accessed 12 October 2009.

Castro, Fidel. "Discurso pronunciado por el Comandante Fidel Castro Ruz, Primer Ministro del Gobierno Revolucionario de Cuba, en la clausura del acto para conmemorar el VI aniversario del asalto al Palacio Presidencial, celebrado en la escalinata de la Universidad de La Habana, el 13 de marzo de 1963." *Discursos e intervenciones del Comandante en Jefe Fidel Castro Ruz, Presidente del Consejo de Estado de la República de Cuba*, http://www.cuba.cu/gobierno/discursos/1963/ esp/f130363e.html, accessed 11 October 2009.

———. *My Life*. Ed. Ignacio Ramonet. Trans. Andrew Hurley. London: Penguin, 2008.

———. "No cayó en el vacío el sacrificio de los mártires: Discurso pronunciado por el Primer Ministro del Gobierno Revolucionario, Comandante Fidel Castro, en la clausura del acto celebrado en la escalinata de la Universidad de La Habana

WORKS CITED

para conmemorar el VI aniversario del asalto al Palacio Presidencial." *El mundo*, 14 March 1963, 5–6.

——. "Only after a Revolution as Profound as the One That Has Taken Place in Our Country Could a Congress Like This Take Place." *Granma Weekly Review*, 9 May 1971, 7–9.

——. "Soy el responsable de la persecución a homosexuales que hubo en Cuba." *La jornada*, 31 August 2010, http://www.jornada.unam.mx/2010/08/31/index .php?section=mundo&article=026e1mun, accessed 18 September 2010.

——. "Speech to the Fighting People." *Fidel Castro Speeches*. Ed. Michael Taber. New York: Pathfinder, 1981. 271–90.

Castro, Fidel, and Tomás Borge. *Face to Face with Fidel Castro: A Conversation with Tomás Borge*. Trans. Mary Todd. Melbourne: Ocean, 1993.

Castro, Raúl. "El diversionismo ideológico, arma sutil que esgrimen los enemigos contra la revolución." *Revolución y cultura* 6 (1972): 2–19.

CENESEX: Centro Nacional de Educación Sexual. http://www.cenesexualidad.sld .cu, accessed 16 August 2011.

Clark, Kenneth. *Leonardo da Vinci*. London: Viking, 1988.

Código Penal. Gaceta Oficial de la República de Cuba, Ministerio de Justicia, http://www.gacetaoficial.cu/html/codigo_penal.html, accessed 10 August 2012.

Cohen, William A. "Manual Conduct in *Great Expectations*." *ELH* 60.1 (1993): 217–59.

"COLEGAS y sus aliados mercenarios: ¿Independientes?" International Lesbian, Gay, Bisexual, Trans and Intersex Association, 8 January 2010, http://ilga.org/ ilga/es/article/mf5M7Sn1sq, accessed 20 August 2011.

Collins, Bradley I. *Leonardo, Psychoanalysis, and Art History: A Critical Study of Psychobiographical Approaches to Leonardo da Vinci*. Evanston: Northwestern University Press, 1997.

Conde, Alfredo. *Una conversación en La Habana*. Madrid: El País/Aguilar, 1989.

Conducta impropia. Dir. Néstor Almendros and Orlando Jiménez Leal. Cinevista, 1984.

"*Consenso* en la polémica intelectual." *Consenso* 11 (2007), http://desdecuba.com/ polemica/, accessed 12 September 2010.

Constitución Política de la República de Cuba (actualizada hasta la Ley de Reforma Constitucional 2002). Political Database of the Americas, http://pdba.georgetown .edu/Constitutions/Cuba/vigente.html, accessed 10 August 2012.

Conte, Antonio. "Memoria de Arenas." *Reinaldo Arenas, aunque anochezca*. Ed. Luis de la Paz. Miami: Universal, 2001. 207–9.

Corral, Wilfrido H. "Ángel Rama y Reinaldo Arenas en Estados Unidos: Intelectuales especularios y la cultura crítica de hoy." *Cuadernos americanos* 78 (1999): 168–206.

Cortiñas, Jorge Ignacio. *Blind Mouth Singing*. Introd. by Coco Fusco. TDR: *The Drama Review* 54.3 (2010): 12–53.

Coste, Didier. Letter to Reinaldo Arenas. Reinaldo Arenas Papers. Box 23, folder 6.

Cotter, Holland. "Art and AIDS: The Stuff Life Is Made Of." *Art in America*, April 1997, 50–56.

Crain, Irving J. *Psychiatry in Cuba*. New York: U.S.–Cuba Health Exchange, 1978.

Crimp, Douglas. *Melancholia and Moralism: Essays on AIDS and Queer Politics*. Cambridge: Massachusetts Institute of Technology Press, 2002.

Cruz-Malavé, Arnaldo. *El primitivo implorante: El "sistema poético del mundo" de José Lezama Lima*. Amsterdam: Rodopi, 1994.

Curbelo, Jesús David. *Diario de un poeta recién cazado*. Santiago de Cuba: Editorial Oriente, 1999.

Cuza Malé, Belkis. "Reinaldo y yo." *El nuevo herald*, 2 March 2001, 17A.

Davis, Natalie Zemon. "Women on Top." *Society and Culture in Early Modern France*. Stanford: Stanford University Press, 1975. 124–51.

"Declaration by the First National Congress on Education and Culture." *Granma Weekly Review*, 9 May 1971, 3–6.

Díaz, Duanel. *Palabras del trasfondo: Intelectuales, literatura e ideología en la Revolución Cubana*. Madrid: Colibrí, 2009.

Díaz, Roberto Ignacio. "Mercedes Merlin, la ópera y Reinaldo Arenas." *Fronteras de la literatura y de la crítica: Actas del XXXV Congreso Internacional de Literatura Iberoamericana*. Ed. Fernando Moreno et al. Poitiers: Centre de Recherches Latino-Américaines–Archivos, 2006. N. pag.

——. "Merlin's Foreign House: The Genres of *La Havane*." *Cuban Studies* 24 (1994): 57–82.

——. "Paratextual Snow; or, The Threshold of Mercedes Merlin." *Colby Quarterly* 32.4 (1996): 237–54.

Díaz Martínez, Manuel. "El caso Padilla: Crimen y castigo." *Encuentro de la cultura cubana* 4–5 (1997): 88–96.

Diccionario de la literatura cubana. 2 vols. Havana: Letras Cubanas, 1980, 1984.

Diego, Eliseo. "El silencio de los elogios: Eliseo Diego habla sobre Reinaldo Arenas." Interview by Camilo Barquet. *Enlace* 1.1 (1994): 1–4.

——. "Sobre *Celestino antes del alba*." *Casa de las Américas* 7.45 (1967): 162–66.

Diego, Josefina de. "Unos poemas de Eliseo Diego y un cuento de Reinaldo Arenas hallados en el estudio del poeta." *Encuentro de la cultura cubana* 12–13 (1999): 97–98.

Doane, Mary Ann. *Femmes Fatales: Feminism, Film Theory, Psychoanalysis*. New York: Routledge, 1991.

Domingo, Jorge. "Un submarino amarillo en el horizonte." *Unión* 7.19 (1995): 89–92.

Donoso, José. *Historia personal del "Boom."* Santiago de Chile: Aguilar Chilena de Ediciones, 1998.

Dos patrias Cuba y la noche. Dir. Christian Liffers. 2006.

Douglas, Mary. *Purity and Danger: An Analysis of the Concepts of Pollution and Taboo.* London: Routledge, 1966.

Dyer, Richard. "It's in His Kiss! Vampirism as Homosexuality, Homosexuality as Vampirism." *The Culture of Queers.* New York: Routledge, 2002. 70–89.

Eakin, Paul John. *Fictions in Autobiography: Studies in the Art of Self-Invention.* Princeton: Princeton University Press, 1985.

Echerri, Vicente. "*Antes que anochezca.*" *El nuevo herald*, 17 February 2001, 18A. Reprint, *CubaEncuentro*, 28 February 2001, http://arch.cubaencuentro.com/espejo/elcriticon/2001/02/28/1322.html, accessed 18 March 2010.

Edwards, Jorge. "Entrevista a Jorge Edwards." Interview by Roberto Valdés Muñoz. *La gaceta de Cuba* 6.63 (1968): 6.

Epps, Brad. "Proper Conduct: Reinaldo Arenas, Fidel Castro, and the Politics of Homosexuality." *Journal of the History of Sexuality* 6.2 (1995): 231–83.

Epstein, Julia. "AIDS, Stigma, and Narratives of Containment." *American Imago* 49.3 (1992): 293–310.

Epstein, William H., ed. *Contesting the Subject: Essays in the Postmodern Theory and Practice of Biography and Biographical Criticism.* West Lafayette: Purdue University Press, 1991.

Erni, John Nguyet. *Unstable Frontiers: Technomedicine and the Cultural Politics of "Curing" AIDS.* Minneapolis: University of Minnesota Press, 1994.

Espinosa Mendoza, Norge. "Historiar en el vacío: Arte, gays y espacio social en Cuba." *Encuentro de la cultura cubana* 41–42 (2006): 83–92.

———. "¿Otro color para una Cuba rosa?" *La Habana elegante* 42–43 (summer–fall 2008), http://www.habanaelegante.com/SummerFall2008/Ecos.html, accessed 4 January 2010.

Estévez, Abilio. "Between Nightfall and Vengeance: Remembering Reinaldo Arenas." *Michigan Quarterly Review* 33.4 (1994): 859–67.

Etter, Roberta, and Stuart Schneider. *Halley's Comet: Memories of 1910.* New York: Abbeville, 1985.

Evenson, Debra. *Revolution in the Balance: Law and Society in Contemporary Cuba.* Boulder: Westview, 1994.

"Exposición 'Clara Morera, Reinaldo Arenas y *El color del verano.*'" *CubaEncuentro*, 23 June 2011, http://www.cubaencuentro.com/cartelera/agenda/exposicion-clara-morera-reinaldo-arenas-y-el-color-del-verano-264515, accessed 4 August 2011.

"Expulsión." *La gaceta de Cuba* 6.66 (1968): 16.

Facio, Ángel. "Estreno de *La casa de Bernarda Alba* en España: Entrevista con Ángel Facio." Interview by M. Pérez Coterillo. *Primer Acto* 152 (1973): 13–16.

Feijóo, Samuel. "Revolución y vicios." *El mundo*, 15 April 1965, 5.

Ferenczi, Sandor. "The Ontogenesis of the Interest in Money." *Sex in Psycho-analysis*. Trans. Ernest Jones. New York: Dover, 1956. 269–79.

Fernández Robaina, Tomás. "Las arenas movedizas." Interview by Eliades Acosta Matos. *La jiribilla* 7 (June 2001), http://www.lajiribilla.co.cu/2001/n7_junio/182_7.html, accessed 24 August 2008.

———. "Carta acerca de *Antes que anochezca*, autobiografía de Reinaldo Arenas." *Journal of Hispanic Research* 1 (1992–93): 152–56.

———. "Los homosexuales y la Revolución." *Encuentro de la cultura cubana* 37–38 (2005): 286–92. A longer version: "El proyecto revolucionario y los homosexuales." *Consenso* 1 (2005), http://www.desdecuba.com/01/articulos/6_01.shtml, accessed 18 May 2008.

———. "Misa para un ángel." *La isla en peso* 18, http://www.uneac.org.cu/LaIslaEnPeso/num18/reverencia.htm, accessed 25 June 2009.

———. *Misa para un ángel*. Havana: Ediciones UNIÓN, 2010.

———. "Rei-surrección: Entrevista a Tomás Fernández Robaina." Interview by Carlos Velazco. *La gaceta de Cuba* 5 (2010): 32–36.

Fernández Soneira, Teresa. "La proximidad de Halley trae recuerdos." *El nuevo herald*, 17 February 1986, 11.

Fornet, Ambrosio. "A propósito de *Las iniciales de la tierra*." *Casa de las Américas* 164 (1987): 148–53.

———. "Una visión crítica." *La jiribilla* 237 (November 2005), http://www.lajiribilla.co.cu/2005/n237_11/237_33.html, accessed 11 April 2010.

Fowler Calzada, Víctor. "Arenas, el irreverente." *La nuez* 4.10–11 (1992): 22–23.

———. "Arenas: Homoerotismo y crítica de la cultura." *Apuntes posmodernos/Postmodern Notes* 6.1 (1995): 20–27.

———. *La maldición: Una historia del placer como conquista*. Havana: Letras Cubanas, 1998.

Freud, Sigmund. "Character and Anal Erotism." *The Standard Edition of the Complete Psychological Works of Sigmund Freud*. 24 vols. Ed. James Strachey. London: Hogarth, 1955–74. 9: 167–73.

———. "Leonardo da Vinci and a Memory of His Childhood." *The Standard Edition of the Complete Psychological Works of Sigmund Freud*. 24 vols. Ed. James Strachey. London: Hogarth, 1955–74. 11: 57–137.

———. "On Transformations of Instinct as Exemplified in Anal Erotism." *The Standard Edition of the Complete Psychological Works of Sigmund Freud*. 24 vols. Ed. James Strachey. London: Hogarth, 1955–74. 17: 125–33.

Fuentes, Oneida. "Donde las arenas son más diáfanas." Interview by Gabriel Pérez. *El caimán barbudo* 318 (2003): 22–23.

———. Letters to Reinaldo Arenas. Reinaldo Arenas Papers. Box 24, folder 8.

Fulleda, Gerardo. "Del pozo ciego a la libertad individual." Interview by Adonis Sánchez Cervera. *El caimán barbudo* 360 (2010), http://www.caimanbarbudo .cu/html_total/simpresas/articulos/360/index_07.html, accessed 27 December 2010.

Fuss, Diana. *Identification Papers*. New York: Routledge, 1995.

Gabriele, John P. "Mapping the Boundaries of Gender: Men, Women and Space in *La casa de Bernarda Alba*." *Hispanic Journal* 15 (1994): 381–92.

Gallo, Rubén. "Reinaldo Arenas and Severo Sarduy: Notes toward a History of a Friendship Gone Awry." *Princeton University Library Chronicle* 67.1 (2005): 86–94.

Gálvez, Joaquín. "Reinaldo Arenas antes que anochezca." *Reinaldo Arenas, aunque anochezca*. Ed. Luis de la Paz. Miami: Universal, 2001. 120.

García, María Cristina. *Havana USA: Cuban Exiles and Cuban Americans in South Florida, 1959–1994*. Berkeley: University of California Press, 1996.

García Buchaca, Edith. *La teoría de la superestructura: La literatura y el arte*. Havana: Ediciones del Consejo Nacional de Cultura, 1961.

García Galló, Gaspar Jorge. *El diversionismo ideológico*. Havana: Ministerio de Salud Pública, Hospital Psiquiátrico de La Habana, 1980.

——. *Nuestra moral socialista*. Havana: Editora del Ministerio de Educación, 1964.

García Lorca, Federico. *La casa de Bernarda Alba*. Ed. Allen Josephs and Juan Caballero. Madrid: Cátedra, 1988.

——. *The House of Bernarda Alba*. *Four Major Plays*. Trans. John Edmunds. New York: Oxford University Press, 1999. 117–72.

García Ronda, Denia et al. "Venturas y desventuras de la narrativa cubana actual." *Temas* 24–25 (2001): 165–92.

García Santos, Daniel. "La intolerancia anula la posibilidad de mutuo reconocimiento." Interview by Manuel Henríquez Lagarde. *La jiribilla* 5 (May 2001), http://www.lajiribilla.co.cu/2001/n5_mayo/087_5.html, accessed 25 July 2010.

Garrandés, Alberto. "El castillo de tierra roja." *CubaLiteraria*, 7 October 2004, http://www.cubaliteraria.com/articuloc.php?idarticulo=11363&idcolumna=22, accessed 24 July 2010.

——. *El concierto de las fábulas: Discursos, historia e imaginación en la narrativa cubana de los años sesenta*. Havana: Letras Cubanas, 2008.

——. "Fray Servando." *CubaLiteraria*, 14 October 2004, http://www.cubaliteraria .com/articuloc.php?idarticulo=11364&idcolumna=22, accessed 24 July 2010.

——, ed. *La ínsula fabulante: El cuento cubano en la Revolución, 1959–2008*. Havana: Letras Cubanas, 2008.

Genette, Gérard. *Palimpsests: Literature in the Second Degree*. Trans. Channa Newman and Claude Doubinsky. Lincoln: University of Nebraska Press, 1997.

Gibson, Ian. *Federico García Lorca: A Life*. New York: Pantheon, 1989.

Gilman, Sander L. "AIDS and Syphilis: The Iconography of Disease." *October* 43 (1987): 87–107.

———. *Picturing Health and Illness: Images of Identity and Difference*. Baltimore: Johns Hopkins University Press, 1995.

Ginsberg, Allen. "Ginsberg." Interview by Allen Young. *Gay Sunshine* 16 (1973): 1, 4–10.

Giralt, P., and M. Gutiérrez Lanza. "El cometa." *El diario de la marina*, 21 May 1910, 2.

Gómez Carriles, Lázaro. "Recordando a Reinaldo." *Reinaldo Arenas: Recuerdo y presencia*. Ed. Reinaldo Sánchez. Miami: Universal, 1994. 39–42.

González, Eduardo. *Cuba and the Fall: Christian Text and Queer Narrative in the Fiction of José Lezama Lima and Reinaldo Arenas*. Charlottesville: University of Virginia Press, 2010.

González, Reynaldo. *Cuba: Una asignatura pendiente*. Binissalem, Illes Balears: Di7 Comunicació, 1998.

González Domínguez, Yomar. "De gusano a mariposa: Crónica por el nacimiento de un infante." *Vitral* 5.25 (1998): 19–20.

González Echevarría, Roberto. "An Outcast of the Island." *New York Times Book Review*, 24 October 1993, 1, 32–33.

González Herrero, Lourdes. "El único extranjero." *Papeles de un naufragio*. Holguín: Ediciones Holguín, 1999. 27–28.

González Martín, Diego. "Algunas consideraciones críticas sobre la teoría freudiana." *Cuba Socialista*, May 1965, 60–78.

———. "Desarrollo de las ideas neurofisiológicas en Cuba en el curso del proceso revolucionario." *Jornada científica internacional: 30 aniversario del asalto al cuartel Moncada*. Ed. María Salomé Morales and Gaspar Quintana. Havana: Editorial de Ciencias Sociales, 1986. 658–74.

"Grandezas y miserias." *La jiribilla* 1 (May 2001), http://www.lajiribilla.co.cu/2001/nro1mayo2001.html, accessed 19 October 2009.

"El gran zoo." *La jiribilla* 1 (May 2001), http://www.lajiribilla.co.cu/2001/nro1mayo2001.html, accessed 19 October 2009.

Griffin, Gabriele. *Representations of HIV and AIDS: Visibility Blue/s*. Manchester: Manchester University Press, 2000.

Gropman, Donald. *Comet Fever: A Popular History of Halley's Comet*. New York: Simon, 1985.

Grover, Jan Zita. "AIDS: Keywords." *October* 43 (1987): 17–30.

Guerra, Lillian. "Gender Policing, Homosexuality and the New Patriarchy of the Cuban Revolution, 1965–70." *Social History* 35.3 (2010): 268–89.

Guevara, Ernesto "Che." "El socialismo y el hombre en Cuba." *El socialismo y el hombre nuevo*. Ed. José Aricó. Mexico City: Siglo Veintiuno, 1982. 3–17.

Halperin, David M. *"One Hundred Years of Homosexuality" and Other Essays on Greek Love*. New York: Routledge, 1990.

Hanson, Ellis. "Undead." *Inside/Out: Lesbian Theories, Gay Theories*. Ed. Diana Fuss. New York: Routledge, 1991. 324–40.

Hasson, Liliane. *Un Cubain libre: Reinaldo Arenas*. Arles: Actes Sud, 2007.

Havana. Dir. Jana Bokova. BBC, 1990.

Henríquez Ureña, Camila. "La literatura cubana en la Revolución." *Panorama de la literatura cubana*. Ed. José A. Portuondo et al. Havana: Centro de Estudios Cubanos, 1970. 209–39.

Heras León, Eduardo, and Desiderio Navarro, eds. *La política cultural del período revolucionario: Memoria y reflexión*. Havana: Centro Teórico-Cultural Criterios, 2008.

Hernández-Reguant, Ariana. "Copyrighting Che: Art and Authorship under Cuban Late Socialism." *Public Culture* 16.1 (2004): 1–29.

Hillson, Jon. *La política sexual de Reinaldo Arenas*. Havana: Letras Cubanas, 2002.

———. "La política sexual de Reinaldo Arenas: Realidad, ficción y el archivo real de la Revolución cubana." *La jiribilla* 1 (May 2001), http://www.lajiribilla.co.cu/2001/nro1mayo2001.html, accessed 19 October 2009. Reprint, *La jiribilla* 37 (January 2002), http://www.lajiribilla.co.cu/2002/nro37enero2002.html, accessed 19 October 2009.

———. "The Sexual Politics of Reinaldo Arenas: Fact, Fiction, and the Real Record of the Cuban Revolution." *Seeing Red* 4.2 (2001), http://www.seeingred.com/Copy/4.2_sexualpolitics.html, accessed 19 October 2009.

Hoffmann, George, ed. *The New Biographical Criticism*. Charlottesville: Rookwood, 2004.

Homer. *Iliad*. Trans. Richmond Lattimore. Chicago: University of Chicago Press, 1961.

Hoz, Pedro de la. *"Antes que anochezca*: ¿Arte o panfleto?" *La jiribilla* 1 (May 2001), http://www.lajiribilla.co.cu/2001/nro1mayo2001.html, accessed 19 October 2009.

Ichikawa, Emilio. "Cándido o el hedonismo." *Encuentro de la cultura cubana* 43 (2006–7): 91–98.

Infante, Rubén Ricardo. "Los diez cuentos del Celestino." *Ahora*, 18 September 2009, http://www.ahora.cu/secciones/cultura/864-los-diez-cuentos-del-celestino.html, accessed 20 August 2010.

"Inicio." *La isla en peso* 18, http://www.uneac.org.cu/LaIslaEnPeso/num18/inicio.htm, accessed 25 June 2009.

Isay, Richard A. *Being Homosexual: Gay Men and Their Development*. New York: Vintage, 2009.

Islas, Maya. "A Reinaldo Arenas: ¿El portero?" *Reinaldo Arenas, aunque anochezca.* Ed. Luis de la Paz. Miami: Universal, 2001. 118–19.

Jambrina, Jesús. "Con los ojos cerrados." *Perverso cubano.* Ed. Claribel Terré Morell. Buenos Aires: Editorial La Bohemia, 1999. 87–91.

———. "Hay que ser escritor." *La gaceta de Cuba* 37.1 (1999): 63.

Janjaque Chivaz, Aliomar. Kilometro Cero (blog), http://kilometro-0.blogspot .com, accessed 18 July 2010.

La jiribilla 1 (May 2001), http://www.lajiribilla.co.cu/2001/nro1mayo2001.html, accessed 19 October 2009.

"Joven literatura cubana." *Dédalo* 9 (2008): 1–8.

King, John. "The Boom of the Latin American Novel." *The Cambridge Companion to the Latin American Novel.* Ed. Efraín Kristal. New York: Cambridge University Press, 2005. 59–80.

Kristeva, Julia. *Powers of Horror: An Essay on Abjection.* Trans. Leon S. Roudiez. New York: Columbia University Press, 1982.

Kundera, Milan. *The Art of the Novel.* Trans. Linda Asher. New York: Harper and Row, 1988.

Kushigian, Julia A. *Reconstructing Childhood: Strategies of Reading for Culture and Gender in the Spanish American Bildungsroman.* Lewisburg, Pa.: Bucknell University Press, 2003.

Laffita, Ramón Elías. "La luz, otra vez la luz." *Palabras hacia la noche.* Guantanamo: Editorial El Mar y La Montaña, 2005. 34–36.

Landers, Timothy. "Bodies and Anti-bodies: A Crisis in Representation." *Global Television.* Ed. Cynthia Schneider and Brian Wallis. Cambridge: Massachusetts Institute of Technology Press, 1988. 281–99.

Laplanche, Jean. *New Foundations for Psychoanalysis.* Trans. David Macey. Cambridge: Basil Blackwell, 1989.

Laplanche, Jean, and Jean-Bertrand Pontalis. "Fantasy and the Origins of Sexuality." *International Journal of Psycho-analysis* 49.1 (1968): 1–18.

———. *The Language of Psychoanalysis.* Trans. Donald Nicholson-Smith. New York: W. W. Norton, 1973.

Laqueur, Thomas W. *Solitary Sex: A Cultural History of Masturbation.* New York: Zone Books, 2003.

Last Address. Dir. Ira Sachs. 2009.

Leiner, Marvin. *Sexual Politics in Cuba: Machismo, Homosexuality, and AIDS.* Boulder: Westview, 1994.

Ley 14. *Gaceta oficial de la República de Cuba,* 30 December 1977, 757–62.

Ley 1262. *Gaceta oficial de la República de Cuba,* 5 January 1974, 63–64.

Ley 1267. *Gaceta oficial de la República de Cuba,* 12 March 1974, 117–18.

Lezama Lima, José. *Cartas a Eloísa y otra correspondencia*. Ed. José Triana. Madrid: Verbum, 1998.

Llovio-Menéndez, José Luis. *Insider: My Hidden Life as a Revolutionary in Cuba*. Trans. Edith Grossman. New York: Bantam, 1988.

Lockwood, Lee. *Castro's Cuba, Cuba's Fidel: An American Journalist's Inside Look at Today's Cuba in Text and Picture*. New York: Macmillan, 1967.

Long, Thomas L. *AIDS and American Apocalypticism: The Cultural Semiotics of an Epidemic*. Albany: State University of New York Press, 2005.

Looby, Christopher. "'The Roots of the Orchis, the Iuli of Chesnuts': The Odor of Male Solitude." *Solitary Pleasures: The Historical, Literary, and Artistic Discourses of Autoeroticism*. Ed. Paula Bennett and Vernon A. Rosario. New York: Routledge, 1995. 163–87.

López, César. "Defender todo lo defendible, que es mucho." Interview by Orlando Castellanos. *La gaceta de Cuba* 2 (1998): 29–31.

———. "Mensajes de César López." *Consenso* 11 (2007), http://www.desdecuba .com/polemica/articulos/10_01.shtml, accessed 18 July 2010.

Loss, Jacqueline. *Cosmopolitanisms and Latin America against the Destiny of Place*. New York: Palgrave, 2005.

Lumsden, Ian. *Machos, Maricones, and Gays: Cuba and Homosexuality*. Philadelphia: Temple University Press, 1996.

Luz, Rodrigo de la. "A Reinaldo." *El ateje: Revista de literatura cubana* 7.19 (2007), http://www.elateje.com/0719/especial071908.htm, accessed 25 December 2010.

Manrique, Jaime. "After Night Falls: The Revival of Reinaldo Arenas." *Village Voice*, 12 December 2000, 67–68, 72.

———. "The Last Days of Reinaldo Arenas: A Sadness as Deep as the Sea." *Eminent Maricones: Arenas, Lorca, Puig, and Me*. Madison: University of Wisconsin Press, 1999. 62–69.

Mario, José. "Allen Ginsberg en La Habana." *Mundo nuevo* 34 (1969): 48–54.

———. "La verídica historia de ediciones El Puente: La Habana, 1961–1965." *Revista hispano cubana* 6 (2000): 89–100.

Marqués de Armas, Pedro. "Psiquiatría para el nuevo estado: algunos documentos." *La Habana elegante* 36 (winter 2006), http://www.habanaelegante .com/Winter2006/Panoptico.html, accessed 13 October 2009.

Marrón, Eugenio. "Un poeta que abre las constelaciones." *La jiribilla* 1 (May 2001), http://www.lajiribilla.co.cu/2001/nro1mayo2001.html, accessed 19 October 2009.

Martí, José. *Cuadernos de apuntes*. Vol. 21 of *Obras completas*. Havana: Editorial Nacional de Cuba, 1965.

Martin, Gerald. *Journeys through the Labyrinth: Latin American Fiction in the Twentieth Century*. New York: Verso, 1989.

Martín, Jorge. *Before Night Falls*. Albany Records, 2010.

Mayhew, Clemmer, III. "Sentenced to Tell the Truth." *Christopher Street* 210 (1994): 13–16.

McGrath, Charles, ed. *Books of the Century: A Hundred Years of Authors, Ideas and Literature*. New York: Times Books, 1998.

Melton, J. Gordon. *The Vampire Book: The Encyclopedia of the Undead*. Detroit: Visible Ink, 1994.

Méndez Rodenas, Adriana. *Gender and Nationalism in Colonial Cuba: The Travels of Santa Cruz y Montalvo, Condesa de Merlin*. Nashville: Vanderbilt University Press, 1998.

———. "Identity and Incest in *Cecilia Valdés*: Villaverde and the Origin(s) of the Text." *Cuban Studies* 24 (1994): 83–104.

Menéndez, Ana. "You Are the Heirs of All My Terrors." *Adios, Happy Homeland!* New York: Black Cat, 2011. 13–19.

Menéndez, Ronaldo. "Money." *El derecho al pataleo de los ahorcados*. Havana: Casa de las Américas, 1997. 63–76.

Menton, Seymour. *Prose Fiction of the Cuban Revolution*. Austin: University of Texas Press, 1975.

Mesa redonda sobre homosexualismo. Havana: Ministerio de Salud Pública, 1972.

Meyer, Richard. "Rock Hudson's Body." *Inside/Out: Lesbian Theories, Gay Theories*. Ed. Diana Fuss. New York: Routledge, 1991. 259–88.

Miller, D. A. "Anal Rope." *Inside/Out: Lesbian Theories, Gay Theories*. Ed. Diana Fuss. New York: Routledge, 1991. 119–41.

Miskulin, Sílvia Cezar. *Os intelectuais cubanos e a política cultural da Revolução, 1961–1975*. São Paulo: Alameda, 2009.

Molloy, Sylvia. "Childhood and Exile: The Cuban Paradise of the Countess of Merlin." *At Face Value: Autobiographical Writing in Spanish America*. New York: Cambridge University Press, 1991. 79–96.

Le Monde hallucinant / El mundo alucinante (video). An opera written by Chazam. Presented by Théâtre Molière, Bordeaux. Videosurf, 20 December 2007, http://www.videosurf.com/video/el-mundo-alucinante-133029878, accessed 25 December 2010.

Morales, Marcelo, Cristina Vives, and Sachie Hernández. "Informe sobre conducta impropia." *CubaEncuentro*, 12 November 2008, http://www.cubaencuentro.com/es/cultura/articulos/informe-sobre-conducta-impropia-131414, accessed 6 December 2009. Reprint, UNEAC: Unión de Escritores y Artistas de Cuba, 18 November 2008, http://www.uneac.org.cu/index.php?act=detalle&id=610&module=noticias, accessed 6 December 2009.

Morrison, James. "The Repression of the Returned: AIDS and Allegory." *AIDS: The Literary Response*. Ed. Emmanuel S. Nelson. New York: Twayne, 1992. 167–74.

Morson, Gary Saul, and Caryl Emerson. *Mikhail Bakhtin: Creation of a Prosaics.* Stanford: Stanford University Press, 1990.

Mudrovcic, María Eugenia. *"Mundo nuevo": Cultura y guerra fría en la década del 60.* Rosario: Beatriz Viterbo, 1997.

Murrieta, Fabio. "Las prisiones de Reinaldo Arenas." *Encuentro de la cultura cubana* 2 (1996): 131–38.

Nagy, Gregory. *The Best of the Achaeans: Concepts of the Hero in Archaic Greek Poetry.* Baltimore: Johns Hopkins University Press, 1979.

Navarrete, William. "Eclipse de sol." *Reinaldo Arenas, aunque anochezca.* Ed. Luis de la Paz. Miami: Universal, 2001. 121.

Negrón-Muntaner, Frances. "'Mariconerías' de Estado: Mariela Castro, los homosexuales y la política cubana." *Nueva sociedad* 218 (2008): 163–79.

"Neutralidad culposa." *La jiribilla* 1 (May 2001), http://www.lajiribilla.co.cu/2001/nro1mayo2001.html, accessed 19 October 2009.

"Notas de la UNEAC." *Unión* 4.4 (1965): 182.

"Noticias de Pueblo Mocho." *La jiribilla* 405 (February 2009), http://www.lajiribilla.co.cu/2009/n405_02/pueblomocho.html, accessed 25 July 2010.

Ocasio, Rafael. *Cuba's Political and Sexual Outlaw: Reinaldo Arenas.* Gainesville: University Press of Florida, 2003.

——. *A Gay Cuban Activist in Exile: Reinaldo Arenas.* Gainesville: University Press of Florida, 2007.

Olivares, Jorge. "Carnival and the Novel: Reinaldo Arenas's *El palacio de las blanquísimas mofetas.*" *Hispanic Review* 53.4 (1985): 467–76.

Olivares Baró, Carlos. *La orfandad del esplendor.* Mexico City: Editorial Aldus, 1995.

Orovio, Helio. *300 boleros de oro.* Havana: UNEAC, 1991.

Ortega, Julio. "La escritura del exilio." *Escandalar* 2.2 (1979): 87–90.

Otero, Lisandro. *Llover sobre mojado: Una reflexión personal sobre la historia.* Havana: Letras Cubanas, 1997.

Ozimek-Maier, Janis. "Power Plays in *La casa de Bernarda Alba.*" *Things Done with Words: Speech Acts in Hispanic Drama.* Ed. Elias L. Rivers. Newark: Juan de la Cuesta, 1986. 73–84.

Padgug, Robert A. "Gay Villain, Gay Hero: Homosexuality and the Social Construction of AIDS." *Passion and Power: Sexuality in History.* Ed. Kathy Peiss and Christina Simmons. Philadelphia: Temple University Press, 1989. 293–313.

Padilla, Heberto. *Fuera del juego: Edición conmemorativa 1968–1998.* Miami: Universal, 1998.

——. *Self-Portrait of the Other.* Trans. Alexander Coleman. New York: Farrar, Straus and Giroux, 1990.

Parker, Andrew. "Grafting David Cronenberg: Monstrosity, AIDS Media, National/Sexual Difference." *Stanford Humanities Review* 3.1 (1993): 7–21.

Pastrana, Déborah. "Un espectáculo flamenco en homenaje a Reinaldo Arenas en el festival de teatro gay." *El mundo*, 15 September 2010, http://www.elmundo.es/ elmundo/2010/09/15/andalucia_malaga/1284544167.html, accessed 25 December 2010.

Pater, Walter. *The Renaissance: Studies in Art and Poetry. The 1893 Text*. Ed. Donald L. Hill. Berkeley: University of California Press, 1980.

Pau-Llosa, Ricardo. "Reinaldo Arenas." *Cuba*. Pittsburgh: Carnegie Mellon University Press, 1993. 87.

Pedraza, Silvia. *Political Disaffection in Cuba's Revolution and Exodus*. New York: Cambridge University Press, 2007.

Pereda, Alcides. *La lluvia que trajo el viento*. Holguín: Ediciones La Luz, 2009.

Pérez, Jorge Ángel. *El paseante Cándido*. Havana: Ediciones UNIÓN, 2001.

Pérez Castillo, Ernesto. "Escribir no es una carrera." Interview by Leopoldo Luis. *El caimán barbudo* 350 (2008): 4–5.

Pérez Galdós, Benito. *Fortunata and Jacinta: Two Stories of Married Women*. Trans. Agnes Moncy Gullón. Athens: University of Georgia Press, 1986.

———. *Fortunata y Jacinta: Dos historias de casadas*. 2 vols. Ed. Santiago Fortuño Llorens. Madrid: Castalia, 2003.

Pérez Rivero, Pedro. *Del portal hacia dentro*. Guantanamo: Editorial El Mar y La Montaña, 2002.

———. *De Sodoma vino un ángel*. Santiago de Cuba: Editorial Oriente, 2004.

Pérez Villar, José, et al. "El afeminamiento en el niño." *Psicología y educación* 8.2 (1965): 55–69.

Piñera Arenas, Óscar [Santiago Martín]. *Amaos los unos a los otros*. Madrid: Betania, 2006.

Pogolotti, Graziella. "Loló, la república, el cometa." *Mujeres latinoamericanas del siglo XX: Historia y cultura*. 2 vols. Ed. Luisa Campuzano. Havana: Casa de las Américas, 1998. 1: 123–29.

———, ed. *Polémicas culturales de los 60*. Havana: Letras Cubanas, 2006.

Ponte, Antonio José. "Un arte de hacer ruinas." Interview by Néstor E. Rodríguez. *Revista iberoamericana* 68.198 (2002): 179–86.

———. *Villa Marista en plata: Arte, política, nuevas tecnologías*. Madrid: Colibrí, 2010.

Portela, Ena Lucía. "El escalofrío y la carcajada." *Babelia* (cultural supplement of *El país*), 28 April 2007, 4. Reprint, *Revista voces* 3 (14 November 2010), http:// vocescuba.com/2010/11/14/el-escalofrio-y-la-carcajada-ena-lucia-portela, accessed 4 February 2011.

———. "No me hagas preguntas capciosas." Interview by Saylín Álvarez Oquendo. *La Habana elegante* 48 (fall–winter 2010), http://www.habanaelegante.com/Fall _Winter_2010/Entrevista_Portela.html, accessed 4 February 2011.

Portuondo, José Antonio. *Itinerario estético de la Revolución cubana*. Havana: Letras Cubanas, 1979.

Prats, Delfín. Letter to Roberto *y demás*. Reinaldo Arenas Papers. Box 25, folder 14.

——. "Yo tengo un mal karma: Entrevista a Delfín Prats." Interview by Leandro Estupiñán Zaldívar. *La gaceta de Cuba* 3 (2006): 22–26.

Prats Sariol, José. "Entrevista con el escritor cubano José Prats Sariol." Interview by Carlos Manuel Estefanía. *CubaNuestra Digital*, 27 September 2005, http://www.cubanuestra.nu/web/article.asp?artID=2797, accessed 18 November 2005.

——. *Guanabo Gay*. Villahermosa, Tabasco, Mexico: Horayveinte, 2004.

——. *Mariel*. Mexico City: Editorial Aldus, 1997.

——. "La voz de *Guanabo Gay*." *CubaEncuentro*, 16 August 2004, http://archi.cubaencuentro.com/cultura/20040816/7f37dca0873677e6f6bb9f180ab442ce.html, accessed 15 February 2010.

"Premio de Cuento." *La gaceta de Cuba* 1 (2009): 14.

"Premio UNEAC de Novela Cirilo Villaverde." *La gaceta de Cuba* 5.53 (1966): 2.

Prendergast, Christopher. *Balzac, Fiction and Melodrama*. London: Edward Arnold, 1978.

Prieto Morales, Abel. "Homosexualismo." *Bohemia*, 21 February 1969, 108–9, 113.

Prieto Taboada, Antonio. "Cómo vivir en ningún sitio: Entrando y saliendo del exilio con Reinaldo Arenas." *Revista hispánica moderna* 55.1 (2002): 168–87.

Prosser, Jay. *Second Skins: The Body Narratives of Transsexuality*. New York: Columbia University Press, 1998.

Quintero Herencia, Juan Carlos. *Fulguración del espacio: Letras e imaginario institucional de la Revolución cubana (1960–1971)*. Rosario: Beatriz Viterbo, 2002.

Quiroga, José. *Cuban Palimpsests*. Minneapolis: University of Minnesota Press, 2005.

Rama, Ángel. *Diario 1974–1983*. Montevideo: Ediciones Trilce, 2001.

——. Letters to Reinaldo Arenas. Reinaldo Arenas Papers. Box 26, folder 4.

——. "Las malandanzas de Reinaldo Arenas." *El universal* (Culturales), 12 September 1982, 3.

——, ed. *Novísimos narradores hispanoamericanos en marcha, 1964–1980*. Mexico City: Marcha, 1981.

——. "Política y naturaleza de los exilios latinoamericanos." *Escandalar* 4.1 (1981): 77–80.

——. "Reinaldo Arenas al ostracismo." *Eco* 231 (1981): 332–36.

——. "La riesgosa navegación del escritor exiliado." *Revista de la Universidad de México* 32.9 (1978): 1–10.

——. "Una nueva política cultural en Cuba." *Cuadernos de Marcha* 49 (1971): 47–68.

Reinaldo Arenas (A True Story). Dir. Lucas Leyva. Borscht Corp., 2011.

Reyes, Dean Luis. "Páginas de Celestino." *La jiribilla* 1 (May 2001), http://www
.lajiribilla.co.cu/2001/nro1mayo2001.html, accessed 19 October 2009.

Rich, Adrienne. *Of Woman Born: Motherhood as Experience and Institution.* New
York: Norton, 1976.

Riverón, Rogelio. "Como quiere que lo vean, se esconde." *La gaceta de Cuba* 1
(2001): 60–61.

———. "Ruptura y tradición." Interview by Johanna Puyol. *La jiribilla* 405 (February 2009), http://www.lajiribilla.co.cu/2009/n405_02/405_13.html, accessed 25
July 2010.

Roberts, Anna. "Queer Fisher King: Castration as a Site of Queer Representation
(*Perceval, Stabat Mater, The City of God*)." *Arthuriana* 11.3 (2001): 49–88.

Rodríguez Feo, José. "Breve recuento de la narrativa cubana." *Unión* 6.4 (1967):
131–36.

Rodríguez Monegal, Emir. *El boom de la novela latinoamericana.* Caracas: Editorial
Tiempo Nuevo, 1972.

Rojas, Rafael. *El estante vacío: Literatura y política en Cuba.* Barcelona: Anagrama,
2009.

———. *Tumbas sin sosiego: Revolución, disidencia y exilio del intelectual cubano.*
Barcelona: Anagrama, 2006.

Romero Tobar, Leonardo. *La novela popular española del siglo XIX.* Madrid: Ariel,
1976.

Ronet, Jorge. *La mueca de la paloma negra.* Ed. Néstor Almendros. Madrid:
Playor, 1987.

Ros, Enrique. *La UMAP: El Gulag castrista.* Miami: Universal, 2004.

Rosen, Ruth. *The Lost Sisterhood: Prostitution in America, 1900–1918.* Baltimore:
Johns Hopkins University Press, 1982.

Rozencvaig, Perla. *Reinaldo Arenas: Narrativa de transgresión.* Mexico City: Oasis,
1986.

Rubio, Lydia. Publicity flyer for her exhibit *Fragments of the Sea.* Museum of Art.
Fort Lauderdale, Florida, 20 February–5 May 1998.

Sadownick, Douglas. "My Father, My Self: Coming Out Inside as the Next Stage
of Gay Liberation." *The Man I Might Become: Gay Men Write about Their Fathers.*
Ed. Bruce Shenitz. New York: Marlowe, 2002. 63–77.

———. *Sex between Men: An Intimate History of the Sex Lives of Gay Men, Postwar to
Present.* San Francisco: HarperSanFrancisco, 1996.

Salas, Luis. *Social Control and Deviance in Cuba.* New York: Praeger, 1979.

Salomón-Beckford, Luis. *La formación del hombre nuevo en Cuba.* Havana: Editorial
de Ciencias Sociales, 1986.

Sánchez-Eppler, Benigno. "Call My Son Ismael: Exiled Paternity and Father/Son
Eroticism in Reinaldo Arenas and José Martí." *differences* 6.1 (1994): 69–97.

———. "Reinaldo Arenas, Re-writer Revenant, and the Re-patriation of Cuban Homoerotic Desire." *Queer Diasporas*. Ed. Cindy Patton and Benigno Sánchez-Eppler. Durham: Duke University Press, 2000. 154–82.

Santa Cruz y Montalvo, María de las Mercedes, Condesa de Merlin. *La Habana*. Trans. Amalia E. Bacardí. Madrid: Cronocolor, 1981.

———. *Mis doce primeros años* and *Historia de Sor Inés*. Havana: Imprenta "El Siglo XX," 1922.

———. *Viaje a La Habana*. Ed. Imeldo Álvarez. Havana: Editorial de Arte y Literatura, 1974.

Santí, Enrico Mario. "Introducción." *El mundo alucinante*. By Reinaldo Arenas. Ed. Enrico Mario Santí. Madrid: Cátedra, 2008. 15–73.

———. "The Life and Times of Reinaldo Arenas." *Michigan Quarterly Review* 23.2 (1984): 227–36.

Santiago, Héctor. "Reinaldo Arenas, las cucarachas y yo." *Reinaldo Arenas, aunque anochezca*. Ed. Luis de la Paz. Miami: Universal, 2001. 194–98.

Sarduy, Severo. "Diario de la peste." *Vuelta* 206 (1994): 33–35.

———. "Escrito sobre Arenas." *Revista de la Universidad de México* 40.39 (1984): 41–43.

———. Letters to Reinaldo Arenas. Reinaldo Arenas Papers. Box 26, folder 7.

———. Telegram to Reinaldo Arenas. Reinaldo Arenas Papers. Box 26, folder 7.

Saslow, James M. "Daddy Was a Hot Number." *The Man I Might Become: Gay Men Write about Their Fathers*. Ed. Bruce Shenitz. New York: Marlowe, 2002. 55–61.

Sassoon, Donald. *Becoming "Mona Lisa": The Making of a Global Icon*. New York: Harcourt, 2001.

Savran, David. *Communists, Cowboys, and Queers: The Politics of Masculinity in the Work of Arthur Miller and Tennessee Williams*. Minneapolis: University of Minnesota Press, 1992.

Schehr, Lawrence R. *Parts of an Andrology: On Representations of Men's Bodies*. Stanford: Stanford University Press, 1997.

Schor, Naomi. "Fiction as Interpretation/Interpretation as Fiction." *The Reader in the Text*. Ed. Susan R. Suleiman and Inge Crosman. Princeton: Princeton University Press, 1980. 165–82.

Schwartz, Debora B. "'A la guise de Gales l'atorna': Maternal Influence in Chrétien's *Conte du Graal*." *Essays in Medieval Studies* 12 (1995): 95–118.

Schwartz, Kessel. *A New History of Spanish American Fiction*. 2 vols. Coral Gables: University of Miami Press, 1971–72.

Schwartz, Lillian. "Leonardo's *Mona Lisa*." *Art and Antiques*, January 1987, 50–54.

Segarra Báez, Iván. "Antes que anochezca." Los-poetas.com, http://www.los-poetas.com/m/ivan1.htm, accessed 25 December 2010.

Seres extravagantes. Dir. Manuel Zayas. Malas Compañías and Doce Gatos, 2004.

Sergent, Bernard. *Homosexuality in Greek Myth*. Trans. Arthur Goldhammer. Boston: Beacon, 1986.

Sierra Madero, Abel. *Del otro lado del espejo: La sexualidad en la construcción de la nación cubana*. Havana: Casa de las Américas, 2006.

Silverman, Kaja. *Male Subjectivity at the Margins*. New York: Routledge, 1992.

Silverstein, Charles. *Man to Man: Gay Couples in America*. New York: Quill, 1982.

Simon, Bennett, and Rachel B. Blass. "The Development and Vicissitudes of Freud's Ideas on the Oedipus Complex." *The Cambridge Companion to Freud*. Ed. Jerome Neu. New York: Cambridge University Press, 1991. 161–74.

Smith, Paul Julian. *Vision Machines: Cinema, Literature, and Sexuality in Spain and Cuba, 1983–1993*. New York: Verso, 1996.

Smith, Verity. "'Obedezco pero no cumplo': An Introduction to the Work of the Holguín Poets." *Cuban Studies* 22 (1992): 173–93.

Smith, Webster. "Observations on the *Mona Lisa* Landscape." *Art Bulletin* 67.2 (1985): 183–99.

Smorkaloff, Pamela Maria. *Readers and Writers in Cuba: A Social History of Print Culture, 1830s–1990s*. New York: Garland, 1997.

Sorensen, Diana. *A Turbulent Decade Remembered: Scenes from the Latin American Sixties*. Stanford: Stanford University Press, 2007.

Soroa, José. "Reinaldo y Selene." *El ateje: Revista de literatura cubana* 7.19 (2007), http://www.elateje.com/0719/especial071910.htm, accessed 25 December 2010.

Soto, Francisco. *Reinaldo Arenas*. New York: Twayne, 1998.

———. *Reinaldo Arenas: The Pentagonía*. Gainesville: University Press of Florida, 1994.

Sprengnether, Madelon. *The Spectral Mother: Freud, Feminism, and Psychoanalysis*. Ithaca: Cornell University Press, 1990.

Stallybrass, Peter, and Allon White. *The Politics and Poetics of Transgression*. Ithaca: Cornell University Press, 1986.

Staten, Henry. *Eros in Mourning: Homer to Lacan*. Baltimore: Johns Hopkins University Press, 1995.

Stoffman, Judy. "Writing Was Reinaldo Arenas's Best Revenge." *Toronto Star*, 3 February 2001, 4.

Stott, Rebecca. *The Fabrication of the Late-Victorian Femme Fatale*. London: Macmillan, 1992.

Strong, Lester. "Openly Gay José Luis Cortés's First Solo Show Tracks an Adventurous Time in the Artist's Life." *Out*, December 2003, 40.

Swanson, Philip. *Latin American Fiction: A Short Introduction*. Oxford: Blackwell, 2005.

Tesis y resoluciones: Primer congreso del Partido Comunista de Cuba. Havana: Departamento de Orientación Revolucionaria del Comité Central del Partido Comunista de Cuba, 1976.

Tobin, Patricia Drechsel. *Time and the Novel: The Genealogical Imperative.* Princeton: Princeton University Press, 1978.

Treichler, Paula A. "AIDS, Homophobia, and Biomedical Discourse: An Epidemic of Signification." *October* 43 (1987): 31–70.

Ubieta Gómez, Enrique. "Arenas y la noche: Notas sobre un libro de memorias." *La jiribilla* 1 (May 2001), http://www.lajiribilla.co.cu/2001/nro1mayo2001.html, accessed 19 October 2009.

Urrea, Beatriz. "Silencio, amor y muerte: El homosexual y la mujer en la obra de García Lorca." *Bulletin of Hispanic Studies* 74 (1997): 37–58.

Valdés, Zoé. *La ficción Fidel.* New York: Rayo, 2008.

Valdés Díaz, Caridad del Carmen. "Acerca de la autoría y la titularidad en el contexto jurídico cubano: ¿El estado como titular del derecho de autor?" *Revista cubana de derecho* 32 (2008): 72–95.

———. "Otra perspectiva: Duración y dominio público de las obras del espíritu en el derecho cubano." *La duración de la propiedad intelectual y las obras en dominio público.* Ed. Carlos Rogel Vide. Madrid: Editorial Reus, 2005. 289–324.

Valero, Roberto. "La tétrica mofeta en su palacio blanquísimo." *Arenas: Recuerdo y presencia.* Ed. Reinaldo Sánchez. Miami: Universal, 1994. 43–49.

———. "Los últimos tiempos de Reinaldo Arenas." *Diario las Américas*, 29 March 1991, 5A, 13A. Reprinted as "'Ay, qué lindo tienes el pelo': Un testimonio de los últimos tiempos de Arenas." *La escritura de la memoria: Reinaldo Arenas: Textos, estudios y documentación.* Ed. Ottmar Ette. Frankfurt am Main: Vervuert, 1992. 29–32.

Valero, Roberto, Liliane Hasson, and Ottmar Ette. "Bibliografía areniana." *La escritura de la memoria: Reinaldo Arenas: Textos, estudios y documentación.* Ed. Ottmar Ette. Frankfurt am Main: Vervuert, 1992. 177–231.

Valle, Amir. "Escribo de la marginalidad porque vivo en esos barrios." Interview by Raúl Tápanes López. *Cuba Underground*, 21 October 2006, http://www.cuba underground.com/revista-de-opinion/entrevista-al-escritor-y-periodista-amir-valle, accessed 17 August 2010.

Varona Roque, Mariela. "Anna Lidia Vega Serova lee un cuento erótico en el patio de un museo colonial." *La gaceta de Cuba* 1 (2002): 3–6.

Velazco, Carlos. "Cópula con Reinaldo Arenas." UNEAC: Unión de Escritores y Artistas de Cuba, http://www.uneac.org.cu/index.php?module=columna_autor&act=columna_autor&id=131, accessed 4 February 2011.

Victoria, Carlos. "La catarata." *Apuntes posmodernos/Postmodern Notes* 6.1 (1995): 36–38.

———. "La estrella fugaz." *El resbaloso y otros cuentos.* Miami: Universal, 1997. 9–39.

"La vida en rosa." *La jiribilla* 37 (January 2002), http://www.lajiribilla.co.cu/2002/nro37enero2002.html, accessed 25 March 2006.

Vidal, Leidy. *Vida vs. crisis: El incesto y la literatura*. Matanzas: Ediciones Matanzas, 2008.

Villaverde, Fernando. "Pugna entre tres escritores en el exilio." *El Miami Herald*, 10 April 1983, 1, 9.

"La voz homoerótica." *La gaceta de Cuba* 5 (2003): 2–24.

Walsh, John K. "A Logic in Lorca's *Ode to Walt Whitman*." *¿Entiendes? Queer Readings, Hispanic Writings*. Ed. Emilie L. Bergmann and Paul Julian Smith. Durham: Duke University Press, 1995. 257–78.

Watney, Simon. *Policing Desire: Pornography, AIDS and the Media*. London: Methuen, 1987.

———. "Short-Term Companions: AIDS as Popular Entertainment." *A Leap in the Dark: AIDS, Art and Contemporary Cultures*. Ed. Allan Klusacek and Ken Morrison. Montreal: Véhicule, 1992. 152–66.

———. "The Spectacle of AIDS." *October* 43 (1987): 71–86.

West, Alan. "Sones peregrinos." *Encuentro de la cultura cubana* 2 (1996): 105–11.

———. *Tropics of History: Cuba Imagined*. Westport, Conn.: Bergin and Garvey, 1997.

White, Edmund. "Gay Autofiction: The Sacred and the Real." *The Dissident Word*. Ed. Chris Miller. New York: Basic Books, 1996. 93–114.

Whitfield, Esther. *Cuban Currency: The Dollar and "Special Period" Fiction*. Minneapolis: University of Minnesota Press, 2008.

Williamson, Judith. "Every Virus Tells a Story: The Meanings of HIV and AIDS." *Taking Liberties*. Ed. Erica Carter and Simon Watney. London: Serpent's Tail, 1989. 69–80.

Wolfgang, Lenora D. "Perceval's Father: Problems in Medieval Narrative Art." *Romance Philology* 34.1 (1980): 28–47.

Wood, Michael. "No Sorrow Left Unturned." *New York Review of Books*, 7 March 1991, 21–23.

Yndurain, Francisco. *Galdós entre la novela y el folletín*. Madrid: Taurus, 1970.

Young, Allen. *Gays under the Cuban Revolution*. San Francisco: Grey Fox, 1981.

Zayas, Manuel. "Mapa de la homofobia." *CubaEncuentro*, 20 January 2006, http://www.cubaencuentro.com/es/cuba/articulos/mapa-de-la-homofobia-10736, accessed 9 July 2009.

·INDEX·

20–21, 27, 33, 63, 134, 157, 177n33; as protégé of Cuba's literati, 16, 24; publishing difficulties of (outside Cuba), 28, 29, 153; rhetoric of indirection in works of, 6, 20, 115, 144; on sex and writing, 33, 177n33; socialist realism and, 5, 17, 20, 41, 152; suicide of, 14, 33–34, 66, 114, 135, 143, 153, 189n6, 194n44; unpublished early novels of, 15, 52, 55; on U.S. gay sexual culture, 27–28; U.S. Latinos and, 26, 27, 28, 150, 153; winner of storytelling competition, 15–16; works of, circulation/reception in Cuba, 6, 154–70, 195n8, 198nn21–22, 198n24, 199nn25–27, 200n28, 200n32; works of, smuggled out of Cuba, 7, 8, 18, 20, 22, 28, 30, 36, 153, 173n1. *See also titles of individual works*

Arencibia Rodríguez, Lourdes, 160–63, 195n8, 198n23

Armand, Octavio, 29, 177n29

Arrufat, Antón, 13

Arturo, la estrella más brillante (*The Brightest Star*) (Arenas), 89, 107–8, 161, 164, 178n34, 195n8; mother figure in, 108, 188n14; Patroclus in, 108. See also *Asalto, El*; *Iliad*

Asalto, El (*The Assault*) (Arenas), 104–5, 108, 153, 155, 161, 164, 178n34, 188n12, 188n14; biographical reading of, 107; Castro, Fidel, in, 106–7; as culmination of *Arturo, la estrella más brillante*, 107–8; the *Iliad* in, 107, 108; incest in, 107, 108; matricide and matrophobia in, 105, 106–7; oedipal telemachy in, 105. See also *Arturo, la estrella más brillante*; *Iliad*; *pentagonía*

Assault, The (Arenas). See *Asalto, El*

Bachelet, Michelle, 166

Badías, María Elena, 132, 133, 142

Bakhtin, Mikhail, 100, 187n3

Bardem, Javier, 154

Barnet, Miguel, 165, 176n19

Barquet, Jesús, 23

Batista, Fulgencio, 15, 24, 36, 38, 45, 46

Bautista, María Luisa, 73, 74, 184n12

Before Night Falls (Arenas). See *Antes que anochezca*

Bejel, Emilio, 173n2

Bellini, Vincenzo: *Norma*, 202n39

"Benítez entra en el juego" (Arenas), 180n9

Benítez Rojo, Antonio, 164, 180n9

Bersani, Leo, 125–26, 193n34

Biblioteca Nacional José Martí, 15–16, 40, 195n8, 200n28

biographical criticism, 2, 3

Bloch, R. Howard, 181n24

Bobes, Marilyn, 198n22

Boom, the (Latin American novel of the 1960s), 1, 148, 150, 151, 152, 154, 193n37

Bosch, Hieronymus, 139

Brightest Star, The (Arenas). See *Arturo, la estrella más brillante*

Browning, Richard L., 58

bugarrones, 21

Bush, Andrew, 180n17

Cabrera, Lydia, 177n29

Cabrera Infante, Guillermo, 1, 3, 8, 19, 148, 150, 152, 164, 184n12; *Tres tristes tigres*, 1, 148, 195n3

Calinescu, Matei, 85

Callen, Michael, 190n16

Camacho, Jorge and Margarita, 17–18, 22, 23, 28, 33, 110, 111, 176n27, 178n34, 194n47

fatherland. See *patria*

Feijóo, Samuel, 8–9

Fernández Robaina, Tomás, 16, 162, 163; *Misa para un ángel*, 163, 182n3

Final de un cuento (Arenas), 178n34, 187n1, 201n37

Fornet, Ambrosio, 12, 155, 160, 162, 165

Fortunata y Jacinta (*Fortunata and Jacinta*) (Pérez Galdós), 4, 38, 39, 40, 41–43, 59, 179nn3–4; paternity in, 39, 41, 42, 43. *See also* Pérez Galdós, Benito

Fowler Calzada, Víctor, 198n22

Freud, Sigmund, 5, 11, 106, 185n18; on anality, 70; on homosexuality, 183n4; on preoedipal mother, 188n17

Freyre de Andrade, María Teresa, 16

Fuentes, Carlos (Arenas's uncle), 186n21

Fuentes, Carlos (writer), 151

Fuentes, Oneida, 4, 5, 6, 14, 15, 66–69, 70, 71, 85, 87, 92, 105, 106, 109, 110, 111, 112–13, 115, 143–47, 163, 181n20, 182n3, 183n5, 183n8, 186n21, 186nn23–24, 188n16, 192n32, 194n46, 195nn48–49

Fundación LGBT Reinaldo Arenas, 167, 200n33

Fuss, Diana, 106

García Buchaca, Edith, 179n8

García Galló, Gaspar Jorge, 10

García Lorca, Federico, 5, 38, 91, 92–93, 94, 97, 98, 100, 101, 102, 104, 111, 112, 113, 160, 188n9. See also *Casa de Bernarda Alba, La*

García Márquez, Gabriel, 32, 148, 150, 151, 177n32, 180n9

Garrandés, Alberto, 163, 195n3, 200n30

gay sexual culture (U.S.), 27–28

Genette, Gérard, 91

Gilman, Sander L., 125, 191n21, 193n33

Ginsberg, Allen, 174n8

Gómez Carriles, Lázaro, 32, 171, 178n35

González, Eduardo, 181n26

González Domínguez, Yomar, 154–55

"Goodbye Mother" (Arenas). *See* "Adiós a mamá"

Graveyard of the Angels (Arenas). See *Loma del Ángel, La*

Guevara, Ernesto (Che), 8, 174n8

Guillén, Nicólas, 164

Halley's Comet, 92, 96, 97, 101, 112; and Cuba in 1910, 111–12, 187n2; history and myth of, 187n2. *See also* "Cometa Halley, El"

"Halley's Comet" (Arenas). *See* "Cometa Halley, El"

Hanson, Ellis, 125, 127, 130, 192n31

Harss, Luis, 30

Hart, Armando, 12

Hasson, Liliane, 31, 32, 68, 137, 185n16

Havana (film), 14, 88, 183n7, 188n17, 201n37

Henríquez Ureña, Camila, 18, 176n21

Hernández, Guillermo, 184n14

Hernández, Ivette, 19

Hillson, Jon, 156, 157, 159, 196n12, 197n19, 198n22

HIV. See AIDS and HIV

homosexuality: anal sex and, 21, 125–26, 127, 134, 193n34; capitalism and, 8, 9; the Cuban Revolution and, 9, 10–11, 12, 17, 20–21, 173n2, 174n8, 174n10, 197n17; as disease, 10, 134; Freud on, 183n4; the law (in Cuba) and, 11, 159, 197n17; the Mariel boatlift and, 14, 24; as monstrosity, 190n10; "phantom father" and,

184n10; revolutionary social hygiene and, 9; as social pathology, 11; as vampirism, 126. *See also* AIDS and HIV

House of Bernarda Alba, The (García Lorca). See *Casa de Bernarda Alba, La*

Hoz, Pedro de la, 156, 157

identity politics, 27

Iliad (Homer): Arenas and, 65, 74–76, 90, 107, 185n15; automourning in, 75, 184nn13–14; fathers and sons in, 75–76; homosexuality in, 107; Patroclus as father figure in, 107. See also *Arturo, la estrella más brillante*; *Asalto, El*

Ill-Fated Peregrinations of Fray Servando, The (Arenas). See *Mundo alucinante, El*

Inferno (Arenas), 178n34

Instituto Cubano del Libro, 18, 161

James, Henry, 38

Jiménez Leal, Orlando, 10; *Conducta impropia* (film), 201n37

Jiribilla, La, 162, 165, 166, 196n12, 198nn21–22, 199n27; inaugural issue of (on Arenas), 156–60

Koch, Dolores, 73, 120, 123

Kristeva, Julia: on abjection, 187n5

Kundera, Milan, 83, 84

Kushigian, Julia, 39, 181n22

Labrador Ruiz, Enrique, 164

Lagarde, Joris, 22

Laplanche, Jean, 71, 74, 185n18

Last Address (film), 201n37

Latcham, Ricardo, 8

laws (Cuban): censorship and, 18, 167;

copyright, 166; *diversionismo ideológico* and, 13, 18; emigration and, 14; employment, 23; homosexuality and, 11, 159, 197n17

Lazarillo de Tormes, 180n11

Lecuona, Ernesto: "Noche azul" (bolero), 54, 55

Leonardo da Vinci, 115, 116, 120, 121, 123, 124, 125, 126, 128, 129, 130, 131, 132, 133, 134, 135, 141, 142, 147, 191n19, 192n30, 192n32. See also *Mona Lisa* (Leonardo da Vinci)

Leprosorio (Arenas), 59, 178n34

Lezama Lima, José, 13, 17, 23, 25, 41, 60–61, 150, 152, 164, 179n7, 184n11; as father figure to Arenas, 72, 73–74; homosexuality and, 72, 184n12; *Paradiso*, 1, 17, 73, 148, 180n11, 195n3; paternal longing and 184n12

"Lezama o el reino de la imagen" (Arenas), 41, 60–61, 179n7

"Literatura cubana dentro y fuera de Cuba, La" (Arenas), 63, 181n27

locas (queens), 21, 27, 123, 139

Loma del Ángel, La (*Graveyard of the Angels*) (Arenas), 89, 164, 178n34, 189n5; incest in, 62; as parody of *Cecilia Valdés*, 38, 41, 62, 63, 101; as a provocative love story, 63. See also *Cecilia Valdés*; Villaverde, Cirilo

López, César, 200n32

Loss, Jacqueline, 193n37, 195n7

MacAdam, Alfred J., 182n28

"Magia y persecución en José Martí" (Arenas), 19

Manrique, Jaime, 31, 32, 34

Mariel: boatlift, 4, 14, 24, 25, 117, 175n16, 176n26, 200n34; generation of writers, 14, 195n8

Mario, José, 174n8, 197n18

Marrón, Eugenio, 157, 160

Martí, José, 19, 20, 102, 185n20, 194n44

Martin, Gerald, 152

Martín, Jorge: *Before Night Falls* (opera), 170–72

Mason, Wes, 171

Melton, J. Gordon, 191n24

Méndez Capote, Renée, 112

Méndez Rodenas, Adriana, 90, 181n27

Menéndez, Ronaldo: "Money," 167–70

Ministerio de Cultura, 12, 156, 158

Molloy, Sylvia, 90

Mona (Arenas), 138, 144, 185n16, 189n4, 189n6, 192n32; as AIDS allegory, 6, 115–35, 138, 142, 147; anal sex in, 116, 123, 128–29, 130, 131, 134; apocalyptic rhetoric in, 122; biographical reading of, 120, 131–35, 142; *El color del verano* and, 135, 138, 141, 142; as discourse of fatality, 122, 125, 129; the ELISA test and, 119, 133; femme fatale in, 124, 125, 129; homophobia in, 120, 125, 134; misogyny in 120, 126; queerness in, 119–20, 121, 127; as transgender/transsexual narrative, 120–21; transphobia in, 120, 121, 134; vampirism in, 126, 127, 130. *See also* AIDS and HIV; Leonardo da Vinci; *Mona Lisa* (Leonardo da Vinci)

Mona Lisa (film), 191n18

Mona Lisa (Leonardo da Vinci), 115, 116, 117, 129, 135, 141, 142, 192n27, 192n32; as femme fatale, 124–25, 191n18; as self-portrait of Leonardo, 116, 120, 131, 142, 192n32; as vampire, 124, 126, 130, 191n19, 192n32. *See also* Leonardo da Vinci; *Mona*

Morera, Clara, 194n44, 201n37

"Morir en junio y con la lengua afuera"

(Arenas), 59–61, 62; mother in, 59; poetic narrator's identification with Perceval, 59; search for father in, 59. *See also* Perceval; *Viaje a La Habana*

Mundo alucinante, El (*The Ill-Fated Peregrinations of Fray Servando*) (Arenas), 2, 3, 23, 73, 150, 153, 161, 165–66, 178n34, 193n37, 195n8; as allegory of the Cuban Revolution, 17, 151; chapters published in Cuba, 18; dedication of, 176n21; French translation of, 7, 18, 20, 151; homosexuality in, 17; honorable mention in UNEAC prize, 7, 17, 173n1; intertextuality in, 1, 38, 101; opera version of, 201n37; publishing history of, 1, 7, 18, 151, 163, 176nn21–22; reception in Cuba after Arenas's death, 163, 165, 195n3; smuggled out of Cuba, 7, 18

Mundo nuevo, 18–19, 176n24

Musil, Robert, 20

Necesidad de libertad (Arenas), 162, 177n32, 178n34, 179n7, 195n8; "Adorada Chelo (carta)," 89; "Arenas disparu?," 22; "Comunicado," 22; "Contra la integridad y estabilidad de la nación: Sentencia contra René Ariza," 175n14; "Cortázar: ¿Senil o pueril?," 32, 177n32; "Delfín Prats Pupo," 89; "Don Miguel Riera," 177n30; "Elogio de las furias," 185n15; "Gabriel García Márquez: ¿Esbirro o es burro?," 32, 177n32; "Grito, luego existo," 19, 175n17, 176n25; "Lezama o el reino de la imagen," 41, 60–61, 179n7; "Martí ante el bosque encantado," 102, 194n44; "La represión (intelectual) en Cuba," 29; "Revista *Mundo nuevo*," 19; "Señor Emir

Rodríguez Monegal," 19; "Severo Sarduy," 177n31; "Un largo viaje de Mariel a Nueva York," 175n17, 176n26

Negrón-Muntaner, Frances, 197n17, 200n33

Oedipus complex, 5, 10–11, 69, 105, 106, 109, 110, 112, 183n4, 188n17

Ortega, Julio, 29

Otero, Lisandro, 176n23

Otra vez el mar (*Farewell to the Sea*) (Arenas), 89, 164, 178n34; French translation of, 31; mothers in, 188n14. See also *pentagonía*

Padgug, Robert A., 134

Padilla, Heberto, 12

Padilla Affair, 12, 22

Padura, Leonardo, 199n26

Palace of the White Skunks, The (Arenas). See *Palacio de las blanquísimas mofetas, El*

Palacio de las blanquísimas mofetas, El (*The Palace of the White Skunks*) (Arenas), 3, 8, 36–41, 43–52, 55–58, 62, 88, 164, 178n34, 181n23; biographical reading of, 52; carnival in, 178n2; character inventory of, 36–37; as family saga, 37, 39; fantasy in, 46, 56, 58, 64; fathers in, 4, 36–46, 55, 56, 57, 58, 59, 61, 179n6; hands in, 46–52, 56, 58; intertextuality in, 4, 38, 39–40, 41, 63; literary realism and, 37, 38, 40; masturbation in, 46, 47, 48, 49, 50, 52; melodrama in, 51; *mise en abyme* in, 55–56; paternal longing in, 45, 46, 56, 57, 63–64; smuggled out of Cuba, 8, 36; writing in, 46, 47, 48, 50, 51, 52, 56. See also *Fortunata y Jac-*

inta; *pentagonía*; Pérez Galdós, Benito; "¡Qué dura es la vida!"

"Páramo en llamas, El" (Arenas), 180n9

Pater, Walter, 124, 130, 191n19

paternal erotics, 5, 59–64

patria (fatherland), 4, 5, 66, 76, 79, 83, 85, 88, 89, 90, 106, 107, 172, 185n20

Pavonato, 175n13

Pavón Tamayo, Luis, 12, 175n13

pentagonía (five-novel cycle) (Arenas), 33, 36, 106, 107, 135, 153, 178n34, 188n14, 194n44, 200n35

Perceval, 59–60, 61, 62; Chrétien de Troyes and, 59; Gerbert de Montreuil and, 60; homoeroticism and, 61; mother of, 59, 60; search for the father by, 59, 60, 61, 181n24; Wagner, Richard, and, 60. *See also* "Morir en junio y con la lengua afuera"

Pereira, Manuel, 184n11

Pérez Castillo, Ernesto, 164

Pérez de Zambrana, Luisa, 140, 141, 142, 194n42

Pérez Galdós, Benito, 4, 38, 39, 40, 41, 50, 179n3, 181n19. See also *Fortunata y Jacinta*; *Palacio de las blanquísimas mofetas, El*

Pérez Rivero, Pedro, 198n22

Persecución (Arenas), 178n34, 195n8

Piñera, Virgilio, 13, 23, 25, 164, 176n21, 184n11; as father figure to Arenas, 72, 73, 74; homosexuality and, 72, 184n12

Pogolotti, Graziella, 112, 179n8

Pogolotti, Marcelo, 112

Pontalis, Jean-Bertrand, 74, 185n18

Ponte, Antonio José, 175n13, 195n8

Portela, Ena Lucía, 199n25

Portero, El (*The Doorman*) (Arenas), 132, 155, 164, 178n34, 189n5

Jorge Olivares

IS THE ALLEN FAMILY PROFESSOR OF
LATIN AMERICAN LITERATURE AT COLBY COLLEGE.

Library of Congress Cataloging-in-Publication Data
Olivares, Jorge.
Becoming Reinaldo Arenas : family, sexuality,
and the Cuban Revolution / Jorge Olivares.
p. cm.
Includes bibliographical references and index.
ISBN 978-0-8223-5382-9 (cloth : alk. paper)
ISBN 978-0-8223-5396-6 (pbk. : alk. paper)
1. Arenas, Reinaldo, 1943–1990 — Criticism and
interpretation. 2. Cuba — History — Revolution,
1959 — Influence. 3. Cuban literature — 20th
century — History and criticism. 4. Politics and
culture — Cuba. 5. Exiles' writings, Cuban.
6. Gay men's writings, Cuban. I. Title.
PQ7390.A72Z826 2013
863'.64 — dc23   2012033711